MW01445148

Unwanted Childbearing and Child Nutritional Status in the Western Balkan Roma Communities

Jelena Čvorović

Unwanted Childbearing and Child Nutritional Status in the Western Balkan Roma Communities

Springer

Jelena Čvorović
Serbian Academy of Sciences and Arts
Institute of Ethnography
Beograd, Serbia

ISBN 978-3-031-91535-2   ISBN 978-3-031-91536-9 (eBook)
https://doi.org/10.1007/978-3-031-91536-9

© The Editor(s) (if applicable) and The Author(s), under exclusive license to Springer Nature Switzerland AG 2025

This work is subject to copyright. All rights are solely and exclusively licensed by the Publisher, whether the whole or part of the material is concerned, specifically the rights of translation, reprinting, reuse of illustrations, recitation, broadcasting, reproduction on microfilms or in any other physical way, and transmission or information storage and retrieval, electronic adaptation, computer software, or by similar or dissimilar methodology now known or hereafter developed.
The use of general descriptive names, registered names, trademarks, service marks, etc. in this publication does not imply, even in the absence of a specific statement, that such names are exempt from the relevant protective laws and regulations and therefore free for general use.
The publisher, the authors and the editors are safe to assume that the advice and information in this book are believed to be true and accurate at the date of publication. Neither the publisher nor the authors or the editors give a warranty, expressed or implied, with respect to the material contained herein or for any errors or omissions that may have been made. The publisher remains neutral with regard to jurisdictional claims in published maps and institutional affiliations.

This Springer imprint is published by the registered company Springer Nature Switzerland AG
The registered company address is: Gewerbestrasse 11, 6330 Cham, Switzerland

If disposing of this product, please recycle the paper.

Acknowledgments

Competing interest: This study received no specific grant from any funding agency, or commercial or not-for-profit instance.
 Conflicts of Interest: None declared.
 Ethical Approval and Informed Consent: This study was performed as a secondary data analysis of the UNICEF MICS 4, 5, and 6, public use data sets, with no identifying information while all procedures involving research study participants were approved by the UNICEF. The data that support the findings of this study are available from Multiple Indicator Cluster Surveys http://mics.unicef.org/surveys.
 The author asserts that all procedures contributing to this work comply with the ethical standards of the relevant national and institutional committees on human experimentation and with the Helsinki Declaration of 1975, as revised in 2008.
 Copyright: Permissions to reprint material have been obtained from Ulster Institute of Social Research and Mankind Quarterly.

Competing Interests The author has no competing interests to declare that are relevant to the content of this manuscript.

Contents

1 **Introduction** 1
   1.1 Parental Investment 2
   1.2 Human Behavior as Part of a Life History 6
       1.2.1 Prenatal Investment 12
       1.2.2 Maternal Age 13
       1.2.3 Parity 14
       1.2.4 Birth Spacing 14
       1.2.5 Socioeconomic Status 15
       1.2.6 Parental Favoritism 16
   References 19

2 **Unwanted Childbearing** 27
   2.1 Unintended Pregnancies and Unwanted Children 27
   2.2 Costs of Unintended Pregnancy in Low-and-Middle-Income Countries 38
       2.2.1 Prenatal Maternal Behavior 38
       2.2.2 Birth Outcomes 39
       2.2.3 Post-Natal Investment 41
   References 44

3 **The Roma: Brief History and Overview** 51
   3.1 Origin 51
   3.2 Nomadism and Traditional Occupations 54
   3.3 Marriage and Reproductive Strategies 55
   3.4 Childbirth and Child Rearming Practices 59
   3.5 Parenting Practices 61
   3.6 Formal Education of Roma Children 63
   3.7 Why Roma Have High Fertility 65
   3.8 Cost of Reproduction for Roma Women 68
       3.8.1 Roma Women's Health 69
       3.8.2 Child Outcomes 70
   References 78

4	**The Roma in the Successor States of Former Yugoslavia**		87
	4.1	The Roma in the Western Balkans........................	87
	4.2	Country Reports......................................	90
		4.2.1 North Macedonia................................	90
		4.2.2 Kosovo..	92
		4.2.3 Bosnia and Herzegovina	95
		4.2.4 Montenegro	98
		4.2.5 Serbia...	100
	References...		103
5	**Parental Care in High-Risk Fertility Settings: Roma Nationally Representative Data from UNICEF MICSs Surveys**..............		107
	5.1	Background to the Research Questions.....................	107
	5.2	Material and Methods	109
		5.2.1 Study Design and Sample	109
		5.2.2 Measures of Parental Investment....................	110
		5.2.3 Child Outcome Variables: Growth and Nutritional Status for Children Aged 0–24 Months	111
		5.2.4 Maternal Direct Care	112
		5.2.5 Maternal and Child Variables.......................	112
		5.2.6 Statistical Analyses	113
	5.3	Sample Characteristics by Country	114
		5.3.1 Bosnia and Herzegovina	114
		5.3.2 Kosovo..	116
		5.3.3 North Macedonia................................	118
		5.3.4 Montenegro	119
		5.3.5 Serbia...	120
		5.3.6 Descriptives and Differences Between the Countries: Roma Children Aged 0–59 Months and their Mothers	122
		5.3.7 Roma Parental Investment for Children Aged 0–24 Months..	127
	5.4	Regression Models.....................................	135
		5.4.1 Predictors of Roma Children's Birthweight, HAZ, WAZ and WHZ Scores	135
		5.4.2 Individual Level HAZ, WAZ and WHZ Scores..........	138
		5.4.3 Roma Parental Investment: Children Aged 25–59 Months .	140
	References...		145
6	**Roma Parental Investment, Unwanted Childbearing and Child Nutritional Status in the Western Balkan Roma Communities**		147
	6.1	Investment in Children Aged 25–59 Months..................	147
		6.1.1 Direct Care.....................................	147
	6.2	Investment in Children Aged 0–24 Months...................	152

		6.2.1	Low Birthweight	152
		6.2.2	Being Unwanted	153
		6.2.3	Nutritional Status of Roma Children	156
	6.3	Instead of Conclusion: How Many Children Is Too Many		159
References				165

Chapter 1
Introduction

Human societies display considerable differences in reproductive and parenting behavior, both between and within cultures, resulting in a variety of family settings in which children are raised. Parents invest and care for their children in numerous ways, but some children may be more invested in than others, and evolutionary models may help explain biases in investment. Among the reasons why one child might receive more parental investment than another may be a difference in child wantedness. Child wantedness is a term used to describe unwanted, live births resulting from unintended pregnancy. Worldwide, unintended pregnancy remains a major public health concern, as it may inflict threats on the health and wellbeing of both the mother and child. However, in both developing and developed countries, whether having a child without wanting to influences parental behavior in ways that result in reduced investments in child nutrition and wellbeing remains an open question. In high fertility populations going through the early stages of fertility decline, stated preference in child wantedness might be recurrently updated to include subsequent births and, thus, exceeding a prior desired number of children may have little effect on child health. The Roma/Gypsies, a historically shunned, largest, poorest and fast-growing minority in many European countries, are well-suited for addressing questions relating to parental care and unwanted childbearing. Today, childbirth and childrearing remain central to the lives of many Roma women to an unprecedented degree in the countries where they reside, but little is known regarding how Roma parents allocate parental investment.

1.1 Parental Investment

Parents every so often sacrifice their own future reproductive success to increase the chances of survival of their offspring, a phenomenon referred to as parental investment (Clutton-Brock, 2019). In 1972, Robert Trivers, an American evolutionary biologist, defined parental investment as "any investment by the parent in an individual offspring that increases the offspring's chance of surviving (and hence reproductive success) at the cost of the parent's ability to invest in other offspring" (Trivers, 1972: 139). In some social mammals, mothers continue to improve the survival of their offspring well into adulthood but whether this extended care comes at a reproductive cost to mothers, and therefore represents maternal investment, is not clear (Weiss et al., 2023). *Homo sapiens* mothers are highly invested in their offspring, with conception and prenatal investment taking place within their bodies, and nursing being the main source of nutrition available to their newborn infants (Bjorklund et al., 2020). Mothers and their offspring have likely evolved psychological mechanisms designed to encourage attachment and thus survival. In humans, as in other primates, it is generally held that long-term mother-offspring bonds provide mutual benefits, and represent maternal care, not necessarily investment (van Noordwijk, 2012).

Human behavior is best understood as part of a life history—a suite of traits genetically organized to meet the trials of life—survival, growth, and reproduction. Human societies display considerable difference in reproductive and parenting behavior, both between and within cultures, resulting in a variety of family settings in which children are raised. Relative to other primates, children require extensive investment by parents because of the extended period of immaturity and dependency (Bjorklund & Myers, 2019).

Parents invest and care for their children in numerous ways, but some children may be more invested in than others: it is expected that parents should respond to their offspring fitness cues, thus parents may favor the healthiest, highest quality children, or a specific sex. Evolutionary models may help explain parental investment and biases in investment. At its core, evolution is about reproduction: natural selection is simply for reproductive success (Trevathan, 2017). Thus, all traits and species behaviors can be evaluated in terms of their reproductive consequences. This, however, does not necessarily imply that "more is better", as there is always an "upper limit," a point at which the costs of producing more far outweigh the benefits of each (Trevathan, 2017:1). In most environments, parental resources are limited, and parents face a trade-off in number of children and allocations of investment per child (quantity-quality trade-off) (Lawson & Mace. 2008). In turn, siblings in large families compete for finite parental resources (quantity-quality trade-off effects), with the negative effects most evident under conditions of resource scarcity and high fertility (Gibson & Lawson, 2011).

A further reason why one child might receive more parental investment than another may be a difference in child wantedness. Child wantedness is a term used to describe unwanted, live births resulting from unintended pregnancy (Čvorović,

2020). Any unplanned, mistimed or unwanted pregnancy at the time of conception is defined as unintended pregnancy. Mistimed pregnancies occur earlier than desired, while unwanted occur when no more children were desired (Zeleke et al., 2021). Worldwide, unintended pregnancy rates are high: in 2010–2014, almost half (44%) of all pregnancies were unintended (Troutman et al., 2020). In spite of the aid of education and family planning services, unintended pregnancy remains a major public health issue.

Contingent on the relative costs of having an abortion and giving birth, more unintended pregnancies lead to higher abortion rates, or birth rates, or both. Unintended pregnancies may inflict threats on the health and wellbeing of both the mother and child, including malnutrition, illness, abuse and neglect, and even death. Unintended pregnancies can further result in cycles of high fertility, as well as poor educational and employment outcomes, and poverty – trials which can span through generations (Bellizzi et al., 2020).

Recent estimates of unintended pregnancy and abortion rates for 150 countries highlight the widely varying unintended pregnancy and abortion rates between countries—even within the same region or geographic area. The greatest variations were found in Latin America and sub-Saharan Africa where, for instance, unintended pregnancy rates in countries ranged from 41 to 107 per 1000 women, and 49 to 145 per 1000 women respectively (Bearak et al., 2022). These differences do not appear to be solely a result of income-level: for example, in Europe, countries with higher unintended pregnancy rates than the regional average are classified as high-income, while the two countries with the lowest estimates of unintended pregnancy are middle-income.

In both developing and developed countries, whether having a child without wanting to influences parental behavior in ways that result in reduced investments in child nutrition and wellbeing is still an open question: research is scant, producing mixed results (Costa et al., 2018; Čvorović, 2020; Deogan et al., 2022). Being unwanted may lead to a wide range of risks for the child: the mother may perceive the child as an additional cost or a burden for which she is not prepared and may invest less in the child either because of limited resources or because of other constraints (Sparks, 2011). On the other hand, especially in high fertility populations living in marginalized, resource-limited settings and undergoing the early stages of fertility decline, stated preference in child wantedness might be updated to include subsequent births where exceeding the prior desired number of children might have little effect on child health and nutrition (Costa et al., 2018). Nonetheless, resource-limited settings have been shown to affect parental conditions which may influence overall parental investment and its weighting per child: parents who have little control of their children's survival and reproductive chances will tend to favor lower levels of parental investment and higher fertility (Quinlan, 2007; Sear, 2011).

To assess parental investment and the costs of unwanted childbearing on the welfare and health in early childhood of "unwanted" children, five poor communities of the Western Balkans Roma were examined. Data were gathered from nationally representative samples of women and children from UNICEF Multiple Indicator Cluster Surveys 4, 5 and 6 (2011–2019) for Roma settlements in Serbia, Montenegro,

Kosovo, North Macedonia and Bosnia and Herzegovina. The study included a review of traditional Roma cultural practices influencing childbirth and childrearing, marriage patterns, and their outcomes for Roma women and their children.

The Roma are a well-suited cohort to explore these issues. Roma/Gypsies are a historically shunned, largest, poorest and fast-growing minority in many European countries. Roma communities are scattered throughout Europe, with the largest concentration in Central and Eastern Europe (Čvorović, 2014). Roma face overwhelming difficulties including limited access to quality education and integration into the labor market, leading to further poverty and social exclusion, and poor living conditions. Additionally, population demographic pyramid of the Roma in Europe are comparable to that of the poorest developing countries in other continents, i.e., poor African or Asian societies. Due to the combination of lower-than-average life expectancy and higher-than-average fertility rates, it is estimated that the average age of Roma population in Central and Eastern Europe is 25 years, in contrast to an average of over 40 years for the non-Roma population (Velux Foundation, 2019).

As in many other traditional ethnic minorities around the world, Roma women experience higher fertility and higher infant and child mortality, compared to non-Roma majority populations. Roma reproductive behavior could be classified as high-risk fertility behavior, characterized by maternal age below 18 years, short birth intervals, and high parity (Singh & Singh, 2024). At the same time, Roma women are over-represented among the disadvantaged: they are often stigmatized, live in poverty within segregated communities, lack adequate education, the skills for and access to jobs, and are subjects to cultural practices that limit women's choices (Coe & Čvorović, 2017).

In the populations of post-communist states, the Roma number between three and ten percent, yet their birth rate is more than twice the national average. At the same time, the so-called "demographic winter" is jeopardizing the future of many nations, especially in the Western Balkans with a substantial Roma minority: population declines are likely to persist in the former Yugoslavia, particularly in Bosnia and Herzegovina and Serbia (Ármás, 2023). The demographic contrast of Roma women with their non-Roma counterparts are the result of the strong regularizing orientations of the Roma: pronatalist and patrilocal marriages are traditionally encouraged early on, followed by adolescent maternity and high fertility (Gamella, 2018; Čvorović, 2014). The Roma ethnic traditional strategy that encourages endogamy and high fertility has probably helped the Roma to create the most favorable strategy of survival and reproduction in a given environment, in response to their historical discrimination, exclusion, shorter life span, and uncertain futures (Čvorović, 2004). However, a by-product of this successful reproductive strategy may be reflected in Roma children health outcomes. Generally, ethnic minority children in marginalized, poor communities are at increased risk of nutritional deprivation. Many of the Roma children grow up in poverty, and suffer from high rates of undernutrition (as indicated by growth stunting, i.e., low height for age), wasting (i.e., low weight for height), underweight (low weight-for-age) and developmental delays compared to their non-Roma counterparts (UNICEF, 2015).

1.1 Parental Investment

Recent data, however, has pointed to changes in the Roma population's reproductive behavior, reflected in a slow decline in birth rate (Nestorová Dická, 2021). Nonetheless, reproduction-- childbirth and childrearing-- remain central to the lives of many Roma women, to a degree unprecedented in countries where Roma reside (Gamella, 2018; Čvorović & Coe, 2017). At the same time, not much is known about the effects that exceeding the desired number of children might have on Roma parental behavior. Recent research suggests that higher unintended pregnancy rates among minorities may be a consequence of unequal access to contraception: unintended pregnancies are often higher among lower income, minority women living in poverty, with an even greater financial impact of such unplanned conceptions than usual (Troutman et al., 2020). Other studies have also found that unintended pregnancy rates are higher in settings where abortion is restricted than where it is broadly legal (Bearak et al., 2020). However, being so poor as not to be able to afford contraception would also imply that another unwanted child is not affordable either (Pritchett, 1994).

Contrary to widespread assumption, however, Roma women in the former Yugoslav republics do have access to health care, possess a relatively good understanding of contraception, and some form of contraception is used by the majority of married women. In addition, abortion is legal and available. The legalization of abortion in the Socialist Federal Republic of Yugoslavia began in the 1950s, and was officially completed with the inclusion of the right to abortion in the highest legislative act in 1974. According to the Law on Abortion of the Federal Republic of Yugoslavia (1974), the right to an abortion can be exercised only at the request of a pregnant woman and this is guaranteed as part of the Constitution. At the time, Yugoslavia was one of only three countries in the world that included the right to terminate pregnancy in its federal Constitution; this was later included in the constitutions of all the republics that made up the former Yugoslavia (Serbia with Kosovo and Metohija, Croatia, Bosnia and Herzegovina, Montenegro, Macedonia and Slovenia). The law, with minor alterations, was subsequently inherited by all the former Yugoslavian states, thus ensuring the freedom and autonomy of the female body.

This manuscript is organized as follows: upon first describing the basic concepts in evolutionary theory and human behavioral ecology, including Life History Theory and reproductive strategy, the various concerns surrounding unintended childbearing are presented, with a special emphasis given to low-and-middle-income countries and high fertility populations. This is followed by a brief history of the emergence of the Roma in Europe, their past and present living conditions, proclaimed traditions, cultural behaviors and beliefs. The next part presents selected country reports: the current situation and reproductive behaviors of the Roma in the five former Yugoslav republics: Serbia, Montenegro, Kosovo, North Macedonia and Bosnia and Herzegovina. The data from UNICEF Multiple Indicator Cluster Surveys 4, 5 and 6 for the Roma settlements in the former Yugoslav republics are then summarized, followed by analyses of the associations between parental investment, maternal behavior and unwanted children, and child nutritional outcomes. Parental investment and parental care are used interchangeably, even though parental care may be the more appropriate term when costs to parental fitness cannot be directly estimated (Hassan et al., 2019).

1.2 Human Behavior as Part of a Life History

One of the fundamental ideas underlying an evolutionary approach to behavior is that organisms become adapted to their environment through the process of natural selection as first proposed in 1858 by Charles Darwin. Darwin was a naturalist who was attempting to explain how organisms came to have the various traits they exhibit, and he discovered that when certain traits that had some chance of being inherited helped individuals leave descendants, those traits in a similar environment tended to increase in frequency, along with the descendants. This discovery of natural selection identified the main cause of the persistence and change in frequencies of inheritable traits (Daly & Wilson, 1983). At that time, Darwin was unaware of the mechanisms of inheritance-- genes, which were yet to be discovered. Genes were discovered by Darwin's contemporary Gregor Mendel, but only after both men were long dead did scientific circles rediscover Mendel's discovery and understand its importance. In 1900s, the discovery of genes became known, and the cause of traits, including behavior, was seen as basically genetic.

In the 1960s and 70s, several biologists formulated what has been termed "the modern synthesis", bringing together Darwin's natural selection theory and biology. G. C. Williams (1966) in his acclaimed book *Adaptation and Natural Selection: A Critique of some Current Evolutionary Thought* refined the traditional Darwinian idea that natural selection acts at the level of the individual as opposed to the group, and inaugurated what has become a major area of empirical and theoretical research in evolutionary behavioral studies. Williams used natural selection, not to explain gene frequencies in gene pools, but to explain the persistence and change in frequencies of inheritable traits. At around the same time William Hamilton (1964) developed the idea that individuals could maximize their fitness not only by maximizing the number of their own offspring but also by extending aid to their genetic relatives. This insight led Robert Trivers (1972, 1974) to develop models of parental investment and parent-offspring conflict. Parent–offspring conflict theory suggests that parents and offspring should disagree over the amount of parental investment in the offspring whereas offspring should always demand more than parents are willing to invest (Trivers, 1974). This conflict reflects an underlying genetic conflict of interest: while parents are equally related to all of their children and disposed to invest equally in them, each individual child is fully related to itself but only half related to its siblings. Parent–offspring conflict has been well documented in both animals and humans and expressed at physiological level during gestation and at the behavioral and psychological level after birth (Traficonte & Maestripieri, 2015).

All these events paved the way for E. O. Wilson's (1975) highly influential work, *Sociobiology: The New Synthesis*. The final chapter of this massive volume as well as Wilson's (1978) *On Human Nature* inaugurated the field of what at the time was

1.2 Human Behavior as Part of a Life History

called human sociobiology, or evolutionary study of human behavior. According to Wilson (1975), since human beings form a species of animals, they follow the same biological laws. Human social and behavioral traits can be seen as universals (common to all people) and these traits can be explained in terms of the same biological principles that apply to other animal species.

The concept of natural selection and adaptation have hitherto been difficult to define, since many biologists use them in quite surprisingly different ways. For many biologists, natural selection is seen as a process in which two alternative alleles compete with each other over time for occupation of a particular place on a chromosome. However, natural selection operates on phenotypes, the actual animals that live and die and breed more or less successfully, but the evolutionary change is transmitted by surviving genes. This is why modern biology equates natural selection with the differential reproduction of genotypes (Daly & Wilson, 1983: 11). The difficulty of recognizing natural selection and adaptation has led to the result that selection and adaptation were defined in terms of their effects on reproductive success or fitness. Fitness is a measure of the extent to which an organism succeeds in passing on its genes to the next generation, compared with other members of the population. Generally, species-typical behavior is usually fit behavior (Symons, 1979). Other concepts central to evolutionary theory are that of function and by-product. Function refers to the purpose for which a character is designed by natural selection; conversely, being the opposite of adaptation, a trait that has no function is referred to as a by-product or artifact. The difficulty in recognizing adaptation for by-products remains one of the key challenges to the evolutionary approach (Symons, 1987).

In the past decades, three separate but complementary branches in the evolutionary study of human behavior have emerged: evolutionary psychology, dual inheritance theory and human behavioral ecology.

Evolutionary psychology combines cognitive science with the theory of natural selection to formulate specific hypotheses about the human psychological makeup. Evolutionary psychologists see the human mind as a set of evolved information processing mechanisms, which are instantiated in the human nervous system. These are adaptations, which produce behavior that solves particular problems, such as mate selection, language, family relations and cooperation (Barkow et al., 1992). Thus, human culture and behavior are generated by a contingent set of functional programs which use and process information from the world, including information that is provided intentionally and unintentionally by other human beings. The questions addressed by evolutionary psychology range from the mundane to the spiritual and touch on just about everything that humans exhibit: sex, love and romance, deception, self-deception, the cooperation, moral and social status, religion, culture, genes, psychology and the conscious and unconscious human mind (review in Buss, 2019).

Dual inheritance theory was first developed by a couple of population geneticists (Cavalli-Sforza & Feldman, 1981) and an anthropologist and an ecologist (Boyd & Richerson, 1985), as a mathematical model to outline the transmission and evolution of culture – beliefs, values, behaviors, technology, and other socially transmitted knowledge within societies around the world. Dual inheritance theory posits that human biology and behavior are influenced by two lines of inheritance, the first being genetic, inherited by parents for all species, and the second, a cultural line, unique to the human species, inherited from other members of society. Much emphasis is laid on the role of social learning in human evolutionary history. Thus, for instance, religion tends to be traditional (i.e., vertically inherited from parents to offspring; see Steadman & Palmer, 2015), and may have evolved as a means to suppress intrafamily conflict through parental/ancestral manipulation, being afterwards extended—both genetically and culturally—within and beyond the family context as a means for social control and encouragement of cooperative behaviors more generally (Crespi & Summers, 2014; Steadman & Palmer, 2015). Additionally, kin selection may have played a role in the evolvement of religiosity, depending on relatedness to social partners (Stucky & Gardner, 2022). Religion influences many aspects of human behavior in ways that could be evolutionarily significant. Religion often serves as a national and cultural identity marker, having strong influence in the lives of families and ethnic groups (Čvorović, 2004). Religion also influences population growth and other demographic parameters: research suggests that an individual's religious affiliation may influence important life history schedules such as timing of reproduction and marriage, childbearing, and desired family size (Blume, 2009). Thus, different religions may have encouraged different traditional reproductive strategies and life histories (Čvorović, 2011). In spite of the significance of religion on family life, there is limited literature on the influence of religion/religiosity on parenting practices (Frosh, 2004). Recent research suggests that religious cultures may function as "cooperative breeding niches" that may encourage alloparenting from large kin networks as well as from unrelated co-religionists to produce successful reproductive strategies, but whether religious cooperation in actuality extends to alloparenting and increases maternal fertility and/or improves child outcomes remains unclear (Shaver, 2017).

Human behavioral ecology broadens the theoretical perspective and methodology of animal behavioral ecology by applying evolutionary models to humans. Behavioral ecology focuses on how efficiently animals use their time and energy in securing resources that may enhance survival and reproduction. The discipline emerged as a paradigm in the early 1970s and was soon followed by evolutionary models applied to human behavior, i.e., human behavioral ecology (Nettle et al., 2013). For both humans and other animals, behavioral ecology underscores the idea that organisms have evolved to respond adaptively to varying ecological environments in ways that are fitness--maximizing, in the sense that fitness represents the total genetic representation of an individual in future generations (Borgerhoff Mulder, 1991). However, behavioral strategies are not directly determined by genes, as an organism's phenotype (observable physiological traits or behavior) is the result of interaction of a given genotype and the environment (Sear, 2015). This interaction may explain human behavioral plasticity: traits can adapt as a result of environmental change, increasing the ability to react to different ecological conditions in flexible ways (Nettle et al., 2013; Sear, 2015).

1.2 Human Behavior as Part of a Life History

As can be appreciated from the above, Life History Theory forms a major branch of behavioral ecology. It organizes research into the evolutionary forces shaping the timing of life events, with a particular focus on age-schedules of fertility and mortality (Kaplan & Gangestad, 2015). Life History traits include such factors as: age at sexual maturity; number and timing of reproductive events; and number and investment per offspring. A basic principle in life history theory is that natural selection, acting on the timing of life events, such as growth, maturation, reproduction, and death, is contingent on the ecology of energy production and mortality risks (Hill & Kaplan, 1999). Thus, each species or subspecies has developed a characteristic life history adapted to the specific ecological problems met by its ancestors (Wilson, 1975). This means that in order to have left descendants, all organisms must have solved the problems of survival, growth, development, and reproduction. These adaptive problems are named somatic effort (survival or maintenance, and growth and development) and reproductive effort (Daly & Wilson, 1983). Reproductive effort consists of mating effort (courtship, locating a mate) and parenting effort (gestation, childbirth itself and postnatal childcare). Thus, the basic tenet of life-history theory is that features of the anatomy, behavioral capacities and development of species arise from natural selection for the optimal allocation of somatic and reproductive effort.

Reproductive strategies are made of sets of coevolved anatomical, physiological and psychological characteristics designed by natural selection for the optimal administration of mating and parenting effort. All species utilize both mating and parenting effort, but comparative research reveals a wide mating-effort continuum in mammalian reproductive strategies (Chisholm et al., 1993). At the high mating-effort end of the continuum, animals tend to mature early and give birth to small offspring in large litters after a short gestation while at the high-parenting-effort end more-or-less opposite traits are prevalent (Promislow & Harvey, 1990). Biologists and psychologists often describe these strategies as different points along a fast-to-slow continuum (the r/K continuum) (Figueredo et al., 2006). Thus, in relation to environmental considerations, Life History Theory asserts that, *ceteris paribus*, species living in unstable and unpredictable environments tend to evolve "fast-selected" traits associated with high reproductive rates, low parental investment and relatively short intergeneration times. At the other end, species living in stable and predictable environments tend to evolve "slow-selected" traits associated with low reproductive rates, high parental investment, and longer intergeneration times (Pianka, 1970).

Compared to other primates and mammals, human life histories are characterized by a long-life span, an extended period of juvenile dependence, support of reproduction by post-reproductive individuals, and often, male support of reproduction through provision for females and their offspring (Hill & Kaplan, 1999). Within-species differences in the human reproductive strategy are, for the most part, due to environmental historical contingencies: decisions (conscious or unconscious) made about the optimum use of reproductive effort are assumed to be dependent on individuals' perceptions of their present socio-ecological condition.

Another key concept in life history theory is that of parental investment. Formulated by Robert Trivers in 1972, parental investment is any cost or investment (such as resources, time, energy) associated with raising offspring that increases the offspring's chances of survival or reproductive success and reduces a parent's ability to invest in other or future offspring (Trivers, 1972). Subsequently, Clutton-Brock (1991, 2019) expanded the definition to include investment in offspring at a cost to any component of a parent's fitness, including mating or somatic maintenance.

Parental investment has multiple domains and can be anything from providing food, protection, shelter or attention, education and financial support. Two types of parental investment can be distinguished: base level, relatively low cost (base) investments, which are essential for greater chances of offspring survival and health, and may include in utero nutritional transfers, practices such as protection, breastfeeding, food allocation, preventing and health seeking behaviors; and so-called surplus resources/investments, whereby parents may decide to invest in their children's education or other investments that may increase their child's wellbeing in addition to those necessary to ensure survival alone (Downey, 2001; Gibson & Sear, 2010). The latter may include intellectual stimulation and other forms of time spent training and teaching children, and interpersonal resources such as providing attention, time, love, affection, and general encouragement (Hertwig et al., 2002).

Parental resources such, for instance, energy and time, spent on one function cannot be spent on another; thus, energy spent on parenting cannot be used for mating or preserving body conditions (Sear, 2015). As such, parents face a number of decisions, or trade-offs, in the appropriate allocation of energy so as to maximize their fitness (Stearns, 1992). Therefore, parents trade-off parenting effort with mating effort, and with somatic maintenance. A further influential concept is the trade-off between current and future reproduction: parents must choose how much to invest in the current offspring so as to preserve energy for future reproductive events. Lastly, parents face a further trade-off in regard to number of children and allocations of investment per child, i.e., between the quality (increasing offspring fitness) and quantity of offspring (increasing offspring number) (Hill & Kaplan, 1999). Thus parents may either produce numerous offspring but invest relatively little in each (the quantity strategy), or produce few offspring but invest substantially in each one (the quality strategy).

In humans, the quality strategy is employed by investing largely in a relatively small number of offspring; however, parents have to decide how they will allocate investment among their offspring, as equal investment in each may not be the best strategy (Sear, 2015).

The female's parental investment in each offspring far exceeds her mate's (Daly & Wilson, 1983). An explanation for this may lie in anisogamy (the difference in size between male and female gametes): the male sex specializes in the production of a large number of small gametes (sperm), while females produce a small number of large gametes (eggs/ova). The female gamete is always the bigger of the two and is a characteristic that defines the sexes. This essential difference has vast implications for male and female roles before and after conception (Williams, 1966). For a male mammal, the necessary sacrifice for reproduction is close to zero, and his role

1.2 Human Behavior as Part of a Life History

can end with copulation. In contrast, for the female, reproduction brings with it an obligatory of burden – that of relatively heavy investment (Trivers, 1972).

Kinship, or enduring close social relationships, according to a number of scholars, was of primary importance to our distant ancestors (Lancaster & Whitten, 1990). The human (and mammalian) strategy of altricial birth and prolonged immaturity of offspring involves intense, long-term maternal (and possibly paternal) care. All parenting, or the bringing in of others, generally kin, to help protect, nurture and teach one's children also appears to have been an important human strategy (Hrdy, 1999). Humans seem to possess a wide range of proximate mechanisms that enhance the probability of their forming nurturing relationships (Silk, 1990) and maintaining these nurturing relationships through time.

Human females, like all mammals, go through considerable sacrifice in order to successfully reproduce: evolutionary life history predicts that the energy invested in reproduction is traded off against investments in maintenance and survival. With regard to short-term cost, the direct costs of reproduction—pregnancy, breastfeeding, and childcare—require energy (Jasienska, 2017). Pregnancy and lactation also involve many physiological changes, including reduced functioning of the maternal immune system. Thus, the metabolic demands associated with these changes mean that women can experience significant physiological costs associated with reproductive effort (Kirkwood & Rose, 1991).

Studies have found that children in traditional societies, who lose their mothers in the first couple of years of life, are at a higher risk of mortality when compared with children with living mothers, pointing to the enormous importance of maternal care for infants (Sear & Mace, 2008). Nevertheless, during human evolutionary history, women did not raise children alone. Biparental care, where both females and males invest in children, varies both across and within human populations (Prall & Scelza, 2020). Just how essential paternal investment was in human evolutionary history still remains uncertain (Shenk, 2011). In comparison to most mammals, human fathers invest along with mothers to provide for children, thus paternal care likely evolved along the course of human life history as a strategy of raising energetically costly, slow-developing offspring (Gettler et al., 2020). Human fathers may offer additional care and protection to their offspring, however, identification of fathers (through marriage) also points out to the possibility that humans obtain far more identifiable kin than any other mammal, which may have played an important role in human cultural and biological evolution (Palmer et al., 2005).

Studies from different ecological environments suggest, however, that fathers have little impact on their children's welfare, and that paternal investment is frequently substituted with care from others (Sear & Mace, 2008; Sear, 2021). This is termed "alloparental care": care that is directed by an individual (an alloparent) toward dependent young who are not their offspring (Wilson, 1975). Furthermore, in raising children, women often get help from relatives, particularly older women and pre-reproductive children, who act as "helpers-at-the-nest", allowing women to raise several children at the same time. This is the essence of the Cooperative Breeding Hypothesis, which derived from the idea that allomaternal assistance was crucial for child survival in the Pleistocene (Hrdy, 1999).

The cooperative breeding system permitted females to produce costly offspring without increasing birth spacing, allowing at the same time migration to new habitats. Studies have shown that allomaternal investment tends to be generally, although not universally, associated with positive child and maternal outcomes, such as improved child growth, nutritional status, survivorship, increased maternal reproductive success and general well-being of mothers and their children (review in Helfrecht et al., 2020).

Due to extensive variation in traditional allomaternal investment, both within and between cultures, research has revealed that humans employ a rather flexible "cooperative breeding strategy", by which "parental" investment may come from other individuals, usually kin, or sources other than parents (Sear, 2015).

In addition to biological constraints and the availability of support from others, maternal investment depends also on the environmental and socioecological context (Helfrecht et al., 2020). Thus, maternal investment decisions may be determined by a number of maternal own factors, such as her developmental environment, age, parity, birth spacing, general resource availability, child characteristics, but also external factors.

1.2.1 Prenatal Investment

Across species, an organism's developmental environment influences growth, development and reproduction, but also has consequences for its descendants. Maternal investment starts in utero: prenatal effort is reflected in the child's birth weight, which is considered to be more representative of maternal expenditure than postnatal effort (postnatal growth or breastfeeding) (Braza, 2004; Coall & Chisholm, 2010). Insufficient fetal nutrition, as a result of inadequate maternal nutrition or a compromised fetal supply line, may be a factor influencing these developmental paths. Child size at birth is mainly dependent on intrauterine factors, reflected in maternal body size and physical rather than genetic factors. Poor uterine environment results in reduced fetal growth, associated with higher rates of infant mortality and, in later life, higher risk of coronary heart disease, hypertension, and diabetes (Barker, 2004). Evolutionary studies have used birth weight as an index of female reproductive effort, with the assumption that there is a positive association between birth weight and offspring fitness, and a negative association between birth weight and residual maternal resources (i.e., investing in increased birth weight involves costs to future reproduction) (Fessler et al., 2005). Put another way, if a woman's reproductive efforts, either over her entire lifetime or only early in her reproductive years, are biased toward increasing number of offspring, there will be a trade-off reflected in the size of offspring i.e., she should produce smaller offspring, corresponding to lower parenting effort and thus lower offspring quality (Promislow & Harvey, 1990; Coall & Chisholm, 2003).

Maternal developmental environment also tends to influence parental investment in the child during pregnancy. For instance, for females who grow up in unfavorable conditions, such as childhood environment characterized by high local mortality rates or psychosocial stress, it may be adaptive to mature earlier and produce more offspring which will each receive reduced investment. Conversely, in a favorable childhood environment, it may be adaptive to mature later and have fewer offspring which will receive more investment (Coall & Chisholm, 2010). Thus, rather than being pathological, low weight at birth can be regarded as an adaptive response to environmental risk and uncertainty (Pike, 2005).

Current psychosocial stress or environmental constraints may also influence investment in utero: numerous studies have documented the trade-offs between investment in current vs. future reproduction, where reproductive potential may be reserved for the future, when conditions might be more favorable. For instance, as pregnancy carries high metabolic costs, lower investment in unborn offspring may occur due to the lack of support (investment) from a mother's partner, especially for women who already have dependent children (Merklinger-Gruchala et al., 2019). This strategy is interpreted as an example of the plasticity of human life history.

1.2.2 Maternal Age

Life history predicts that maternal age influences the amount of parental investment. This prediction is referred to as "the terminal investment hypothesis": females tend to adjust investment in regard to remaining age-related reproductive potential, i.e., investment tends to increase with age (Clutton-Brock, 1984; Fessler et al., 2005). According to this hypothesis, it is expected that older mothers, with limited opportunities to bear an additional child, have higher investment in a particular child than younger mothers who have greater number of reproductive years ahead (Uggla & Mace, 2016). However, previous studies on the relationship of maternal age and child investment were inconclusive with older mothers either more or less likely to invest in children (review in Tifferet et al., 2007). Studies have generally shown that younger mothers tend to have higher rates of infanticide in both traditional and modern societies, while post-partum depression levels tend to be lower among older mothers and interpreted as a lower disposition to reduce investment in new offspring. For children born to older mothers, there may be additional advantages over children born to younger mothers. Studies have found that higher maternal age is associated with a more favorable offspring phenotype (height), better survival outcome for multiple pregnancies, and improved child health and development (Savage et al., 2013). Conversely, older maternal age (≥ 35 years) may be linked to higher rates of low birth weight (lower investment) owing to the theoretically predicted greater biological risk associated with extremes of reproductive age and reproductive outcomes.

1.2.3 Parity

In life history, parity is often taken to be a rough measure of maternal investment, i.e., there is an inverse scaling between number and size of offspring across and within species (Walker et al., 2008). Growing up with many siblings (parental trade-off between number of children and investment per offspring) results in reduced parental investment but also economic difficulties, as the birth of each additional child limits the time, attention and other resources parents can provide to any one of their children (Lawson & Mace, 2011).

Nonetheless, studies have shown that high parity women tend to have heavier offspring due to variation in maternal body condition and reproductive experiences. Thus, physiologically, high parity women have more vascularized uteri, which leads to infants of higher birth weight: the first pregnancy prepares the body, and with each subsequent pregnancy, the body becomes more efficient (Hinkle et al., 2014). Age tends to be strongly correlated with parity, i.e., reproductive effort increases with age. However, for high-parity women, poverty, inadequate nutrition, successive pregnancies, short intervals between deliveries and lactation may, separately or in combination, all contribute to poor maternal and child health outcomes, including low weight at birth (King, 2003).

1.2.4 Birth Spacing

Birth spacing is the duration of time between two successive live births, and represents a key component of fertility behavior and family planning (Rutstein, 2005). In hunter–gatherer societies, the typical birth interval tended to be three to 4 years (Kaplan et al., 2000).

In regard to health, the World Health Organization (WHO) endorses a minimum inter-pregnancy interval of 2 years or an inter-birth interval of 33 months or more to ensure the optimal benefits for mothers and their newborns. However, in both developing and developed countries, significant variation in birth spacing was found, with women from developing countries usually having shorter birth spacing: Research from 52 developing countries showed that over two-thirds of births occurred within 30 months from the preceding live birth (Rutstein, 2005).

Furthermore, studies have found that in most populations, but more commonly in developing countries with inadequate health care, closely spaced siblings are at a higher risk of mortality, poor birth outcomes, including preterm birth, small for gestational age, and low birthweight. These costs may be explained by poor recovery of maternal somatic resources between births (maternal depletion syndrome) and a decrease in the intense child care given in the first years of life to successive siblings (King, 2003). In turn, the converse has been reported in developed Western countries with advanced health care systems and good maternal nutritional status. A recent study from low-and middle-income countries found shorter breastfeeding and female sex of the previous child to be the only factors consistently associated with short birth spacing (Pimentel et al., 2020). In addition, short birth spacing may be associated with poor parental care practices, reduced investment and fast life history strategy (Dhingra & Pingali, 2021; Berg et al., 2020).

1.2.5 Socioeconomic Status

The effects of environmental quality and risk, and parental own condition will affect parental ability to invest, investment itself, and the possible payoffs to investment. Poor conditions of local environment affect parental conditions and overall parental investment and how biased that investment is (Quinlan, 2007). Under high risk poor conditions, there may be limited differential investment between children, as parents may have little control of children's survival and reproductive chances, and may favor low levels of investment and higher fertility (Sear, 2015). When risk factors appear low, parents may increase their investment, expecting greater returns from their efforts in terms of child survival, development, and eventual reproductive success, which in turn may result in a reduction of fertility rates (Gibson & Lawson, 2011; Winterhalder & Leslie, 2002).

The socioeconomic status of parents has been shown to significantly influence their capacity to invest in offspring. Most of the research on parenting and socioeconomic status has come from economic studies of the modern family (review in Fan & Porter, 2020). Generally, these studies have found that the lower the socioeconomic status, the lower the level of actual or potential investment—as evidenced by higher levels of child abuse and neglect (Garbarino, 1985). In contrast, families of higher socioeconomic position tend to increase their investment in each child rather than increase the number (Fingerman et al., 2015). Parents' childrearing knowledge may also vary along socioeconomic and cultural gradients, with negative effects on parenting (Roubinov & Boyce, 2017).

Modern economic phenomena, such as state policies, public health improvements and care, or food, by reducing external environmental risks and improving resources, have the potential to strongly impact parental behavior (Gibson & Lawson, 2011). In countries with well-established welfare systems (e.g. a welfare state) policies supporting the family, such as cash transfers/financial social assistance in particular, may modify parental behavior (Čvorović, 2024). By providing parents access to certain resources, the welfare incentives may increase the reliability of parental investment returns and thus increase opportunities to invest in offspring quality vs. quantity, i.e., encourage greater engagement per child and eventually a drop in fertility.

In low-and middle-income countries, cash transfers in particular may alleviate parental conditions in large families by compensating for the additional costs of an extra child, and in this way decrease or mask the effects of a trade-off between family size (quantity) and child quality (Gibson & Lawson, 2011). On the other hand, cash benefits have been shown to encourage tighter sibling spacing in more generous welfare states, and to increase fertility (Halla et al., 2016). Generally, therefore, people tend to have more children when costs of childrearing are lower, or when the state– rather than the parent(s)– bears the cost of rearing children (Bergsvik et al., 2021; Čvorović, 2024).

1.2.6 Parental Favoritism

Biases in parental investment by child's characteristics have been documented across cultures: maternal investment (motherly love) is not unconditional, but tends to depend on maternal and child characteristics (Hrdy, 1999). Some children may receive more investment than others: parents tend to favor specific children with a higher likelihood of contributing to parental fitness (Uggla & Mace, 2016; Quinlan, 2007). In behavioral ecology, offspring "quality" is defined as individual fitness. Thus, parental favoritism may be adaptive: depending on the environment, the specific child characteristics that may lead to parental biases in investment usually include child's sex, age (birth order), or other child quality/endowments, such as general health.

1.2.6.1 Child's Sex

Parental investment theory suggests that natural selection will favor equal parental investment for sons and daughters when childrearing of both sexes is equally costly (Fisher, 1999). However, the costs and benefits of investing in each sex are hardly ever uniform and biased parental behavior by child sex is documented across human cultures (Hassan et al., 2019). This is known as the Trivers-Willard hypothesis (TWH): parents in good conditions will invest more in sons, while parents in poor conditions will invest more in daughters, i.e., high-quality sons are expected to outreproduce high quality daughters, while low-quality daughters are expected to outreproduce low quality sons (Trivers & Willard, 1973). TWH has been subject of numerous studies, and while studies on mammals in general provide support for the hypothesis, studies on humans provide markedly inconsistent results (Cameron & Dalerum, 2009). The human-studies mixed results provoked continuing debates around the suitability of the species or population being studied, or when such biases are more likely to occur, and the validity of various measures of parental investment proxies and parental and offspring conditions (Lynch et al., 2018). The preference is often measured by the sex ratio at birth, or as post-natal investment. Sex-biases in post-natal care may include such factors as discriminatory feeding, supervision, expenditure on healthcare and schooling, and differential allocation of resources throughout life, including the transfer of inheritance.

When sex-biased parental investment is found, it is usually biased in favor of sons, especially in some East and South Asian countries, but also in sub-Saharan Africa societies (review in Hassan et al., 2019). This is especially prevalent in polygynous marriages or when males are expected to care for their aging parents. In turn, when parents favor daughters it is usually explained by the shortage of the particular sex or "helpers at the nest", where daughters are considered the more helpful sex: girls tend to more chores than boys and help more with housework and care for younger children, which benefits the family economically (Bereczkei & Dunbar, 1997; Quinlan et al., 2005). Daughter-biased investment has been observed in several populations, including the American Hutterites communities in Tibet and China, the !Kung in Botswana, and the Hungarian and Serbian Roma (Hassan et al., 2019; Bereczkei & Dunbar, 1997; Čvorović, 2022).

1.2.6.2 Birth Order

The relevance of birth order to parental investment is largely related to age of offspring (Hertwig et al., 2002). Evolutionary theory suggests that parents tend to place much greater value in older offspring as offspring reproductive value increases with higher age. Age is correlated with reproductive value, defined as the expected future reproductive output of an individual at a given age. In social sciences, this is explained by the resource dilution hypothesis, an assumption that having more siblings implies a dilution of parental resources (Downey, 2001). However, the results are not always consistent with either of the two models. Extensive literature among Western populations documents the effects of birth order on various individual outcomes, with later-born children faring worse than their siblings: for instance, there is a negative relationship between child birth order and height, education and IQ, and income and survival (review in Lin et al., 2020). Recent studies also show an association between birth order and parental investment, as first-born children tend to receive greater attention and cognitive stimulation in early childhood (Pruckner et al., 2021). Furthermore, pre- and post-natal maternal behavior appears to favor first-borns: prenatal care and breastfeeding seem to be greater in the first pregnancy (Lehmann et al., 2018). Conversely, younger siblings in developing countries may fare better (Andersen & Mine Gunes, 2023). Among non-Western populations, higher birth order is associated with higher birth weight and early child survival, possibly as a consequence of "helpers-at-the-nest", i.e., older siblings engaging in childcare or other work, or through increased parental experience in child care and increased effort with parental age (Hertwig et al., 2002). Birth order and parental investment outcomes may have a non-linear association, with first and last born offspring benefiting from periods of exclusive parental investment, with middle-born offspring being at a disadvantage.

1.2.6.3 Child Health

From a parental investment perspective, it is expected that higher reproductive value of a child should correspond to higher levels of investment. Thus, it is expected that children with low reproductive value are more likely to be neglected, maltreated, and at greater at risk of infanticide (Daly & Wilson, 1983, 1988). Furthermore, parents living in poverty are expected to display low investment in at-risk infants (Scheper-Hughes, 2012), while parents in more affluent environments (as in many Western countries) are expected to show high investment in at-risk infants (Beaulieu & Bugental, 2008). Evolutionary theory suggests that maternal decisions are dependent on complex computations around a child's probable reproductive outcomes and maternal own ability (cognitively, emotionally, or in terms of actual resources) to provide care for the child (Hrdy, 1999; Beaulieu & Bugental, 2008).

Generally, all things being equal, parents will favor healthier children. Child's weight at birth has been often used as an indicator for initial health (Lynch & Brooks, 2013). Low birthweight is expected to influence a child's reproductive value, being a significant predictor of early childhood growth and development but also later life outcomes, including education, employment, and life-long health (Gillion, 2017). Children born with a low birthweight (<2500 g) are at a higher risk of chronic diseases later in life, which are likely to be detrimental to an individual's fitness (Thomas et al., 2004). At the same time, lower birth weight is one of the key indicators of reduced maternal investment in pregnancy (Coall & Chisholm, 2003). Studies have found that parents tend to favor fitter, healthier children, i.e., children with normal birth weight tend to receive more parental investment than children with low birth weight, while the negative effects may be mitigated by increased maternal education and socioeconomic status (SES) (Restrepo, 2016; Gillion, 2017).

Research has found both compensating as well as reinforcing parental behavior in regard to birthweight, by SES. For instance, the current literature shows great variability across the SES gradients, yielding contradictory results. Studies have found that the lower the socioeconomic status, the lower the biases in investment (Gibson & Sear, 2010). Others have found that higher SES mothers tend to invest more in less-advantaged children (Fan & Porter, 2020). Thus, high-SES parents tend to compensate for a child's disadvantage in birth weight by investing more in low-birth weight children as they can afford the more costly efforts (Bugental & Beaulieu, 2003; Hsin, 2012). In turn, lower-SES parents, in order to reduce the risk of investment, tend to reinforce birth differences by investing in more advantaged children (normal birth weight). In contrast, some studies found the opposite: economically advantaged parents tended to provide more investment to more advantaged children, while others found no parental responses to birth weight or other advantage-related differentials (Grätz & Torche, 2016; Abufhele et al., 2017).

Literature and research on the effects of child advantage at birth on parental investment in developing countries is scant, and may vary across different ethnic groups (Prevoo & Tamis-LeMonda, 2017). Ethnic-minority parents are more likely than majority parents to be from low SES, albeit that there is considerable variation in parental behavior within socioeconomic strata (Knauer et al., 2018).

References

Abufhele, A., Behrman, J., & Bravo, D. (2017). Parental preferences and allocations of investments in children's learning and health within families. *Social Science and Medicine, 194,* 76–86. https://doi.org/10.1016/j.socscimed.2017.09.051

Andersen, D. C., & Mine Gunes, P. (2023). Birth order effects in the developed and developing world: Evidence from international test scores. IZA Discussion Papers, No. 15931, Institute of Labor Economics (IZA), Bonn https://docs.iza.org/dp15931.pdf.

Ármás, J. (2023). Lost generations losing generation: The consequences of the demographic crisis in the Western Balkans. *Foreign Policy Review, 16*(1), 109–120. https://doi.org/10.47706/KKIFPR.2023.1.109-120

Barker, D. J. (2004). The developmental origins of well–being. *Philosophical Transactions of the Royal Society of London. Series B: Biological Sciences, 359*(1449), 1359–1366. https://doi.org/10.1098/rstb.2004.1518

Barkow, J. H., Cosmides, L., & Tooby, J. (Eds.). (1992). *The adapted mind: Evolutionary psychology and the generation of culture.* Oxford University Press.

Bearak, J. M., Popinchalk, A., Beavin, C., Ganatra, B., Moller, A. B., Tunçalp, Ö., & Alkema, L. (2022). Country-specific estimates of unintended pregnancy and abortion incidence: A global comparative analysis of levels in 2015–2019. *BMJ Global Health, 7*(3), e007151. https://doi.org/10.1136/bmjgh-2021-007151

Bearak, J., Popinchalk, A., Ganatra, B., Moller, A. B., Tunçalp, Ö., Beavin, C., ... and Alkema, L. (2020). Unintended pregnancy and abortion by income, region, and the legal status of abortion: Estimates from a comprehensive model for 1990–2019. *Lancet Global Health, 8*(9), e1152-e1161. https://doi.org/10.1016/S2214-109X(20)30315-6

Beaulieu, D. A., & Bugental, D. (2008). Contingent parental investment: An evolutionary framework for understanding early interaction between mothers and children. *Evolution and Human Behavior, 29*(4), 249–255. https://doi.org/10.1016/j.evolhumbehav.2008.01.002

Bellizzi, S., Mannava, P., Nagai, M., & Sobel, H. L. (2020). Reasons for discontinuation of contraception among women with a current unintended pregnancy in 36 low and middle-income countries. *Contraception, 101*(1), 26–33. https://doi.org/10.1016/j.contraception.2019.09.006

Bereczkei, T., & Dunbar, R. I. (1997). Female-biased reproductive strategies in a Hungarian Gypsy population. *Proceedings of the Royal Society of London Series B: Biological Sciences, 264*(1378), 17–22. https://doi.org/10.1098/rspb.1997.0003

Berg, V., Miettinen, A., Jokela, M., & Rotkirch, A. (2020). Shorter birth intervals between siblings are associated with increased risk of parental divorce. *PLoS One, 15*(1), e0228237. https://doi.org/10.1371/journal.pone.0228237

Bergsvik, J., Fauske, A., & Hart, R. K. (2021). Can policies stall the fertility fall? A systematic review of the (quasi-) experimental literature. *Population and Development Review, 47*(4), 913–964. https://doi.org/10.1111/padr.12431

Bjorklund, D. F., & Myers, A. J. (2019). The evolution of parenting and evolutionary approaches to childrearing. In M. H. Bornstein (Ed.), *Handbook of parenting: Biology and ecology of parenting* (pp. 3–29). Routledge/Taylor and Francis Group.

Bjorklund, D. F., Myers, A. J., & Bartolo-Kira, A. (2020). Human child-rearing and family from an evolutionary perspective. In F. J. R. van de Vijver & W. K. Halford (Eds.), *Cross-cultural family research and practice* (pp. 13–55). Elsevier.

Blume, M. (2009). The reproductive benefits of religious affiliation. In E. Voland & W. Schiefenhövel (Eds.), *The biological evolution of religious mind and behavior* (pp. 117–126). Springer Science + Business Media.

Borgerhoff Mulder, M. (1991). Human behavioural ecology. In J. R. Krebs & N. B. Davies (Eds.), *Behavioural ecology: An evolutionary approach* (pp. 69–98). Blackwell Scientific.

Boyd, R., & Richerson, P. J. (1985). *Culture and the evolutionary process.* University of Chicago Press.

Braza, F. (2004). Human prenatal investment affected by maternal age and parity. *Human Ecology, 32*, 163–175. https://doi.org/10.1023/B:HUEC.0000019761.98723.af

Bugental, D. B., & Beaulieu, D. A. (2003). A bio-social cognitive approach to understanding and promoting the outcomes of children with medical and physical disorders. In R. Kail (Ed.), *Advances in child development and behavior* (Vol. 31, pp. 129–258). Academic.

Buss, D. (2019). *Evolutionary psychology: The new science of the mind*. Routledge.

Cameron, E. Z., & Dalerum, F. (2009). A Trivers-Willard effect in contemporary humans: Male-biased sex ratios among billionaires. *PLoS One, 4*(1), e4195. https://doi.org/10.1371/journal.pone.0004195

Cavalli-Sforza, L. L., & Feldman, M. W. (1981). *Cultural transmission and evolution: A quantitative approach*. Princeton University Press.

Chisholm, J. S., Ellison, P. T., Evans, J., Lee, P. C., Lieberman, L. S., Pavlik, Z., et al. (1993). Death, hope, and sex: Life-history theory and the development of reproductive strategies [and comments and reply]. *Current Anthropology, 34*(1), 1–24. https://doi.org/10.1086/204131

Clutton-Brock, T. H. (1984). Reproductive effort and terminal investment in iteroparous animals. *The American Naturalist, 123*(2), 212–229. https://doi.org/10.1086/284198

Clutton-Brock, T. H. (1991). *The evolution of parental care* (Vol. 368). Princeton University Press.

Clutton-Brock, T. H. (2019). *The evolution of parental care*. Princeton University Press.

Coall, D. A., & Chisholm, J. S. (2003). Evolutionary perspectives on pregnancy: Maternal age at menarche and infant birth weight. *Social Science and Medicine, 57*(10), 1771–1781. https://doi.org/10.1016/S0277-9536(03)00022-4

Coall, D. A., & Chisholm, J. S. (2010). Reproductive development and parental investment during pregnancy: Moderating influence of mother's early environment. *American Journal of Human Biology, 22*(2), 143–153. https://doi.org/10.1002/ajhb.20965

Coe, K., & Čvorović, J. (2017). The health of Romanian gypsy women in Serbia. *Health Care for Women International, 38*(4), 409–422. https://doi.org/10.1080/07399332.2017.1292278

Costa, M. E., Trumble, B., Kaplan, H., & Gurven, M. D. (2018). Child nutritional status among births exceeding ideal family size in a high fertility population. *Maternal and Child Nutrition, 14*(4), e12625. https://doi.org/10.1111/mcn.12625

Crespi, B., & Summers, K. (2014). Inclusive fitness theory for the evolution of religion. *Animal Behaviour, 92*, 313–323. https://doi.org/10.1016/j.anbehav.2014.02.013

Čvorović, J. (2004). Sexual and reproductive strategies among Serbian Gypsies. *Population and Environment, 25*(3), 217–242. https://doi.org/10.1007/s11111-004-4485-y

Čvorović, J. (2011). The differential impact of religion on life history and reproductive strategy: Muslim and orthodox gypsies in Serbia. *Mankind Quarterly, 51*(3), 330–348. https://doi.org/10.46469/mq.2011.51.3.5

Čvorović, J. (2014). *The Roma: A Balkan underclass*. Ulster Institute for Social Research.

Čvorović, J. (2020). Child wantedness and low weight at birth: Differential parental investment among Roma. *Behavioral Sciences, 10*(6), 102. https://doi.org/10.3390/bs10060102

Čvorović, J. (2022). Maternal age at marriage and child nutritional status and development: Evidence from Serbian Roma communities. *Public Health Nutrition, 25*(5), 1183–1193. https://doi.org/10.1017/S1368980022000544

Čvorović, J. (2024). The impact of welfare on maternal investment and sibling competition: Evidence from Serbian Roma communities. *Journal of Biosocial Science, 56*(3), 560–573. https://doi.org/10.1017/S0021932023000184

Čvorović, J., & Coe, K. (2017). Reproductive investment and health costs in Roma women. *International Journal of Environmental Research and Public Health, 14*(11), 1337. https://doi.org/10.3390/ijerph14111337

Daly, M., & Wilson, M. (1983). *Sex, evolution and behavior: Adaptions for reproduction*. Willard Grant Press.

Daly, M., & Wilson, M. (1988). *Homicide*. NY: Aldine.

References

Deogan, C., Abrahamsson, K., Mannheimer, L., & Björkenstam, C. (2022). Having a child without wanting to? Estimates and contributing factors from a population-based survey in Sweden. *Scandinavian Journal of Public Health, 50*(2), 215–222. https://doi.org/10.1177/1403494820965762

Dhingra, S., & Pingali, P. L. (2021). Effects of short birth spacing on birth-order differences in child stunting: Evidence from India. *Proceedings of the National Academy of Sciences, 118*(8), e2017834118. https://doi.org/10.1073/pnas.2017834118

Downey, D. B. (2001). Number of siblings and intellectual development: The resource dilution explanation. *American Psychologist, 56*(6–7), 497. https://doi.org/10.1037/0003-066x.56.6-7.497

Fan, W., & Porter, C. (2020). Reinforcement or compensation? Parental responses to children's revealed human capital levels. *Journal of Population Economics, 33*(1), 233–270. https://doi.org/10.1007/s00148-019-00752-7

Fessler, D. M., Navarrete, C. D., Hopkins, W., & Izard, M. K. (2005). Examining the terminal investment hypothesis in humans and chimpanzees: Associations among maternal age, parity, and birth weight. *American Journal of Physical Anthropology, 127*(1), 95–104. https://doi.org/10.1002/ajpa.20039

Figueredo, A. J., Vásquez, G., Brumbach, B. H., Schneider, S. M., Sefcek, J. A., Tal, I. R., et al. (2006). Consilience and life history theory: From genes to brain to reproductive strategy. *Developmental Review, 26*(2), 243–275. https://doi.org/10.1016/j.dr.2006.02.002

Fingerman, K. L., Kim, K., Davis, E. M., Furstenberg, F. F., Jr., Birditt, K. S., & Zarit, S. H. (2015). "I'll give you the world": Socioeconomic differences in parental support of adult children. *Journal of Marriage and Family, 77*(4), 844–865. https://doi.org/10.1111/jomf.12204

Fisher, R. A. (1999). *The genetical theory of natural selection: A complete variorum edition*. Oxford University Press.

Frosh, S. (2004). Religious influences on parenting. In M. Hoghugh, N. Long, & N. (Eds.), *Handbook of parenting: Theory and research for practice* (pp. 98–109). SAGE Publications.

Gamella, J. F. (2018). Marriage, gender and transnational migrations in fertility transitions of Romanian Roma women. *Intersections. East European Journal of Society and Politics, 4*(2), 57–85. https://doi.org/10.17356/ieejsp.v4i2.389

Garbarino, J. (1985). An ecological approach to child maltreatment. In L. H. Pelton (Ed.), *The social context of child abuse and neglect* (pp. 228–267). Human Sciences Press, Inc.

Gettler, L. T., Boyette, A. H., & Rosenbaum, S. (2020). Broadening perspectives on the evolution of human paternal care and fathers' effects on children. *Annual Review of Anthropology, 49*(1), 141–160. https://doi.org/10.1146/annurev-anthro-102218-011216

Gibson, M. A., & Lawson, D. W. (2011). "Modernization" increases parental investment and sibling resource competition: Evidence from a rural development initiative in Ethiopia. *Evolution and Human Behavior, 32*(2), 97–105. https://doi.org/10.1016/j.evolhumbehav.2010.10.002

Gibson, M. A., & Sear, R. (2010). Does wealth increase parental investment biases in child education? Evidence from two African populations on the cusp of the fertility transition. *Current Anthropology, 51*(5), 693–701.

Gillion, L. (2017). Birth weight as Destiny? How parental investment reinforces the birth weight educational gap. *Journal of Social, Behavioral, and Health Sciences, 11*(1), 6. https://doi.org/10.5590/JSBHS.2017.11.1.6

Grätz, M., & Torche, F. (2016). Compensation or reinforcement? The stratification of parental responses to children's early ability. *Demography, 53*(6), 1883–1904. https://doi.org/10.1007/s13524-016-0527-1

Halla, M., Lackner, M., & Scharler, J. (2016). Does the welfare state destroy the family? Evidence from OECD member countries. *The Scandinavian Journal of Economics, 118*(2), 292–323. https://doi.org/10.1111/sjoe.12144

Hassan, A., Schaffnit, S. B., Sear, R., Urassa, M., & Lawson, D. W. (2019). Fathers favour sons, mothers don't discriminate: Sex-biased parental care in northwestern Tanzania. *Evolutionary Human Sciences, 1*, e13. https://doi.org/10.1017/ehs.2019.14

Helfrecht, C., Roulette, J. W., Lane, A., Sintayehu, B., & Meehan, C. L. (2020). Life history and socioecology of infancy. *American Journal of Physical Anthropology, 173*(4), 519–629. https://doi.org/10.1002/ajpa.24145

Hertwig, R., Davis, J. N., & Sulloway, F. J. (2002). Parental investment: How an equity motive can produce inequality. *Psychological Bulletin, 128*(5), 728. https://doi.org/10.1037/0033-2909.128.5.728

Hill, K., & Kaplan, H. (1999). Life history traits in humans: Theory and empirical studies. *Annual Review of Anthropology, 28*(1), 397–430. https://doi.org/10.1146/annurev.anthro.28.1.397

Hinkle, S. N., Albert, P. S., Mendola, P., Sjaarda, L. A., Yeung, E., Boghossian, N S., & Laughon, S. K. (2014). The association between parity and birthweight in a longitudinal consecutive pregnancy cohort. *Paediatric and Perinatal Epidemiology, 28*(2), 106–115. https://doi.org/10.1111/ppe.12099

Hrdy, S. B. (1999). *Mother nature*. Chatto and Windus.

Hsin, A. (2012). Is biology destiny? Birth weight and differential parental treatment. *Demography, 49*, 1385–1405. https://doi.org/10.1007/s13524-012-0123-y

Jasienska, G. (2017). Costs of reproduction, health, and life span in women. In G. Jasienska, D. Sherry, & D. Holmes (Eds.), *The arc of life: Evolution and health across the life course* (pp. 159–176). Springer.

Kaplan, H., Hill, K., Lancaster, J., & Hurtado, A. M. (2000). A theory of human life history evolution: Diet, intelligence, and longevity. *Evolutionary Anthropology, 9*(4), 156–185. https://doi.org/10.1002/1520-6505(2000)9:4<156::AID-EVAN5>3.0.CO;2-7

Kaplan, H. S., & Gangestad, S. W. (2015). Life history theory and evolutionary psychology. In D. Buss (Ed.), *The handbook of evolutionary psychology* (pp. 68–95). Wiley. https://doi.org/10.1002/9780470939376.ch2

King, J. C. (2003). The risk of maternal nutritional depletion and poor outcomes increases in early or closely spaced pregnancies. *The Journal of Nutrition, 133*(5), 1732S–1736S. https://doi.org/10.1093/jn/133.5.1732S

Kirkwood, T. B., & Rose, M. R. (1991). Evolution of senescence: Late survival sacrificed for reproduction. *Philosophical Transactions of the Royal Society of London. Series B: Biological Sciences, 332*(1262), 15–24. https://doi.org/10.1098/rstb.1991.0028

Knauer, H. A., Ozer, E. J., Dow, W., & Fernald, L. C. (2018). Stimulating parenting practices in indigenous and non-indigenous Mexican communities. *International Journal of Environmental Research and Public Health, 15*(1), 29. https://doi.org/10.3390/ijerph15010029

Lancaster, J., & Whitten, P. (1990). *Sharing in human evolution. Anthropology: Contemporary perspectives* (6th ed.). Scott, Foresman/Little Brown Higher Education.

Lawson, D. W., & Mace, R. (2008). Sibling configuration and childhood growth in contemporary British families. *International Journal of Epidemiology, 37*(6), 1408–1421. https://doi.org/10.1093/ije/dyn116

Lawson, D. W., & Mace, R. (2011). Parental investment and the optimization of human family size. *Philosophical Transactions of the Royal Society B: Biological Sciences, 366*(1563), 333–343. https://doi.org/10.1098/rstb.2010.0297

Lehmann, J. Y. K., Nuevo-Chiquero, A., & Vidal-Fernandez, M. (2018). The early origins of birth order differences in children's outcomes and parental behavior. *Journal of Human Resources, 53*(1), 123–156. https://doi.org/10.3368/jhr.53.1.0816-8177

Lin, W., Pantano, J., & Sun, S. (2020). Birth order and unwanted fertility. *Journal of Population Economics, 33*(2), 413–440.

Lynch, R., Wasielewski, H., & Cronk, L. (2018). Sexual conflict and the Trivers-Willard hypothesis: Females prefer daughters and males prefer sons. *Scientific Reports, 8*(1), 15463. https://doi.org/10.1038/s41598-018-33650-1

Lynch, J. L., & Brooks, R. (2013). Low birth weight and parental investment: Do parents favor the fittest child? *Journal of Marriage and Family, 75*(3), 533–543. https://doi.org/10.1111/jomf.12028

References

Merklinger-Gruchala, A., Jasienska, G., & Kapiszewska, M. (2019). Paternal investment and low birth weight—the mediating role of parity. *PLoS One, 14*(1), e0210715. https://doi.org/10.1371/journal.pone.0210715

Nestorová Dická, J. (2021). Demographic changes in Slovak Roma Communities in the new millennium. *Sustainability, 13*(7), 3735. https://doi.org/10.3390/su13073735

Nettle, D., Gibson, M. A., Lawson, D. W., & Sear, R. (2013). Human behavioral ecology: Current research and future prospects. *Behavioral Ecology, 24*(5), 1031–1040. https://doi.org/10.1093/beheco/ars222

Palmer, C. T., Steadman, L., & B. and Coe, K. (2005). More kin: An effect of the tradition of marriage. *Structure and Dynamics, 1*(2).

Pianka, E. R. (1970). On r-and K-selection. *The American Naturalist, 104*(940), 592–597. https://doi.org/10.1086/282697

Pike, I. L. (2005). Maternal stress and fetal responses: Evolutionary perspectives on preterm delivery. *American Journal of Human Biology, 17*(1), 55–65. https://doi.org/10.1002/ajhb.20093

Pimentel, J., Ansari, U., Omer, K., et al. (2020). Factors associated with short birth interval in low- and middle-income countries: A systematic review. *BMC Pregnancy and Childbirth, 20*, 156. https://doi.org/10.1186/s12884-020-2852-z

Prall, S. P., & Scelza, B. A. (2020). Why men invest in non-biological offspring: Paternal care and paternity confidence among Himba pastoralists. *Proceedings of the Royal Society B, 287*(1922), 20192890. https://doi.org/10.1098/rspb.2019.2890

Prevoo, M. J., & Tamis-LeMonda, C. S. (2017). Parenting and globalization in western countries: Explaining differences in parent–child interactions. *Current Opinion in Psychology, 15*, 33–39. https://doi.org/10.1016/j.copsyc.2017.02.003

Pritchett, L. H. (1994). Desired fertility and the impact of population policies. *Population and Development Review, 20*, 1–55. https://doi.org/10.2307/2137605

Promislow, D. E., & Harvey, P. H. (1990). Living fast and dying young: A comparative analysis of life-history variation among mammals. *Journal of Zoology, 220*(3), 417–437. https://doi.org/10.1111/j.1469-7998.1990.tb04316.x

Pruckner, G. J., Schneeweis, N., Schober, T., & Zweimüller, M. (2021). Birth order, parental health investment, and health in childhood. *Journal of Health Economics, 76*, 102426. https://doi.org/10.1016/j.jhealeco.2021.102426

Quinlan, R. J. (2007). Human parental effort and environmental risk. *Proceedings of the Royal Society B: Biological Sciences, 274*(1606), 121–125. https://doi.org/10.1098/rspb.2006.3690

Quinlan, R., Quinlan, M., & Flinn, M. (2005). Local resource enhancement and sex-biased breastfeeding in a Caribbean community. *Current Anthropology, 46*(3), 471–480. https://doi.org/10.1086/430017

Restrepo, B. J. (2016). Parental investment responses to a low birth weight outcome: Who compensates and who reinforces? *Journal of Population Economics, 29*(4), 969–989. https://doi.org/10.1007/s00148-016-0590-3

Roubinov, D. S., & Boyce, W. T. (2017). Parenting and SES: Relative values or enduring principles? *Current Opinion in Psychology, 15*, 162–167. https://doi.org/10.1016/j.copsyc.2017.03.001

Rutstein, S. O. (2005). Effects of preceding birth intervals on neonatal, infant and under-five years mortality and nutritional status in developing countries: Evidence from the demographic and health surveys. *International Journal of Gynecology & Obstetrics, 89*, S7–S24. https://doi.org/10.1016/j.ijgo.2004.11.012

Savage, T., Derraik, J. G., Miles, H. L., Mouat, F., Hofman, P. L., & Cutfield, W. S. (2013). Increasing maternal age is associated with taller stature and reduced abdominal fat in their children. *PLoS One, 8*(3), e58869. https://doi.org/10.1371/journal.pone.0058869

Scheper-Hughes, N. (Ed.). (2012). *Child survival: Anthropological perspectives on the treatment and maltreatment of children* (Vol. 11). Springer Science and Business Media.

Sear, R. (2011). Parenting and families. In V. Swami (Ed.), *Evolutionary psychology: A critical introduction* (pp. 215–250). BPS Blackwell.

Sear, R. (2015). Evolutionary contributions to the study of human fertility. *Population Studies, 69*(Suppl 1), S39–S55. https://doi.org/10.1080/00324728.2014.982905

Sear, R. (2021). The male breadwinner nuclear family is not the 'traditional' human family, and promotion of this myth may have adverse health consequences. *Philosophical Transactions of the Royal Society B, 376*(1827), 20200020. https://doi.org/10.1098/rstb.2020.0020

Sear, R., & Mace, R. (2008). Who keeps children alive? A review of the effects of kin on child survival. *Evolution and Human Behavior, 29*(1), 1–18. https://doi.org/10.1016/j.evolhumbehav.2007.10.001

Shaver, J. H. (2017). Why and how do religious individuals, and some religious groups, achieve higher relative fertility? *Religion, Brain and Behavior, 7*(4), 324–327. https://doi.org/10.1080/2153599X.2016.1249920

Shenk, M. K. (2011). Our children: Parental decisions—how much to invest in your offspring. In U. J. Frey et al. (Eds.), *Essential building blocks of human nature* (The Frontiers collection) (pp. 17–38). Springer.

Silk, J. B. (1990). Human adoption in evolutionary perspective. *Human Nature, 1*, 25–52.

Singh, P., & Singh, K. K. (2024). Trends, patterns and predictors of high-risk fertility behaviour among Indian women: Evidence from National Family Health Survey. *BMC Public Health, 24*(1), 626. https://doi.org/10.1186/s12889-024-18046-3

Sparks, C. S. (2011). Parental investment and socioeconomic status influences on children's height in Honduras: An analysis of national data. *American Journal of Human Biology, 23*(1), 80–88. https://doi.org/10.1002/ajhb.21104

Steadman, L. B., & Palmer, C. T. (2015). *Supernatural and natural selection: Religion and evolutionary success*. Routledge.

Stearns, S. (1992). *The evolution of life histories*. Oxford University Press.

Stucky, K., & Gardner, A. (2022). The evolution of religiosity by kin selection. *Religion, Brain and Behavior, 12*(4), 347–364. https://doi.org/10.1080/2153599X.2022.2076727

Symons, D. (1979). *The evolution of human sexuality*. Oxford University Press.

Symons, D. (1987). Darwin and human nature. *Behavioral and Brain Sciences, 10*(1), 89–89. https://doi.org/10.1017/S0140525X00056508

Thomas, F., Teriokhin, A. T., Budilova, E. V., Brown, S. P., Renaud, F., & Guegan, J. F. (2004). Human birthweight evolution across contrasting environments. *Journal of Evolutionary Biology, 17*(3), 542–553. https://doi.org/10.1111/j.1420-9101.2004.00705.x

Tifferet, S., Manor, O., Constantini, S., Friedman, O., & Yoel, E. (2007). Parental investment in children with chronic disease: The effect of child's and mother's age. *Evolutionary Psychology, 5*(4), 844–859. https://doi.org/10.1177/147470490700500413

Traficonte, D. M., & Maestripieri, D. (2015). Parent–offspring conflict. In P. Whelehan & A. Bolin (Eds.), *The international encyclopedia of human sexuality* (pp. 861–1042). Wiley.

Trevathan, W. R. (2017). *Human birth: An evolutionary perspective*. Routledge.

Trivers, R. L. (1972). Parental investment and sexual selection. In B. Campbell (Ed.), *Sexual selection and the descent of man, 1871–1971* (pp. 136–179). Aldine.

Trivers, R. L. (1974). Parent-offspring conflict. *American Zoologist, 14*(1), 249–264. https://doi.org/10.1093/icb/14.1.249

Trivers, R. L., & Willard, D. E. (1973). Natural selection of parental ability to vary the sex ratio of offspring. *Science, 179*, 90–92. https://doi.org/10.1126/science.179.4068.90

Troutman, M., Rafique, S., & Plowden, T. C. (2020). Are higher unintended pregnancy rates among minorities a result of disparate access to contraception? *Contraception and Reproductive Medicine, 5*, 1–6. https://doi.org/10.1186/s40834-020-00118-5

Uggla, C., & Mace, R. (2016). Parental investment in child health in sub-Saharan Africa: A cross-national study of health-seeking behaviour. *Royal Society Open Science, 3*(2), 150460. https://doi.org/10.1098/rsos.150460

UNICEF. (2015). Early childhood development. The analysis of Multiple Indicator Cluster Survey data. https://www.unicef.org/serbia/media/1201/file/MICS%20ECD.pdf accessed July 2024.

References

van Noordwijk, M. A. (2012). From maternal investment to lifetime maternal care. In J. C. Mitani, J. Call, P. M. Kappeler, R. A. Palombit, & J. B. Silk (Eds.), *The evolution of primate societies* (pp. 321–342). Chicago.

Velux Foundation. (2019). Roma in Europe. https://www.researchgate.net/publication/341111319_2019_Roma_in_Europe. Accessed October 2024.

Walker, R. S., Gurven, M., Burger, O., & Hamilton, M. J. (2008). The trade-off between number and size of offspring in humans and other primates. *Proceedings of the Royal Society B: Biological Sciences, 275*(1636), 827–834. https://doi.org/10.1098/rspb.2007.1511

Weiss, M. N., Ellis, S., Franks, D. W., Nielsen, M. L. K., Cant, M. A., Johnstone, R. A., et al. (2023). Costly lifetime maternal investment in killer whales. *Current Biology, 33*(4), 744–748. https://doi.org/10.1016/j.cub.2022.12.057

Williams, G. (1966). *Adaptation and natural selection: A critique of some current evolutionary thought*. Princeton University Press.

Wilson, E. O. (1975). *Sociobiology: The new synthesis*. Harvard University Press.

Wilson, E. O. (1978). *On human nature*. Harvard University Press.

Winterhalder, B., & Leslie, P. (2002). Risk-sensitive fertility: The variance compensation hypothesis. *Evolution and Human Behavior, 23*(1), 59–82.

Zeleke, L. B., Alemu, A. A., Kassahun, E. A., Aynalem, B. Y., Hassen, H. Y., & Kassa, G. M. (2021). Individual and community level factors associated with unintended pregnancy among pregnant women in Ethiopia. *Scientific Reports, 11*(1), 12699. https://doi.org/10.1038/s41598-021-92157-4

Chapter 2
Unwanted Childbearing

The concept of unintended pregnancy has been used by demographers, public health and social science researchers to investigate maternal and, in the case of live birth, child outcomes. Recent data show that an estimated 34% in Western Europe to 54% in Eastern Europe of pregnancies are unintended, despite 50 years of available effective contraception. In fact, contraception prevalence has been found to have no effect on excess fertility, while the challenge of reducing fertility has translated into one of reducing fertility desire rather than reducing unwanted fertility. Unwanted childbearing-- the mismatch between actual and desired fertility-- is extensive in high-fertility societies. Anthropological studies and ethnographies among traditional societies provide an in-depth insight into the socioeconomic and cultural circumstances relating to why some children are deemed undesirable, how and why unwanted children are treated by their mothers and caregivers, and the physical and mental consequences of being an unwanted child. Disinvesting in unwanted children has occurred in our species since its origin, and occurs in many cultures and populations. Throughout history and across cultures, mothers have chosen various ways to disinvest in unwanted children, e.g. infanticide, abandonment, giving the child to kin to raise, and leaving the child at foundling hospitals or orphanages. Maternal decision-making is dependent on specific demographic, ecological, and cultural contexts, where maternal options are additionally restricted by fitness trade-offs.

2.1 Unintended Pregnancies and Unwanted Children

One important factor, albeit that it has received limited attention when investigating birth differentials and parental biases in investment, is unwanted childbearing. Childbearing intentions are predicated on wantedness: unintended/unplanned or mistimed pregnancies may result in unwanted childbearing and unwanted births (Santelli et al., 2003). The differences between wanted and unwanted fertility has long been a focus of fertility research, reflecting theoretical as well as policy concerns (Casterline & El-Zeini, 2022). The policy goals tend to be women-centered, concentrating on fulfilling an unmet need for contraception and family planning in order to reduce unwanted conception, which, in the absence of abortion, leads to unwanted childbearing.

Unintended childbearing may be associated with adverse maternal behavior during pregnancy and low investment in utero as it may result in consequent poor perinatal outcomes, such as low birthweight (defined as birth weight less than 2500 gr), infant mortality, postnatal child malnutrition, illness, abuse and neglect, and even death (Shah et al., 2011).

The concept of unintended pregnancy has been used by demographers, public health and social science researchers to address maternal and, in the case of live births, child outcomes. Unintended pregnancies are further classified as unwanted pregnancies (occurring when no more children were wanted) or mistimed pregnancies (occurring at a different time than desired (Santelli et al., 2003). Despite the increased use of contraceptives over the years, unintended pregnancy remains a public health concern throughout the world. Globally, nearly half of all pregnancies, totaling 121 million each year, are unintended (Hall et al., 2017). Recent data show that an estimated 34% in Western Europe to 54% in Eastern Europe of pregnancies are unintended, despite 50 years of effective, available contraception (ESHRE Capri Workshop Group, 2018).

Numerous studies have highlighted that unmet need for contraception may be an underlying reason for unintended pregnancies: in several low-resource settings, the findings suggest a strong positive association between unmet need for contraception and unwanted pregnancy (Bishwajit et al., 2017; Yaya & Ghose, 2018). Thus, unmet need for contraception is used to explain persistent high fertility: often, there is a significant disparity between women's intention and their actual use of contraception, which leads to many women having unintended pregnancies (Lutalo et al., 2018). This intention discrepancy-women who stated in surveys that they wanted no more children but were doing nothing about it—was first termed the "KAP-Gap" but later replaced by "unmet need for contraception" (Cleland et al., 2014). In the past decades, unmet need for contraception has been regarded as a key indicator for monitoring the progress of family planning programs. The concept, however, was greeted with considerable criticism: many have argued that using unmet need as a measure of contraceptive demand may be misleading, mostly because a substantial proportion of women identified in surveys as having an unmet need would not use contraceptives even if they were available (Oas, 2016; Callahan & Becker, 2014). Additionally, studies from the field of economics have questioned the effectiveness of increased contraceptive access alone in reducing fertility and unwanted births (Pritchett, 1994). In a study of more than 40 countries, data show that fertility tends to be largely driven by differences in fertility preferences and not by differences in family planning programs and/or contraceptive access (Pritchett, 1994). In fact, almost all the observed variation in fertility across countries can be explained by differences in fertility desire, with one desired child leading to one additional birth. Furthermore, data from a number of countries show that fertility planning reduces average fertility rates by not more than one child per woman (Pritchett, 1994). Thus, contraceptive usage was found to have no effect on excess fertility, whereas the challenge of reducing fertility translates into one of reducing fertility desire, not unwanted fertility. This argument remains the current explanation for fertility decline. In other words, fertility decline for the most part tends to be driven by a decline in the desire for fertility, which, in turn, is influenced by improvements in socio-economic development, infant and child survival rates, and a shifting balance of childbearing costs and benefits (Galor, 2012).

As a consequence of modernization and overall socio-economic development, educational status, especially in women, may play the key role in fertility reduction (Bongaarts & Hodgson, 2022). Everywhere, education is being seen as one of the most powerful predictors of demographic behavior in that, for women, education tends to be positively associated with greater autonomy in decision-making, more knowledge about contraception, higher potential for earnings, reduced infant and child mortality and fewer children (Pritchett, 1994; Cleland et al., 2014; Sandiford et al., 1991).

However, it remains an open question as to whether developmental or family planning programs are truly effective in driving down fertility and unwanted births (Günther & Harttgen, 2016). Overall, demographers typically argue that unwanted childbearing (the mismatch between actual and desired fertility) is widespread in high-fertility societies and can only be reduced by family planning programs, while economists, by and large, maintain that fertility can be reduced through economic development which increases the opportunity costs of raising children. The latter argument is often summed up as a slogan: "Development is the best contraceptive" (Knodel & Van de Walle, 1979:217).

Aside from policy and scientific debates, the drivers of unintended and unwanted pregnancies appear to differ between developed and developing countries. In Western countries, unintended pregnancy may result from non-use of contraceptive methods, contraceptive failure, and sometimes rape (ESHRE Capri Workshop Group, 2018). Abortion is a frequent outcome of unintended pregnancy, which may lead to serious, long-term negative and psychological health effects, including infertility and maternal death. At present, in several high-income countries, unintended pregnancy is in decline: it is estimated that between 12% in Sweden and around 30% in USA of pregnancies carried to term are unplanned; i.e., are either mistimed or unwanted (Brzozowska et al., 2021). In Western countries, women who report that their pregnancies have been unplanned, tend to be young (in their teens or early twenties), of low socioeconomic status, and without a steady partner (ESHRE Capri Workshop Group, 2018). The majority of these pregnancies are the result of contraceptive failure.

In contrast, a large body of literature from low-and-middle income countries has shown that a number of individual, family, community, and program factors impact the incidence of an unintended pregnancy (Gipson et al., 2008). Moreover, qualitative studies from low-and-middle income countries suggest that the desire to maintain a relationship, poor contraceptive knowledge, and misinformation about contraceptive side effects appear to be some of the main reasons for experiencing unintended pregnancies (Ajayi et al., 2021). Additionally, intimate partner violence was found to be a strong risk factor in predicting unintended pregnancy across a variety of settings: according to population risk estimates for 10 countries (Bangladesh, Brazil, Ethiopia, Japan, Namibia, Peru, Samoa, Serbia and Montenegro, Thailand, and United Republic of Tanzania) and studies from 17,518 ever-partnered women, reducing intimate partner violence by 50% would potentially reduce unintended pregnancy by 2–18% (Pallitto et al., 2013).

There are, however, several problems associated with studies of unintended pregnancies. Many countries, including high-income countries, lack data on the proportions of births that are from unintended pregnancies. Even more problematic is the method used to measure unintended pregnancies (ESHRE Capri Workshop Group, 2018). A single, valid measure or common definition does not exist, and studies typically use interchangeable terms, such as whether the pregnancy was planned or unplanned, intended or unintended, wanted or unwanted. Furthermore, measures typically only account for surviving children, and if disadvantaged children suffer higher mortality, this may skew the actual number of unwanted children (Flatø, 2018). The majority of studies use cross-sectional, retrospective reports of pregnancy intention by asking mothers to recall their feelings at the time of conception, or to relate their feelings about their most recent live birth. Retrospective questions about desired family size, timing of pregnancy or "wantedness" are complicated by the fact that desired family size is to some extent likely a rationalization of actual family size, and parents are understandably reluctant to retrospectively report their existing children as unwanted or mistimed.

Most importantly, too, are the significant differences between an unwanted pregnancy and an unwanted child (Guterman, 2015). Maternal feelings about a pregnancy, or assessments of intention, tend to be especially fluid, and may become more supportive of the pregnancy and the child over time. As the pregnancy progresses, mothers may become more likely to embrace the pregnancy more positively and adopt pro-developmental behaviors. For instance, studies in Morocco and India have found that women were more likely to switch to a more positive response in retrospective reports of pregnancy intention, re-categorizing "unwanted" to "wanted" child (Gipson et al., 2008). In contrast, when a mother continues to assess the pregnancy, and especially later on, the child as "unwanted," this reflects an even more extreme sentiment than what she initially described as an unwanted pregnancy (Guterman, 2015). Additionally, parental preferences may also play a part in the assessment: studies have found that parents may also shift from a "wanted" child to an "unwanted" one, if the child's characteristics differ from those the parent was expecting or desiring (Rosenzweig & Wolpin, 1993).

Across cultures, sons and early born children tend to be more desirable than their counterparts, as moderated by family composition (Levine, 1987; Das Gupta et al., 2003). An extreme example of son preference is sex selective abortion, i.e., the systematic elimination of girls-- female fetuses. A large body of literature has documented the phenomenon of "missing" women in countries with a strong social and

2.1 Unintended Pregnancies and Unwanted Children

cultural preference for sons (Rastogi & Sharma, 2022). The usual explanation for son preferences is that frequently, in patriarchal societies, cultural and economic value of sons exceeds those of daughters, whereas son preference may manifest in many ways, ranging from differential allocation of parental and household resources, health seeking behaviors and neglect, abuse of female children, to infanticide (Oomman & Ganatra, 2002). With the increasing availability of ultrasound since the mid-1980s, to present day non-invasive prenatal testing, sex selective abortion began to become widespread (Bowman-Smart et al., 2020). Skewed sex ratios at birth for humans is around 104–106 boys per 100 girls; however, some Asian and European countries have seen sex ratios well in excess of this: numerous studies have documented skewed sex ratios in births in China, Viet Nam, in certain regions of Central Asia and Europe, as well as parts in India, with significant outcome implications for girls (Channon et al., 2021). In India, starting from infancy, daughters receive less parental investment: they are breastfed for a shorter period, receive less childcare, fewer vaccinations and vitamin supplements, they are less likely to be hospitalized, they tend to be shorter in stature, and suffer excess mortality through abortion, infanticide and neglect (Ebert & Vollmer, 2022). In families without the achieved desired number of sons, daughters tend to be even more unwanted at higher birth order and among parents with fewer reproductive opportunities ahead. Some families may engage in son-biased fertility behavior and exceed the planned family size in trying to conceive a boy, thus creating more unwanted children (Bongaarts & Hodgson, 2022).

Explanations of son preference generally highlight cultural customs, religious and social traditions, and economic incentives: sons tend to be preferred because they have a greater wage-earning capacity, especially valued in agrarian subsistence; in addition, sons continue the family line and are expected to provide care to parents in illness and old age (Hesketh & Xing, 2006). In India, there are cultural, local reasons influencing son preference, such as the expense of the dowry, and in China and South Korea, patriarchal family systems (Das Gupta et al., 2003).

In Europe, Montenegro, along with Albania, top of the list of the countries with the greatest skewed sex ratio at birth. For instance, in 2009, there were 114 boys born for every 100 girls; it is estimated that 50 female fetuses were intentionally aborted in Montenegro annually from 2000 until 2014, despite the strict prohibitions against sex-selective abortions (Davidović, 2023). Thus far, sex-selective abortions have created a scarcity of 3000 females in Montenegro, while future projections caution that by 2035, there could be even greater scarcity numbering 8000 females.

Previous systematic reviews showed that research on the relationships between pregnancy intentions (unwanted births) and pregnancy outcomes is limited, while the focus has been on high-income countries (Hall et al., 2017). Overall, results have been mixed, with the gaps in literature suggesting a need for more studies especially from developing populations. The current evidence implies that an unintended pregnancy may influence pre-and -post natal maternal behaviors in ways that can result in poor birth outcomes and infant and child well-being, contingent on environmental and cultural context. The effects of unintended pregnancy may affect child health outcomes for one particular time period, for instance, in the prenatal period, while impacts of unwanted childbearing may also be persistent and cumulative, extending into early childhood and beyond (Gipson et al., 2008).

Anthropological single culture studies and evolutionary theory may contribute to our better understanding of the meaning of unwanted childbearing at the species, individual and cultural levels. Anthropological studies and ethnographies provide in-depth insights into the socioeconomic circumstances and cultural contexts as to why some children are deemed undesirable, and how and why the unwanted children are treated by their mothers and caregivers, along with physical and mental manifestations of being an unwanted child (Scheper-Hughes, 1992; Levine, 1987; Čvorović, 2013). Cross-cultural analyses of human parental investment decisions have found that children who are unlikely to survive and reproduce and, thus, unlikely to be contributors to their parents' fitness, are killed at birth in many societies and, if they are not killed, may experience higher risk of physical abuse and neglect (Daly & Wilson, 1983).

Disinvestment in unwanted children has occurred in our species since its origin, in many cultures and many populations. Throughout history and across cultures, mothers have chosen from a number of ways to disinvest in some of their children: through infanticide, abandonment, passing the child to kin to raise, or leaving the child at foundling hospitals or orphanages. Infanticide (the intentional killing of infants or offspring) of undesired children is documented in all human populations, although to varying degrees, ranging from near zero to over 40% of live births. Infanticide includes death to children less than 1 year; the act termed as filicide when parents commit infanticide of an offspring (Pitt & Bale, 1995). Infanticide is perhaps the most extreme method of failure to invest in early life health (Fenske & Wang, 2023). According to estimates, infanticide may have been the most commonly used method of fertility control during much of human history (Harris & Ross, 1987).

In mammals, female infanticide is widespread and varies in relation to social organization and life history (Lukas & Huchard, 2019). Infanticide by mothers also occurs under similar conditions in non-human primates and several other species, although for primates, unrelated males tend to be the most likely perpetrators. Among humans, biological parents are usually the ones responsible for the largest percentage of infanticides (Hrdy, 1992). Evolutionary theory postulates that the maternal killing of offspring may, under certain conditions, represent an evolved behavioral pattern that increases the reproductive fitness of the mother (Trivers, 1985). Mothers may commit infanticide when an offspring's life expectancy is reduced and, as a result, mothers may benefit from reduced or ceased investment and dedicate resources to future pregnancies. And even though thresholds for maternal investment were likely created by evolving motivational processes, modifications in parental investment are to this day deliberately calculated to achieve economic, cultural, as well as biologically-based ends (Hausfater & Hrdy, 2017). Maternal decision-making is highly dependent on specific demographic, ecological and cultural contexts, where maternal options are additionally constrained by fitness trade-offs (Hrdy, 1992). Mothers committing infanticide tend to be very young, i.e., mothers with high reproductive values are significantly more likely to commit infanticide than are older mothers nearing the end of their reproductive careers. Furthermore, they tend to be affected by adverse economic and social conditions that may jeopardize the survival and thriving of an offspring (Daly & Wilson, 1988). Thus, the child may be killed or left to die if it possesses severe disabilities, or is unwanted for any other reasons.

Historical accounts document how common it was, for instance in ancient Rome and medieval Europe, for children to be abandoned due to adverse circumstances, wrong timing, high fertility, poverty or distinctive child characteristics (Hrdy, 1999). In Europe, prior to the fertility transition, child abuse and general neglect seems to have been common, signifying that some children were not necessarily wanted (Knodel & Van de Walle, 1979). Historically, infanticide was common among unmarried mothers; however, far more common were traditional infant unhygienic and childrearing practices in many parts of Europe, termed by historians as "concealed infanticide" or "infanticide by neglect" Such negligent child-rearing practices may collectively have contributed to the high infant and child mortality rates in much of Europe during the eighteenth and nineteenth centuries. For example, in much of central Europe, the custom of hand feeding, instead of breastfeeding of infants, was commonly practiced, which significantly affected infant mortality, given the inadequate nutritional content of the food fed to infants and the unhygienic environment of the day. Among poor segments of the society, mothers were expected to work alongside other family members and assume primary responsibility for child care, yet infant death was frequently met with indifference or, in some cases, relief from a burden. In the absence of contraceptives, some women continued having unwanted children, as there were few options to do otherwise. The usual explanation is that high fertility persisted as a response to high infant and child mortality; however, high infant mortality rates may also have been, at least in part, the maternal response to unwanted births (Knodel & Van de Walle, 1979:232). Maternal decision-making is dependent on specific demographic, ecological, and cultural contexts, where maternal options are additionally constrained by fitness trade-offs (Hrdy, 1992). Hence, marriage and inheritance rules, religious beliefs and social norms regarding family honor influence parental decision to cease investment in the human infant. The main motives for parents committing infanticide include reduction of family size, family composition and change of the timing of parental investment by the mother (and/or father). In addition to infanticide, mothers may engage in what the literature refers to as "selective neglect", "benign neglect", "masked deprivation", or "passive infanticide'", with all these terms implying the possibility that highly stressed mothers may themselves be contributing to the high rates of infant death as a form of post-partum abortion or indirect family planning (Scheper-Hughes, 1992). "Selective neglect" refers to the gradual reduction of food, attention and curative care necessary for survival of a specific infant or child. The type of neglect chosen may be based on cultural preferences involving the child's sex, birth order or physical characteristics, such as health. In addition, parents may sell off unwanted offspring, abandon the infant to where someone else can take care of it, or give it away to an institution or for adoption (Hrdy, 1992). According to

Hausfater and Hrdy (2017), abandonment of a child should be considered the default "disinvestment strategy" for parents terminating the investment, with infanticide being the last resort when all other options have failed.

Yet infanticide, passive infanticide and reduced investment in an offspring are still common. Among the Nankani of northern Ghana, certain children—usually those who are disabled, abnormal, or developmentally delayed—are treated by their parents with ambivalence and, eventually, aggression (Denham, 2020). It is believed that these children are "spirit children", sent from the bush to provoke misfortune and destroy the family. Upon being identified, some of them are subject to infanticide, either through the administration of herbal decoctions or prolonged parental neglect. Among the !Kung San who live mostly on the western edge of the Kalahari desert, around one in a hundred babies were abandoned at birth and left to die; in many hunter-gatherer societies, anthropologists have documented abandoning of a newborn because it arrived too soon after a still-nursing sibling (Howell, 2017). In some Canadian Eskimo tribes, anthropological studies and sex ratios of children, suggest a female infanticide rate of 66 percent (Pitt & Bale, 1995).

A striking example comes via the work of Nancy Scheper-Hughes (1992). Her ethnography was focused on three generations of shantytown women in northern Brazil, whose lives were characterized by hunger, deprivation and high mortality of their children. Usually, a woman who has lost at least one infant or a child is illiterate, a rural migrant, marginally employed in urban area, and likely to have given birth to four or more other, living children. The women in the study had an average of 9.5 pregnancies; of which 1.4 on average ended in spontaneous or induced abortion or stillbirth; 43% of the live born children died between the ages of 0 to 5 years (3.5 on average per woman); and a further 5% of children died between the ages of 6 and 12 years. Seventy percent of the reported child deaths occurred between birth and 6 months, and 82% of the deaths had occurred by the end of the first year. Breastfeeding was usually sporadic, and weaning often completed as early as the second week of life, and seldom any later than the third or fourth month. Furthermore, children who survived, as well as those who died, usually suffered their first "crisis" (vomiting and diarrhea) by the time they were a month old. Sex preferences existed but were not dominant. In about a third of the families, childhood deaths came in close sequence, occurring either at the start or at the end of the mother's reproductive career. Early childbearing seemed to contribute to the deaths, while at the other end, a number of physical, economic and psychological factors seemed to influence the bias in survivability of later born children. Some women were quite candid in expressing that their last-born children represented a particular burden and that it was in fact a "blessing" that they died in infancy. In this particular setting, maternal preference for stronger, healthier children was obvious ("fighters and survivors"). These women are, as Scheper-Hughes (1992:535) termed them, "family strategists, necessarily allocating scarce resources so that some of their children may be more or less favored for survival".

Moreover, in this particular setting, the death of a child did not evoke much grief, either maternal or public. According to Scheper-Hughes (1992:541), weeping mothers may be chastised by her neighbors and community, reminding her that the death of her child "was for the best". Cause of death was usually explained as *doença de criança* (child's disease, i.e., malnutrition and dehydration), and the suffering child was usually left to die a gradual death, meaning a child was let to fade away without adequate care. This practice, the child's disease in interaction with maternal selective inattention, represents, in other words, "death by gradual neglect" (Scheper-Hughes, 1992:540). The folk illness, *doença de criança* is the major cause of infant and childhood mortality in Northeast Brazil; it is a sociocultural term, developed by the folk medicine and applied to the end stages of severe childhood infectious diseases and malnutrition (Nations, 1992).

Thus, the conventionally understood culture of motherhood and motherly love has in these poverty-stricken slums, assumed a new meaning: many women cannot expect that their children will survive and many use passive infanticide as means to an end. Under these adverse economic and cultural conditions, mothers are prevented from rearing healthy offspring, and infant and child death typically carries with it little expressed grieving or even contemplation, to the extent that child mortality appears accepted and even fated. Scheper-Hughes (1992) explained the selective neglect of children as a direct consequence of women's non-participation in the national economy.

Even so, the Brazilian shantytown women are not alone in their experiences. In many other cultures, such as for instance, several Tibetan communities, differential treatment of more- and less-valued children (wanted and unwanted children) begins at birth, with the wanted ones receiving better, and the latter (unwanted) poorer child care, with these attitudes and behaviors being locally understood and accepted as such (Levine, 1987). Emotional attachment, if any, tends to follow upon assessed child value as either desired/wanted or undesired/unwanted. Thus, local people say they tend to care less about their daughters, and grieve less when they die, these remarks expressed even in front of children. Thus, attitudes of "It doesn't matter if a girl dies" introduce different patterns of child care, based on the value of a given child (Levine, 1987:290).

In these Tibetan communities, after childbirth, mothers are usually allowed much-needed rest and exemption from work; however, when after a less-valued child is born, the mother is denied the customary rest and more nutritional diet. For a desired child, even poor families often go into debt to buy groceries like meat and butter for the benefit of a highly valued child (usually a son); however, even well-off families will withhold buying more expensive goods for the mother of a daughter, or a less-valued son, while the mother is immediately sent to work in the fields. Tibetan women often complain that these customs reduce lactation. When the mother of the unwanted child goes to work, the child is often left alone and hungry for prolonged periods of time, or under the care of less-able caretakers. Even in the situation of illness, the unwanted child will not have the benefit of its mother's presence, since it is not considered as worthy of the mother's lost work time. In contrast, a wanted son will not be left alone when ill but will be attended to by its mother for a full year and, afterwards, whenever he is ill. Less-valued or unwanted children also tend to receive less emotional support from family members, while the mother in effect is punished for giving birth to a child of the wrong sex. More-valued children, especially if they were wanted boys, are fed better foods, and because mothers spend more time at home more with wanted children, these children receive more frequent meals.

In these Tibetan communities, a child may be unwanted for several characteristics in addition to preferred sex (male): boys who have healthy older brothers, illegitimate children of either sex, who are frequently subject to immediate infanticide, and children born to parents whose marriages are unstable. Additionally, the health of the child, attractiveness and general disposition, as well as the household wealth, also influence the quality of care a child receives. Illegitimate children are at greatest risk of all for receiving reduced, if any, childcare, due to both local morality and economic pressure. Unmarried women with a child may kill the baby at birth, or she may try to rear it and, faced with hardships, provide less than optimal care. In Ladog, one of the three studied communities, the majority of illegitimate newborns die at birth, while in other two communities, "accidents" and direct neglect cause detriment in later life. As in other traditional cultures around the world, these occurrences may go hand in hand with cultural beliefs and practices that serve to mask maternal responsibility for the death of a child (Levine, 1987; Čvorović, 2013).

In the past twin infanticide practice was widely prevalent in sub-Saharan Africa. In Africa as a whole, twins are a growing share of child deaths: they are three times as likely to die as children than singletons, with the mortality concentrated in the first year of life, particularly in the first month (Fenske & Wang, 2023). In some subsistence societies, twins are seen as a bad omen; they are often born prematurely, and tend to be weaker, therefore less likely to survive and thrive (Ball & Hill, 1996). Traditionally, either one or both infants may be abandoned or killed. "Bad omens" function as cues to terminate parental investment, and as markers of biological conditions that will threaten the survival of infants (Ball & Hill, 1996). For instance, among the Yoruba of Southwestern Nigeria, newborn twins used to be rejected and even sacrificed (Leroy et al., 2002). As in many other African societies, twins are ascribed supernatural origins and may provoke strong emotional reactions, from fear and repugnance to hope and respect. Mostly for genetic reasons, Yoruba have the highest dizygotic twinning rate in the world (4.4 percent of all maternities). In Yoruba traditional settings, a high rate of premature delivery, lack of adequate medical care, and the former practice of twin infanticide caused the perinatal mortality of twins to be very high. The high mortality rate associated with twins has contributed to the development of a special twin belief system: the twins share one soul, and if one twin dies, a carved statue, holding the deceased's soul, is made and cared for by the remaining twin so they may always be united. The carved stature made of wood is called *the Iibeji*, or Yoruba Twin Figure(s), usually commissioned upon the birth of twins in a family. If both twins have died, two of these figures are made.

Twin infanticide did not occur in isolation: in fact, societies, which kill twins also kill infants mainly due to reduced survival chances of the infants; such practice may ultimately be an adaptive strategy to increase reproductive success (Ball & Hill, 1996).

Maternal love and investment appears to be conditional (Hrdy, 1999). Females everywhere face different reproductive challenges than males, as they are limited in the number of children they can produce. This difference may have promoted a reproductive strategy whereby women try to maximize the quality rather than the quantity of offspring: maternal reproductive success reflects in the number of children she successfully raises to reproductive maturity. Maternal disinvestment, including infanticide, is a response to circumstances – environmental or social constraints—and the characteristics of the child.

In addition to a single-culture ethnographic focus, studies frequently use large cross-national and national data sets to investigate rates and consequences of unintended pregnancy and childbirth across the globe. Large surveys, such as the Demographic and Health Surveys (DHS) and UNICEF Multiple Indicator Cluster Surveys (MICS), ask whether recent births (for instance, in the past 2 years prior to the survey), or the current pregnancy, were wanted at the time, wanted later, or not at all.

Research using large surveys on the maternal behavior in response to unintended pregnancy and unwanted childbearing resulting in a live birth (child wantedness), and the effects on child's outcomes, has produced contradictory results (review in Hall et al., 2017). Presently, in low-and middle-income countries, the rates of unintended pregnancies remain high: in some regions unintended pregnancy accounts for more than half of all pregnancies (Aragaw et al., 2023). In low-and middle-income countries, more than 70 million women experience unintended pregnancies each year (Hajizadeh & Nghiem, 2020).

In many low-and middle-income countries, wanted childbearing almost always declines as countries move through the fertility transition; however, unwanted childbearing tends to rise in the first half of the transition, declining near the end of the transition (Bongaarts & Hodgson, 2022). It is commonly accepted that among populations undergoing fertility transition, fertility preferences are unstable and influenced by external factors such as overall development, child mortality, family-composition preferences, and couple's various motivations for childbearing. In low- and middle-income countries, the increased use of modern contraception during the past 50 years ranks among the most important changes in the demography as a whole (Ibitoye et al., 2022). Despite these changes, it is estimated that by the end of this century, most of the world's live births will be occurring in less-developed countries, while in nearly all others fertility rates will be too low to sustain population levels (Bhattacharjee et al., 2024). Moreover, for the 2015–2019 period, low-income countries had the highest unintended pregnancy rate and the lowest proportion of unintended pregnancies ending in abortions (Bearak et al., 2020).

For instance, in Kenya, data have shown that young and unmarried women, irrespective of their educational attainment and household wealth status, have a greater likelihood of experiencing unintended pregnancy (Ikamari, 2024). Several studies have also documented associations between unintended pregnancy and child's birth order. A cross-country study in sub-Saharan Africa found that adolescent girls and young women with three or more births are more likely to have unintended pregnancies compared to women with single birth (Ahinkorah et al., 2020). This is a common finding: children higher in the birth order are much more likely to be unwanted

(Lin et al., 2020). In Ethiopia, multiparous (more than one child) and grand multiparous (has given birth 5 or more times) women are more likely to experience unintended pregnancy compared to nulliparous women (Zeleke et al., 2021). These findings were confirmed in a cross-national sample of 36 low and middle-income countries: unintended pregnancies often lead to further cycles of high fertility and unwanted childbearing (Bellizzi et al., 2020). In turn, high fertility influences maternal and child health outcomes, including infant mortality, and it may often reduce from human capital investment, slow economic growth, and mitigate environmental threats (Reda et al., 2020). Presently, the highest child mortality remains concentrated in the poor African regions (Sapkota et al., 2020). Several studies have established the association between child mortality and unintended pregnancy: studies from Ethiopia, Nigeria, Nepal and Kenya document that among women, death of a child may create fear of losing more children which often results in having an unintended higher number of children (Reda et al., 2020). Findings from other studies also indicate that mortality exposure could increase women's unintended fertility through several psychological, relational, and behavioral mechanisms, and as a result, mortality exposure can influence fertility, not by shaping women's desires, but by disrupting the realization of those desires (Smith-Greenaway et al., 2022).

2.2 Costs of Unintended Pregnancy in Low-and-Middle-Income Countries

When pregnancies that are reported as unwanted or unintended result in a live birth, what are the particular risks to wellbeing for an unwanted child? Pre-natal investment and maternal behavior during an unwanted pregnancy can strongly impact the health of infants, including birth outcomes, and may be influenced by mother's attitude toward the pregnancy (Kost et al., 1998). Postnatal parenting practices and investment may be reflected in measures of infant and child mortality, preventive and feeding practices, child nutritional outcomes and development.

2.2.1 Prenatal Maternal Behavior

A number of studies have found a positive association between unwanted pregnancy and late initiation of antenatal care and/or decreased number of antenatal care visits (Hajizadeh & Nghiem, 2020; Singh et al., 2015; Rahman et al., 2016; Ochako & Gichuhi, 2016; Amo-Adjei & Anamaale Tuoyire, 2016; Yargawa et al., 2021), while others have found no association or mixed effects (Marston & Cleland, 2003). Most of these studies were based on women's retrospective recall of the timing of their antenatal care visits and retrospective assessments of pregnancy intention. However, both the initiation and the frequency of antenatal care visits varied by country's context. For instance, the effect of pregnancy intention in five-countries: Peru, the Philippines, Egypt, Kenya and Bolivia yielded mixed results (Marston & Cleland, 2003). In some countries (Peru and the Philippines), unwanted pregnancies were significantly associated with delayed antenatal care; in other countries (e.g. Egypt), women with unwanted pregnancies were less likely to delay antenatal care compared with women having wanted pregnancies, while mistimed births were also associated with a higher risk of late antenatal care in other countries (Kenya, Peru, and the Philippines). In these five countries, in addition to unwanted pregnancy, birth order (three and higher) had a significant influence on health care utilization. Moreover, some studies found that women with unwanted pregnancies were less likely to use professional delivery services (Marston & Cleland, 2003; Rahman et al., 2016), but this association was found to be non-significant in a number of countries (Egypt, Kenya, Bolivia, the Philippines and Ethiopia (Marston & Cleland, 2003; Wado et al., 2013). The inconsistencies in these results may be due to differences in the studied populations, and the design and timing of the studies (Hajizadeh & Nghiem, 2020).

2.2.2 Birth Outcomes

For low-and-middle-income countries, the evidence for the relationships between pregnancy intention and child outcomes: stillbirth, infant mortality, and low birth weight, is mixed.

2.2.2.1 Miscarriage or Stillbirth

There are limited data regarding pregnancy intention and miscarriage or stillbirth. A recent study from Malawi found no relationship between pregnancy intention and miscarriage or stillbirth (Hall et al., 2017). In contrast, a study in Ethiopia found a higher odds of pregnancy loss for unintended compared to intended pregnancies (Assefa et al., 2012). However, also in several other countries (Ghana, Guinea-Bissau, Ethiopia, Uganda and Bangladesh), an association was found between unintended pregnancy and stillbirths (Yargawa et al., 2021).

2.2.2.2 Infant Mortality

In high fertility settings, unwanted births, but also infant and child mortality, remains high. High mortality among very young children may in part reflect mothers' reactions to unwanted births (Knodel & Van de Walle, 1979). Thus, neglectful child-rearing practices and the resulting infant and child deaths could serve as a means to limit family size in the absence of birth control. From this perspective, the high infant and child mortality rates can be considered as much an accommodation to high fertility as the opposite.

Evidence of the association between pregnancy intendedness and early childhood mortality, however, is limited and inconclusive (Gipson et al., 2008). Studies from India, Bangladesh, Ghana, Guinea-Bissau, Ethiopia, and Uganda found increased risk of infant mortality in unintended pregnancies (Yargawa et al., 2021; Singh et al., 2012; Chalansani et al., 2007). Another study from India found the association between pregnancy intendedness and infant mortality to be only marginally significant (Singh et al., 2013). A study from rural Banglaseh, found higher odds of mortality among unwanted children (neonatal and postneonatal) because they were the undesired sex (Chalansani et al., 2007). However, a study from Bangladesh found no significant relationship between unwanted children and childhood mortality (Montgomery et al., 1997). Among adolescent mothers in Kenya, Uganda, and Tanzania there was increased risk of infant mortality if the pregnancy was unwanted (Ochieng Arunda et al., 2022). In contrast, a Malawi study found no relationship at all (Hall et al., 2017).

Most of these/the above studies relied on retrospective reports; thus women may be less likely to report deceased children if they were unwanted, i.e., from unintended pregnancies, and this may explain why some longitudinal studies have found that children from unintended pregnancies have lower odds of survival, but that cross-sectional studies have produced opposite results (Smith-Greenaway & Sennott, 2016).

2.2.2.3 Low Birthweight

A number of studies examined the effects of unwanted pregnancy on the risk of low birth weight. Maternal investment starts in utero, and low birth weight is one of the main indexes of lower maternal investment during pregnancy (Coall & Chisholm, 2003). In a study from rural southwestern Ethiopia, unwanted pregnancy was associated with low birthweight, while this association was also found for mean birthweight: the mean birth weight of babies after unwanted pregnancy was 114 g lower compared with births from intended pregnancy (Wado et al., 2014). Also, in studies from Bangladesh and Ecuador, low birthweight was strongly associated with unintended pregnancy (Rahman et al., 2019; Eggleston et al., 2001). In Peru, unplanned and mistimed pregnancies were significantly associated with low birth weight, while birth weight and gestational age were also lower in unplanned, mistimed and unwanted pregnancies (Ticona et al., 2024). However, the findings are inconclusive, as some studies had mixed results or found no association at all (Joyce et al., 2000; Hall et al., 2017): A study in Tehran, Iran, also showed no significant association between unintended pregnancy and low birth weight (Omani-Samani et al., 2019). The inconsistency in these results may be explained by confounders such as socioeconomic position, maternal risk behavior (smoking), maternal nutrition or previous birth history (Wado et al., 2014; Omani-Samani et al., 2019).

2.2.3 Post-Natal Investment

2.2.3.1 Breastfeeding

Studies in developing countries generally have found that women who have had unplanned pregnancies were less likely to breastfeed and to continue breastfeeding, compared to women with planned pregnancies (Chatterjee & Sennott, 2021; Thaithae et al., 2023; Mamo et al., 2020; Pérez-Escamilla et al., 1999; Berra et al., 2001; Chinebuah & Pérez-Escamilla, 2001).

2.2.3.2 Child Preventive Care

Mixed results have been produced from developing countries in regard to the effect of unintended pregnancy on preventive care. Some studies found that unwanted children may be disadvantaged with respect to vaccinations, but the effect appears to be country- and context- specific (Marston & Cleland, 2003). For mistimed and unwanted children, vaccinations were lower in Nepal, Egypt, Kenya and Peru compared with wanted children, while this was not found for Bolivia and the Philippines (Marston & Cleland, 2003; Singh et al., 2015; Echaiz et al., 2018). A large study from India shows that unwanted children were less likely to be immunized (Chatterjee & Sennott, 2021). However, a recent study from 48 Demographic Health Surveys conducted in Africa, Asia, Latin America and Europe, found no significant differences in childhood vaccination between children born from unwanted and wanted pregnancies (Hajizadeh & Nghiem, 2020). In Indonesia, children unwanted at birth were more likely than other children to become ill, and less likely to receive treatment for illnesses (Jensen & Ahlburg, 2002).

2.2.3.3 Child Nutritional Status

Child undernutrition contributes to approximately one-half of all childhood mortalities, and remains a major public health concern, particularly in resource-poor environments (Gausman et al., 2022). Nutritional status in children is usually expressed in terms of z-scores based on the WHO reference population. z-scores are indicators for child nutritional status as they measure the number of standard deviations from the median of the reference population by child's age.

Childhood undernutrition includes fetal growth restriction (defined as birthweight for gestational age and sex below the 10th centile of the Inter-Growth Standards, stunting, wasting, and underweight. An abnormally slow rate of gain in child's height or length represents an important aspect of the poor health and social conditions of many children in low-income and middle-income countries. Deficit in HAZ (stunting/when a child is short for his/her age), may lead to chronic malnutrition with long-term developmental risks (de Onis & Branca, 2016). WAZ or under-weight (undernutrition) refers to low weight-for-age, when a child can be either thin or short for his/her age, as a result of a combination of chronic and acute malnutrition. WHZ refers to low weight-for-height (wasting) when a child is thin for his/her/their height, but not necessarily short, resulting from acute malnutrition, and carrying an increased risk of morbidity and mortality. Longer-term consequences of undernutrition include reduced stature in adulthood, cognitive impairment and chronic disease (Hoddinott et al., 2013). Stunting and wasting represent different biological processes but share many of the same causes (Gausman et al., 2022). Children may pass through different states of anthropometric failure and experience one or more failures at different times during their lives. In fact, literature searches have failed to find any independent causes of wasting that are not also associated with stunting. Additionally, studies have found that wasted children are more likely to develop stunting, and in certain areas, these conditions are a reaction to seasonal trends and environmental stressors. However, stunting is largely regarded as relatively unresponsive to marginal or short-term nutritional insufficiency. In contrast, underweight and wasting are considered the result of acute starvation and/or disease, but neither indicator can clearly differentiate between recent and chronic nutritional deficiencies. Infectious diseases, through reducing appetite, increasing metabolic requirements, and increasing nutrient loss, can further exacerbate these conditions.

The causes of early childhood undernutrition in low- and middle-income countries are complex and poorly understood, and may not merely be a consequence of nutritional inadequacy (Roth et al., 2017). Many epidemiological studies have primarily concentrated on individual or household-level risk factors, such as certain exposures varying between individuals and households. Several risk factors for stunting have been identified: maternal low levels of education, infections and micronutrient deficiencies, among others, but without clearly identified causal relationships (Black et al., 2013). Biological risk factors for stunting include fetal growth restriction and maternal height, while socio-economic determinants of child nutrition are being increasingly recognized (Danaei et al., 2016). Thus, given the declines in mean HAZ with age due to a downward shift in the entire HAZ distribution, the main underlying causes of postnatal linear growth faltering may be population-wide exposures to e.g. community-level or shared environmental factors to which nearly all children in the population are exposed (Roth et al., 2017).

A recent review found that in low and middle-income countries, boys have a consistently higher risk of all forms of growth faltering than girls, and children with multiple anthropometric deficits had higher mortality rates from birth to 2 years than those without deficits (Mertens et al., 2023). Another recent study found that in low- and middle- income countries, the odds of a child being malnourished increase as the age of the mother increases, being married, being a girl, and having a rural residency, while the practice of breastfeeding reduced the risk (Chilot et al., 2023). Older children under five were more likely to be malnourished when compared to younger ones. Furthermore, as household income and family size increase, the odds of malnutrition increase too, explained by consumption of relatively cheap, energy-dense foods and dilution of family resources.

2.2 Costs of Unintended Pregnancy in Low-and-Middle-Income Countries

In addition to macro-level social and environmental conditions, maternal characteristics and parental investment may be reflected in various measures of child nutrition (Costa et al., 2018; Leroy & Frongillo, 2019): It has been suggested that a psychological factor associated with child stunting may be either unwanted or mistimed unintended pregnancy (Kinyoki et al., 2015; Shaka et al., 2020). Studies investigating the relationship between being unwanted and nutritional outcomes have been focused on low and middle-income countries, where malnutrition remains a major problem. Estimated childhood stunting across low-and middle-income countries decreased from 36.9% in 2000 to 26.6% in 2017, while wasting was at 14.2%, with both conditions remaining unacceptably high (Victora et al., 2021). Recent data indicates that stunting and wasting might already be present at birth, and that the incidence of both conditions reach a peak during the first 6 months of life.

In a Peruvian study, it was also found that there was a 15% higher risk of stunting among children from unwanted pregnancies compared with those from wanted pregnancies (Marston & Cleland, 2003). Studies from Ethiopia and Bolivia confirmed this finding (Shaka et al., 2020; Shapiro-Mendoza et al., 2005). In contrast, the findings of a study from Egypt were opposite: the likelihood of stunting was lower if a pregnancy was mistimed or unwanted than if it was wanted (Barber et al., 1999). Other studies have found limited or no evidence of the influence of child wantedness on child nutritional outcomes. A study on Malawian children found that, after controlling for age no there was no significant difference in probability of being stunted by mother's pregnancy intention. (Baschieri et al., 2017). Similarly, in a cross-national study of 48 Demographic Health Surveys conducted in Africa, Asia, Latin America and Europe, no significant influences of unwanted pregnancy on child health indicators, i.e., stunting (height-for-age), underweight (weight-for-age) and wasting (weight-for-height) were found (Hajizadeh & Nghiem, 2020). Given the limited number of studies and mixed results documented in the existing literature, recent systematic reviews have called for further studies investigating the outcomes of unintended pregnancies in LMICs (Hall et al., 2017).

An aspect that has received only limited attention in studies assessing the impact of unintended pregnancy and health outcomes is family size, or the sibship size (number of siblings). A cross-national study from 15 developing countries (Bolivia, north east Brazil, Colombia, the Dominican Republic, Guatemala, and Trinidad and Tobago in Latin America and the Caribbean region; Egypt, Morocco, Sri Lanka, and Thailand in Asia and North Africa, and Burundi, Ghana, Mali, Senegal, and Zimbabwe in sub-Saharan Africa) assessed siblings' impact on younger children's nutritional status (Desai, 1995). The findings of this study suggests that both sibship size and unintended pregnancy (being unwanted) have a marked impact on children's health outcomes, with negative impact of sibship size being greater for families that exceeded their desired size than among families that were planned.

2.2.3.4 Child's Emotional and Cognitive Development

Findings from high-income countries generally indicate that unwanted children are more likely to have difficulties with social and interpersonal relationships, mental health, and occupational spheres, including involvement in criminal activity, which can extend into later life and adulthood (Guterman, 2015). According to U.S. data from a longitudinal birth cohort study, one of the earliest potentially identifiable risk-factors for child maltreatment and abuse is the intentions of the pregnancy, where maternal reports of unintended pregnancy were found to be associated with psychological aggression and neglect. The study also stressed the importance of paternal perspectives in pregnancy intentions, as these reports also documented physical aggression towards the unwanted children (Guterman, 2015).

Studies from Sweden and Finland have also found that unwantedness is frequently associated with later-life disadvantageous socio-economic circumstances, including need for psychiatric care, poor-quality social life, and crime-registered offenses (review in Gipson et al., 2008). In Czechoslovakia, a study of unwanted children whose mothers had been denied abortion, documented that these children, though brought up under relatively good socioeconomic conditions and within their biological families, performed more poorly in school, and had more psychological problems and delinquency than a matching group of children born to families who wanted them (David, 2006).

Studies identifying the potential risks of maltreatment and abuse of unwanted children in low-and-middle-income countries are presently unavailable.

References

Ahinkorah, B. O., Seidu, A. A., Appiah, F., Oduro, J. K., Sambah, F., Baatiema, L., et al. (2020). Effect of sexual violence on planned, mistimed and unwanted pregnancies among women of reproductive age in sub-Saharan Africa: A multi-country analysis of demographic and health surveys. *SSM-Population Health, 11*, 100601. https://doi.org/10.1016/j.ssmph.2020.100601

Ajayi, A. I., Odunga, S. A., Oduor, C., Ouedraogo, R., Ushie, B. A., & Wado, Y. D. (2021). "I was tricked": Understanding reasons for unintended pregnancy among sexually active adolescent girls. *Reproductive Health, 18*, 1–11. https://doi.org/10.1186/s12978-021-01078-y

Amo-Adjei, J., & Anamaale Tuoyire, D. (2016). Effects of planned, mistimed and unwanted pregnancies on the use of prenatal health services in sub-Saharan Africa: A multicountry analysis of demographic and health survey data. *Tropical Medicine and International Health, 21*(12), 1552–1561. https://doi.org/10.1111/tmi.12788

Aragaw, F. M., Amare, T., Teklu, R. E., Tegegne, B. A., & Alem, A. Z. (2023). Magnitude of unintended pregnancy and its determinants among childbearing age women in low and middle-income countries: Evidence from 61 low and middle-income countries. *Frontiers in Reproductive Health, 5*, 1113926. https://doi.org/10.3389/frph.2023.1113926

Assefa, N., Berhane, Y., Worku, A., & Tsui, A. (2012). The hazard of pregnancy loss and stillbirth among women in Kersa, East Ethiopia: A follow up study. *Sexual and Reproductive Healthcare, 3*(3), 107–112. https://doi.org/10.1016/j.srhc.2012.06.002

Ball, H. L., & Hill, C. M. (1996). Reevaluating "twin infanticide". *Current Anthropology, 37*(5), 856–863. https://doi.org/10.1086/204569

References

Barber, J. S., Axinn, W. G., & Thornton, A. (1999). Unwanted childbearing, health, and mother-child relationships. *Journal of Health and Social Behavior*, 231–257. https://doi.org/10.2307/2676350

Baschieri, A., Machiyama, K., Floyd, S., Dube, A., Molesworth, A., Chihana, M., et al. (2017). Unintended childbearing and child growth in northern Malawi. *Maternal and Child Health Journal, 21*, 467–474. https://doi.org/10.1007/s10995-016-2124-8

Bearak, J., Popinchalk, A., Ganatra, B., Moller, A. B., Tunçalp, Ö., Beavin, C., et al. (2020). Unintended pregnancy and abortion by income, region, and the legal status of abortion: Estimates from a comprehensive model for 1990–2019. *Lancet Global Health, 8*(9), e1152–e1161. https://doi.org/10.1016/S2214-109X(20)30315-6

Bellizzi, S., Mannava, P., Nagai, M., & Sobel, H. L. (2020). Reasons for discontinuation of contraception among women with a current unintended pregnancy in 36 low and middle-income countries. *Contraception, 101*(1), 26–33. https://doi.org/10.1016/j.contraception.2019.09.006

Berra, S., Rajmil, L., Passamonte, R., Fernandez, E., & Sabulsky, J. (2001). Premature cessation of breastfeeding in infants: Development and evaluation of a predictive model in two Argentinian cohorts: The CLACYD study*, 1993–1999. *Acta Paediatrica, 90*(5), 544–551. https://doi.org/10.1111/j.1651-2227.2001.tb00796.x

Bishwajit, G., Tang, S., Yaya, S., & Feng, Z. (2017). Unmet need for contraception and its association with unintended pregnancy in Bangladesh. *BMC Pregnancy and Childbirth, 17*, 1–9. https://doi.org/10.1186/s12884-017-1379-4

Bhattacharjee, N. V., Schumacher, A. E., Aali, A., Abate, Y. H., Abbasgholizadeh, R., Abbasian, M., et al. (2024). Global fertility in 204 countries and territories, 1950–2021, with forecasts to 2100: A comprehensive demographic analysis for the global burden of disease study 2021. *The Lancet, 403*(10440), 2057–2099. https://doi.org/10.1016/S0140-6736(24)00550-6

Black, R. E., Victora, C. G., Walker, S. P., Bhutta, Z. A., Christian, P., De Onis, M., et al. (2013). Maternal and child undernutrition and overweight in low-income and middle-income countries. *Lancet, 382*(9890), 427–451. https://doi.org/10.1016/S0140-6736(13)60937-X

Bongaarts, J., & Hodgson, D. (2022). Socio-economic determinants of fertility. In *Fertility transition in the developing world* (pp. 51–62). Springer.

Bowman-Smart, H., Savulescu, J., Gyngell, C., Mand, C., & Delatycki, M. B. (2020). Sex selection and non-invasive prenatal testing: A review of current practices, evidence, and ethical issues. *Prenatal Diagnosis, 40*(4), 398–407. https://doi.org/10.1002/pd.5755

Brzozowska, Z., Buber-Ennser, I., & Riederer, B. (2021). Didn't Plan One but got One: Unintended and sooner-than-intended Parents in the East and the West of Europe. *European Journal of Population, 37*(3), 727–767.

Callahan, R., & Becker, S. (2014). Unmet need, intention to use contraceptive and unwanted pregnancy in rural Bangladesh. *International Perspectives on Sexual and Reproductive Health, 40*(1), 4–10. https://doi.org/10.1363/4000414

Casterline, J. B., & El-Zeini, L. O. (2022). Multiple perspectives on recent trends in unwanted fertility in low-and middle-income countries. *Demography, 59*(1), 371–388. https://doi.org/10.1215/00703370-9644472

Chalansani, S., Casterline, J., & Koenig, M. (2007). Consequences of unwanted childbearing: A study of child outcomes in Bangladesh. Paper presented at the annual meeting of the population Association of America, New York. https://www.researchgate.net/profile/John-Casterline/publication/228602916_Unwanted_Childbearing_and_Child_Survival_in_Bangladesh/links/53da425b0cf2e38c633669cd/Unwanted-Childbearing-and-Child-Survival-in-Bangladesh.pdf.

Channon, M. D., Puri, M., Gietel-Basten, S., Stone, L. W., & Channon, A. (2021). Prevalence and correlates of sex-selective abortions and missing girls in Nepal: Evidence from the 2011 population census and 2016 demographic and health survey. *BMJ Open, 11*(3), e042542. https://doi.org/10.1136/bmjopen-2020-042542

Chatterjee, E., & Sennott, C. (2021). Fertility intentions and child health in India: Women's use of health services, breastfeeding, and official birth documentation following an unwanted birth. *PLoS One, 16*(11), e0259311. https://doi.org/10.1371/journal.pone.0259311

Chilot, D., Belay, D. G., Merid, M. W., Kibret, A. A., Alem, A. Z., Asratie, M. H., et al. (2023). Triple burden of malnutrition among mother–child pairs in low-income and middle-income countries: A cross-sectional study. *BMJ Open, 13*(5), e070978. https://doi.org/10.1136/bmjopen-2022-070978

Chinebuah, B., & Pérez-Escamilla, R. (2001). Unplanned pregnancies are associated with less likelihood of prolonged breast-feeding among primiparous women in Ghana. *The Journal of Nutrition, 131*(4), 1247–1249. https://doi.org/10.1093/jn/131.4.1247

Cleland, J., Harbison, S., & Shah, I. H. (2014). Unmet need for contraception: Issues and challenges. *Studies in Family Planning, 45*(2), 105–122. https://doi.org/10.1111/j.1728-4465.2014.00380.x

Coall, D. A., & Chisholm, J. S. (2003). Evolutionary perspectives on pregnancy: Maternal age at menarche and infant birth weight. *Social Science and Medicine, 57*(10), 1771–1781. https://doi.org/10.1016/S0277-9536(03)00022-4

Costa, M. E., Trumble, B., Kaplan, H., & Gurven, M. D. (2018). Child nutritional status among births exceeding ideal family size in a high fertility population. *Maternal and Child Nutrition, 14*(4), e12625. https://doi.org/10.1111/mcn.12625

Čvorović, J. (2013). Serbian gypsy witch narratives: 'Wherever Gypsies Go, There the Witches Are, We Know!'. *Folklore, 124*(2), 214–225. https://doi.org/10.1080/0015587X.2013.798535

Davidović, J. (2023). "My dear unwanted": Media discourse on sex-selective abortion in Montenegro. *Feminist Media Studies, 23*(3), 937–959. https://doi.org/10.1080/14680777.2021.2018620

Daly, M., & Wilson, M. (1983). *Sex, evolution and behavior: Adaptions for reproduction*. Willard Grant Press.

Daly, M., & Wilson, M. (1988). *Homicide*. NY: Aldine.

Danaei, G., Andrews, K. G., Sudfeld, C. R., Fink, G., McCoy, D. C., Peet, E., et al. (2016). Risk factors for childhood stunting in 137 developing countries: A comparative risk assessment analysis at global, regional, and country levels. *PLoS Medicine, 13*(11), e1002164. https://doi.org/10.1371/journal.pmed.1002164

Das Gupta, M., Zhenghua, J., Bohua, L., Zhenming, X., Chung, W., & Hwa-Ok, B. (2003). Why is son preference so persistent in East and South Asia? A cross-country study of China, India and the Republic of Korea. *The Journal of Development Studies, 40*(2), 153–187.

David, H. P. (2006). Born unwanted, 35 years later: The Prague study. *Reproductive Health Matters, 14*(27), 181–190. https://doi.org/10.1016/S0968-8080(06)27219-7

Denham, A. R. (2020). Of house or bush: The cultural psychodynamics of infanticide in northern Ghana. *Current Anthropology, 61*(1), 77–99. https://doi.org/10.1086/706989

De Onis, M., & Branca, F. (2016). Childhood stunting: A global perspective. *Maternal and Child Nutrition, 12*, 12–26. https://doi.org/10.1111/mcn.12231

Desai, S. (1995). When are children from large families disadvantaged? Evidence from cross-national analyses. *Population Studies, 49*(2), 195–210. https://doi.org/10.1080/0032472031000148466

Ebert, C., & Vollmer, S. (2022). Girls unwanted–the role of parents' child-specific sex preference for children's early mental development. *Journal of Health Economics, 82*, 102590. https://doi.org/10.1016/j.jhealeco.2022.102590

Echaiz, J., Blas, M., & Kancherla, V. (2018). Unintended pregnancy and its impact on childhood rotavirus immunization in Peru. *Revista Panamericana de Salud Pública, 42*, e96. https://doi.org/10.26633/RPSP.2018.96

Eggleston, E., Tsui, A. O., & Kotelchuck, M. (2001). Unintended pregnancy and low birthweight in Ecuador. *American Journal of Public Health, 91*(5), 808. https://doi.org/10.2105/ajph.91.5.808

ESHRE Capri Workshop. (2018). Why after 50 years of effective contraception do we still have unintended pregnancy? A European perspective. *Human Reproduction, 33*(5), 777–783. https://doi.org/10.1093/humrep/dey089

References

Flatø, M. (2018). The differential mortality of undesired infants in sub-Saharan Africa. *Demography, 55*(1), 271–294. https://doi.org/10.1007/s13524-017-0638-3

Fenske, J., & Wang, S. (2023). Tradition and mortality: Evidence from twin infanticide in Africa. *Journal of Development Economics, 163*, 103094. https://doi.org/10.1016/j.jdeveco.2023.103094

Galor, O. (2012). The demographic transition: Causes and consequences. *Cliometrica, 6*(1), 1–28. https://doi.org/10.1007/s11698-011-0062-7

Gausman, J., Kim, R., Li, Z., Tu, L., Rajpal, S., Joe, W., & Subramanian, S. V. (2022). Comparison of child undernutrition anthropometric indicators across 56 low-and middle-income countries. *JAMA Network Open, 5*(3), e221223. https://doi.org/10.1001/jamanetworkopen.2022.1223

Gipson, J. D., Koenig, M. A., & Hindin, M. J. (2008). The effects of unintended pregnancy on infant, child, and parental health: A review of the literature. *Studies in Family Planning, 39*(1), 18–38. https://doi.org/10.1111/j.1728-4465.2008.00148.x

Günther, I., & Harttgen, K. (2016). Desired fertility and number of children born across time and space. *Demography, 53*, 55–83. https://doi.org/10.1007/s13524-015-0451-9

Guterman, K. (2015). Unintended pregnancy as a predictor of child maltreatment. *Child Abuse and Neglect, 48*, 160–169. https://doi.org/10.1016/j.chiabu.2015.05.014

Hall, J. A., Benton, L., Copas, A., & Stephenson, J. (2017). Pregnancy intention and pregnancy outcome: Systematic review and meta-analysis. *Maternal and Child Health Journal, 21*, 670–704. https://doi.org/10.1007/s10995-016-2237-0

Harris, M., & Ross, E. B. (1987). *Death, sex, and fertility. Population regulation in preindustrial and developing societies.* Columbia University Press.

Hajizadeh, M., & Nghiem, S. (2020). Does unwanted pregnancy lead to adverse health and healthcare utilization for mother and child? Evidence from low-and middle-income countries. *International Journal of Public Health, 65*, 457–468. https://doi.org/10.1007/s00038-020-01358-7

Hesketh, T., & Xing, Z. W. (2006). Abnormal sex ratios in human populations: Causes and consequences. *Proceedings of the National Academy of Sciences, 103*(36), 13271–13275. https://doi.org/10.1073/pnas.0602203103

Hrdy, S. B. (1992). Fitness tradeoffs in the history and evolution of delegated mothering with special reference to wet-nursing, abandonment, and infanticide. *Ethology and Sociobiology, 13*(5–6), 409–442. https://doi.org/10.1016/0162-3095(92)90011-R

Hrdy, S. B. (1999). *Mother nature.* Chatto and Windus.

Hausfater, G., & Hrdy, S. B. (2017). *Infanticide: Comparative and evolutionary perspectives.* Routledge.

Hoddinott, J., Behrman, J. R., Maluccio, J. A., Melgar, P., Quisumbing, A. R., Ramirez-Zea, M., et al. (2013). Adult consequences of growth failure in early childhood. *American Journal of Clinical Nutrition, 98*(5), 1170–1178. https://doi.org/10.3945/ajcn.113.064584

Howell, N. (2017). *Demography of the Dobe! kung.* Routledge.

Ibitoye, M., Casterline, J. B., & Zhang, C. (2022). Fertility preferences and contraceptive change in low-and middle-income countries. *Studies in Family Planning, 53*(2), 361–376. https://doi.org/10.1111/sifp.12202

Ikamari, L. (2024). A multilevel analysis of factors associated with unintended pregnancy in Kenya. *Journal of African Population Studies, 37*(1), 5291. https://doi.org/10.59147/jg3nxVbP

Jensen, E. R., & Ahlburg, D. A. (2002). Family size, unwantedness, and child health and health care utilisation in Indonesia. *Bulletin of Indonesian Economic Studies, 38*(1), 43–59. https://doi.org/10.1080/000749102753620275

Joyce, T. J., Kaestner, R., & Korenman, S. (2000). The effect of pregnancy intention on child development. *Demography, 37*(1), 83–94. https://doi.org/10.2307/2648098

Kinyoki, D. K., Berkley, J. A., Moloney, G. M., Kandala, N. B., & Noor, A. M. (2015). Predictors of the risk of malnutrition among children under the age of 5 years in Somalia. *Public Health Nutrition, 18*(17), 3125–3133. https://doi.org/10.1017/S1368980015001913

Knodel, J., & Van de Walle, E. (1979). Lessons from the past: Policy implications of historical fertility studies. *Population and Development Review*, 217–245. http://www.jstor.org/stable/1971824

Kost, K., Landry, D. J., & Darroch, J. E. (1998). Predicting maternal behaviors during pregnancy: Does intention status matter? *Family Planning Perspectives*, 79–88. https://doi.org/10.2307/2991664

Leroy, F., Olaleye-Oruene, T., Koeppen-Schomerus, G., & Bryan, E. (2002). Yoruba customs and beliefs pertaining to twins. *Twin Research and Human Genetics*, *5*(2), 132–136. https://doi.org/10.1375/twin.5.2.132

Leroy, J. L., & Frongillo, E. A. (2019). Perspective: What does stunting really mean? A critical review of the evidence. *Advances in Nutrition*, *10*(2), 196–204. https://doi.org/10.1093/advances/nmy101

Levine, N. E. (1987). Differential child care in three Tibetan communities: Beyond son preference. *Population and Development Review*, 281–304. https://doi.org/10.2307/1973194

Lin, W., Pantano, J., & Sun, S. (2020). Birth order and unwanted fertility. *Journal of Population Economics*, *33*(2), 413–440. https://doi.org/10.1007/s00148-019-00747-4

Lukas, D., & Huchard, E. (2019). The evolution of infanticide by females in mammals. *Philosophical Transactions of the Royal Society B*, *374*(1780), 20180075. https://doi.org/10.1098/rstb.2018.0075

Lutalo, T., Gray, R., Santelli, J., Guwatudde, D., Brahmbhatt, H., Mathur, S., et al. (2018). Unfulfilled need for contraception among women with unmet need but with the intention to use contraception in Rakai, Uganda: A longitudinal study. *BMC Women's Health*, *18*, 1–7. https://doi.org/10.1186/s12905-018-0551-y

Mamo, K., Dengia, T., Abubeker, A., & Girmaye, E. (2020). Assessment of exclusive breastfeeding practice and associated factors among mothers in west Shoa zone, Oromia, Ethiopia. *Obstetrics and Gynecology International*, *1*, 3965873. https://doi.org/10.1155/2020/3965873

Marston, C., & Cleland, J. (2003). Do unintended pregnancies carried to term lead to adverse outcomes for mother and child? An assessment in five developing countries. *Population Studies*, *57*(1), 77–93. https://doi.org/10.1080/0032472032000061749

Mertens, A., Benjamin-Chung, J., Colford, J. M., Jr., Coyle, J., Van der Laan, M. J., Hubbard, A. E., et al. (2023). Causes and consequences of child growth faltering in low-resource settings. *Nature*, *621*(7979), 568–576. https://doi.org/10.1038/s41586-023-06501-x

Montgomery, M. R., Lloyd, C. B., Hewett, P. C., & Heuveline, P. (1997). The consequences of imperfect fertility control for children's survival, health, and schooling. In *Demographic and health surveys analytical reports no.7*. Macro International.

Nations, M. (1992). The child's disease (*Doença de criança*): Popular paradigm of persistent diarrhea? *Acta Paediatrica*, *81*, 55–65. https://doi.org/10.1111/j.1651-2227.1992.tb12373.x

Oas, R. (2016). Is there unmet need for family planning? *The New Atlantis*, 61–76.

Ochako, R., & Gichuhi, W. (2016). Pregnancy wantedness, frequency and timing of antenatal care visit among women of childbearing age in Kenya. *Reproductive Health*, *13*, 1–8. https://doi.org/10.1186/s12978-016-0168-2

Ochieng Arunda, M., Agardh, A., Larsson, M., & Asamoah, B. O. (2022). Survival patterns of neonates born to adolescent mothers and the effect of pregnancy intentions and marital status on newborn survival in Kenya, Uganda, and Tanzania, 2014–2016. *Global Health Action*, *15*(1), 2101731. https://doi.org/10.1080/16549716.2022.2101731

Oomman, N., & Ganatra, B. R. (2002). Sex selection: The systematic elimination of girls. *Reproductive Health Matters*, *10*(19), 184–188. https://doi.org/10.1016/S0968-8080(02)00029-0

Omani-Samani, R., Ranjbaran, M., Mohammadi, M., Esmailzadeh, A., Sepidarkish, M., Maroufizadeh, S., & Almasi-Hashiani, A. (2019). Impact of unintended pregnancy on maternal and neonatal outcomes. *The Journal of Obstetrics and Gynecology of India*, *69*, 136–141. https://doi.org/10.1007/s13224-018-1125-5

Pallitto, C. C., García-Moreno, C., Jansen, H. A., Heise, L., Ellsberg, M., & Watts, C. (2013). Intimate partner violence, abortion, and unintended pregnancy: Results from the WHO multi-

References

country study on women's health and domestic violence. *International Journal of Gynecology & Obstetrics, 120*(1), 3–9. https://doi.org/10.1016/j.ijgo.2012.07.003

Pérez-Escamilla, R., Cobas, J. A., Balcazar, H., & Benin, M. H. (1999). Specifying the antecedents of breast-feeding duration in Peru through a structural equation model. *Public Health Nutrition, 2*(4), 461–467. https://doi.org/10.1017/S1368980099000646

Pitt, S. E., & Bale, E. M. (1995). Neonaticide, infanticide, and filicide: A review of the literature. *Journal of the American Academy of Psychiatry and the Law, 23*(3), 375–386.

Pritchett, L. H. (1994). Desired fertility and the impact of population policies. *Population and Development Review, 20*, 1–55. https://doi.org/10.2307/2137605

Rahman, M. M., Rahman, M. M., Tareque, M. I., Ferdos, J., & Jesmin, S. S. (2016). Maternal pregnancy intention and professional antenatal care utilization in Bangladesh: A nationwide population-based survey. *PLoS One, 11*(6), e0157760. https://doi.org/10.1371/journal.pone.0157760

Rahman, M., Nasrin, S. O., Rahman, M., Rahman, A., Mostofa, G., Jesmin, S. S., & Buchanan, F. (2019). Maternal pregnancy intention and its association with low birthweight and pregnancy complications in Bangladesh: Findings from a hospital-based study. *International Health, 11*(6), 447–454. https://doi.org/10.1093/inthealth/ihz010

Rastogi, G., & Sharma, A. (2022). Unwanted daughters: The unintended consequences of a ban on sex-selective abortions on the educational attainment of women. *Journal of Population Economics, 35*(4), 1473–1516. https://doi.org/10.1007/s00148-022-00896-z

Reda, M. G., Bune, G. T., & Shaka, M. F. (2020). Epidemiology of high fertility status among women of reproductive age in Wonago District, Gedeo zone, Southern Ethiopia: A community-based cross-sectional study. *International Journal of Reproductive Medicine, 2020*(1), 2915628. https://doi.org/10.1155/2020/2915628

Rosenzweig, M. R., & Wolpin, K. I. (1993). Maternal expectations and ex post rationalizations: The usefulness of survey information on the wantedness of children. *Journal of Human Resources*, 205–229. https://doi.org/10.2307/146201

Roth, D. E., Krishna, A., Leung, M., Shi, J., Bassani, D. G., & Barros, A. J. (2017). Early childhood linear growth faltering in low-income and middle-income countries as a whole-population condition: Analysis of 179 demographic and health surveys from 64 countries (1993–2015). *The Lancet Global Health, 5*(12), e1249–e1257. https://doi.org/10.1016/S2214-109X(17)30418-7

Sandiford, P., Morales, P., Gorter, A., Coyle, E., & Smith, G. D. (1991). Why do child mortality rates fall? An analysis of the Nicaraguan experience. *American Journal of Public Health, 81*(1), 30–37. https://doi.org/10.2105/ajph.81.1.30

Santelli, J., Rochat, R., Hatfield-Timajchy, K., Gilbert, B. C., Curtis, K., Cabral, R., et al. (2003). The measurement and meaning of unintended pregnancy. *Perspectives on Sexual and Reproductive Health*, 94–101.

Sapkota, N., Gautam, N., Lim, A., & Ueranantasun, A. (2020). Estimation of under-5 child mortality rates in 52 low-migration countries. *Child Health Nursing Research, 26*(4), 463. https://doi.org/10.4094/chnr.2020.26.4.463

Scheper-Hughes, N. (1992). *Death without weeping: The violence of everyday life in Brazil*. University of California Press.

Shah, P. S., Balkhair, T., Ohlsson, A., Beyene, J., Scott, F., & Frick, C. (2011). Intention to become pregnant and low birth weight and preterm birth: A systematic review. *Maternal and Child Health Journal, 15*(2), 205–216. https://doi.org/10.1007/s10995-009-0546-2

Shaka, M. F., Woldie, Y. B., Lola, H. M., Olkamo, K. Y., & Anbasse, A. T. (2020). Determinants of undernutrition among children under-five years old in Southern Ethiopia: Does pregnancy intention matter? A community-based unmatched case-control study. *BMC Pediatrics, 20*, 1–10. https://doi.org/10.1186/s12887-020-2004-7

Shapiro-Mendoza, C., Selwyn, B. J., Smith, D. P., & Sanderson, M. (2005). Parental pregnancy intention and early childhood stunting: Findings from Bolivia. *International Journal of Epidemiology, 34*(2), 387–396. https://doi.org/10.1093/ije/dyh354

Singh, A., Chalasani, S., Koenig, M. A., & Mahapatra, B. (2012). The consequences of unintended births for maternal and child health in India. *Population Studies, 66*(3), 223–239. https://doi.org/10.1080/00324728.2012.697568

Singh, A., Singh, A., & Mahapatra, B. (2013). The consequences of unintended pregnancy for maternal and child health in rural India: Evidence from prospective data. *Maternal and Child Health Journal, 17*, 493–500.

Singh, A., Singh, A., & Thapa, S. (2015). Adverse consequences of unintended pregnancy for maternal and child health in Nepal. *Asia Pacific Journal of Public Health, 27*(2), NP1481–NP1491. https://doi.org/10.1177/1010539513498769

Smith-Greenaway, E., & Sennott, C. (2016). Death and desirability: Retrospective reporting of unintended pregnancy after a child's death. *Demography, 53*(3), 805–834. https://doi.org/10.1007/s13524-016-0475-9

Smith-Greenaway, E., Yeatman, S., & Chilungo, A. (2022). Life after loss: A prospective analysis of mortality exposure and unintended fertility. *Demography, 59*(2), 563–585. https://doi.org/10.1215/00703370-9807961

Thaithae, S., Yimyam, S., & Polprasarn, P. (2023). Prevalence and predictive factors for exclusive breastfeeding at six months among Thai adolescent mothers. *Children, 10*(4), 682. https://doi.org/10.3390/children10040682

Ticona, D. M., Huanco, D., & Ticona-Rendón, M. B. (2024). Impact of unplanned pregnancy on neonatal outcomes: Findings of new high-risk newborns in Peru. *International Health, 16*(1), 52–60. https://doi.org/10.1093/inthealth/ihad018

Trivers, R. L. (1985). *Social evolution*. The Benjamin Cummings Publishing Company.

Victora, C. G., Christian, P., Vidaletti, L. P., Gatica-Domínguez, G., Menon, P., & Black, R. E. (2021). Revisiting maternal and child undernutrition in low-income and middle-income countries: Variable progress towards an unfinished agenda. *The Lancet, 397*(10282), 1388–1399. https://doi.org/10.1016/S0140-6736(21)00394-9

Wado, Y. D., Afework, M. F., & Hindin, M. J. (2013). Unintended pregnancies and the use of maternal health services in southwestern Ethiopia. *BMC International Health and Human Rights, 13*, 1–8. https://doi.org/10.1186/1472-698X-13-36

Wado, Y. D., Afework, M. F., & Hindin, M. J. (2014). Effects of maternal pregnancy intention, depressive symptoms and social support on risk of low birth weight: A prospective study from southwestern Ethiopia. *PLoS One, 9*(5), e96304. https://doi.org/10.1371/journal.pone.0096304

Yargawa, J., Machiyama, K., Ponce Hardy, V., Enuameh, Y., Galiwango, E., Gelaye, K., et al. (2021). Pregnancy intention data completeness, quality and utility in population-based surveys: EN-INDEPTH study. *Population Health Metrics, 19*, 1–18. https://doi.org/10.1186/s12963-020-00227-y

Yaya, S., & Ghose, B. (2018). Prevalence of unmet need for contraception and its association with unwanted pregnancy among married women in Angola. *PLoS One, 13*(12), e0209801. https://doi.org/10.1371/journal.pone.0209801

Zeleke, L. B., Alemu, A. A., Kassahun, E. A., Aynalem, B. Y., Hassen, H. Y., & Kassa, G. M. (2021). Individual and community level factors associated with unintended pregnancy among pregnant women in Ethiopia. *Scientific Reports, 11*(1), 12699. https://doi.org/10.1038/s41598-021-92157-4

Chapter 3
The Roma: Brief History and Overview

The best available estimate is that about ten million to twelve million Roma live in Europe, with large concentrations in Central and Eastern Europe. The majority of Roma live in extended families within segregated communities characterized by poverty, unemployment, poor education, and poor-quality housing. Roma communities are closely knit, characterized by limited social contact with non-Roma, while rules of behavior are culturally prescribed with distinct gender roles. Since coming to Europe, the Roma have been received with hostility and much of their history has been characterized by persecution by non-Roma. Despite their presence in the Balkans for centuries, integration of the Roma into their host societies is poor. During the communist era in Central and South-Eastern Europe, many Roma benefited from the system, whereas in the period of transition to capitalism the Roma have become the biggest losers. Currently, in the populations of the post-communist states, the Roma number between three and ten percent, and are the population group worst affected by unemployment in all countries. Thus, they have high levels of unemployment, substandard housing, lack of education and skills, and increasing dependence on state benefits and services. At the same time, their birth rate is more than twice the national average. In most countries, the Roma have remained a separated and distinctive ethnic group, retaining their group identity by not cooperating in one very important way: marriage.

3.1 Origin

Roma/Gypsies are a diverse population of South Asian origin which migrated to Europe from central northern India; they arrived in the Byzantine Empire some 900–1100 years ago and became one of the peoples of Europe (Fraser, 1992). It is most likely that the Roma major migration route went through Persia, Armenia,

Greece and the Slavic-speaking parts of the Balkans, as evident from linguistic influences preserved in all Romani dialects. Early European historical sources refer to the Gypsies as Egyptians, and the term "Gypsy" is thought to mirror that assumption. Historical sources reveal that the Gypsies themselves spread legend about their Egyptian origin; they presented themselves as dukes, kings and princes from Egypt. The term Gypsy is today considered pejorative, and the appellation "Roma" is used instead. However, not all Roma people refer to themselves as Roma, and some prefer the European term *cigani* or *zigeuner* (Čvorović, 2010).

Today, the best estimate is that about ten million to twelve million Roma live in Europe, with a large concentration in Central and Eastern Europe (Čvorović, 2014). The precise number of the Roma in Europe is virtually impossible to determine, with contributing factors such as under-sampling of Roma settlements, inability to locate unregistered Roma, frequent migrations, self-declaration of themselves as other ethnic groups, and frequent change of their preferred ethnic identity for opportunistic reasons (Crețan & Turnock, 2008).

Despite the difficulties in estimating their number, all reports and studies agree that, throughout Europe, the majority of Roma live in extended families, in segregated communities characterized by poverty, unemployment, poor education, and poor-quality housing. Usually, communities are close-knit and have limited social contact with non-Roma, while rules of behavior are culturally prescribed with distinct gender roles (Engebrigtsen, 2016). They experience social exclusion, lower life expectancy (ten to fifteen years lower than the European average), higher infant mortality and birth rates, and unemployment up to 80 percent in certain areas (Van Baar, 2021). Many Roma lack education and skills, thus face limited formal employment opportunities, while the majority survive through a combination of social benefits and informal work (Čvorović & Vojinović, 2020). In wealthier European countries, many live exclusively on social assistance (Engebrigtsen, 2016).

Genetic studies, historical and linguistic data suggest that the European Roma, comprised of a large number of socially different endogamous groups, may be a complex aggregation of genetically isolated founder populations (Ena et al., 2022). Research suggest that the Roma are genetically closer to Indians than to European populations, with a strong internal diversity, being far more heterogeneous than autochthonous European populations (Mendizabal et al., 2011). Divisions of the Roma founder population continued during its history in Europe, resulting in numerous socially separated and geographically dispersed endogamous groups. Thus, today, within Europe, there are several Roma metagroups. The classification of the groups/tribes as such is not uniform all over Europe but, generally, there are the Roma of East European extraction; the Sinti in Germany, Manouches in France and Catalonia; the Kaló in Spain, Ciganos in Portugal and Gitans of southern France; and the Romanichals of Britain (Kalaydjieva et al., 2001). The greatest variety of Roma groups is found in the Balkans, where many groups/tribes with distinct social boundaries still exist (Čvorović, 2010).

Since their coming to Europe, Roma have been received with hostility, and much of their history has been overshadowed by persecution from non-Roma (Čvorović, 2014). Upon their arrival in Europe, the Roma, regardless of the countries to which

3.1 Origin

they migrated, share a similar history. At first, they were free to move about and work unmolested for a century or more, before social and economic factors forced them into a situation of enslavement (Fraser, 1992). In the fifteenth century, Roma were traded as slaves in the principalities of Moldavia and Wallachia (present day Romania). In Central and Eastern Europe, the policies of the Austrian Empire and the Ottoman Empire shaped Roma communities in important ways. Under Empress Maria Theresa, Habsburg strategies in the eighteenth century aimed to put an end to the Roma's nomadic lifestyle and encourage assimilation. These strategies involved barring Roma from engaging in most of their traditional occupations and forcibly removing their children and sending them to school. These efforts were ultimately unsuccessful, along with many similar attempts initiated by later rulers in various European nations (Lauwagie, 1979).

During the Ottoman invasion and the establishment of the Empire in the Balkans in the fourteenth and fifteenth centuries, a large number of Roma settled in the region where some served as craftsmen in the army. By that point, however, there was already a Roma population in the Balkans from an earlier wave of migrations (Marushiakova & Popov, 2001). Policies in the Ottoman Empire toward the Roma were more relaxed on the whole and Roma were mostly allowed free movement across borders. However, they were pressed by the Turkish administration into a gray zone between Muslims and non-Muslims and subsequently formed a group of their own (Ginio, 2004). Still, the Roma were greatly influenced by the Ottomans, and many Roma converted to Islam to take advantage of the opportunities offered to Muslims during the Ottoman period, such as tax benefits (Crowe, 2000). The tax register at the time of Sultan Suleiman I the Magnificent (1522–1523), recorded approximately 66,000 Roma in the Balkans, of which about 47.000 were Christian. Over time, the numbers changed in favor of the Muslim Roma as a result of the continuing conversion to Islam. Historical and political circumstances in the nineteenth and twentieth century forged the formation of new ethno-national states throughout the Balkans, where Eastern Orthodoxy became the official religion, and which in turn profoundly altered the status and position of the Roma, These circumstances influenced the variety of Roma groups found in the Balkans (Čvorović, 2010). For example, in the former Yugoslavia, almost each local Roma community had a distinct name even when there was no apparent difference in dialect and occupation between them (Vukanović, 1983).

Despite their presence in the Balkans for centuries, integration of the Roma into their host societies is poor (Čvorović, 2014). During the socialist/communist era in Central and South-Eastern Europe, many Roma benefited from the system. The general policy of socialist governments was to assimilate the Roma, and they were targeted for low-skilled employment within the centrally planned economy (Crowe, 1996). In the post-war years, efforts were made to help the Roma to settle down and to improve their economic and cultural status, which often included the banning of nomadism in most of the countries in the region. Decrees and policies aimed at socioeconomic integration by providing housing and jobs for the Roma were issued by the Communist rulers. Some countries set up workshops to support traditional Roma crafts such as coppersmithing. However, the Roma were not attracted to these low-paying and physically demanding jobs and opted instead to be employed in state-owned enterprises, frequently in unskilled positions, but nonetheless with certain benefits. This created "a culture of dependency" for many Roma (Ringold et al., 2005).

With the fall of communism and the period of transition to capitalism, the living standards and general quality of life have declined for many, but most acutely for the Roma: while largely protected by the socialist regimes, the Roma have been the biggest losers during this transition (Ladányi & Szelényi, 2002). Reflecting their often deplorable life conditions since the fall of communism, they have been called as the "orphans of transition", the "Blacks of East Europe'" and '"the underclass'" (Barany, 1998; Čvorović, 2014). At present, in the populations of the post-communist states, the Roma number between three and ten percent, and are the population group worst hit by unemployment in these states. Thus, they have high levels of unemployment, substandard housing, lack of education and skills, and an escalating dependence on state benefits and services. At the same time, their birth rate is more than twice the national average.

In Europe, various Roma groups are today divided on the basis of religion and language used. They have no common territory and their cultural models often vary from country to country. In many countries, as a result of assimilation processes and manipulation with their ethnicity, many Roma deny their Roma ancestry and altogether reject a connection with Roma people in general (Barany, 2002). Others identify with the country's majority group. Frequently, they have adopted their hosts' culture as a response to the different requirements of prevailing social and environmental settings (Čvorović, 2004). It is for these reasons that Roma culture in general is so diverse and difficult to pinpoint, yet, despite this, a number of generalizations can still be made about their traditional behaviors and culture.

3.2 Nomadism and Traditional Occupations

In the past, nomadism was an important feature of many Roma groups. Typically, due to their flexibility and willingness to move location, they were able to exploit marginal opportunities within their hosts' economy but never attained economic self-sufficiency (Oakley, 1983). They frequently engaged in trade with outsiders in the surrounding society, or undertook whatever occupations they found available, mostly in jobs on the margins of the non-Roma economy. Still, the occupational niches Roma filled made them part of the host country's economy, which benefited both them and the non-Roma (Čvorović, 2014). The traditional Roma occupations included crafts such as trough-making, basket-making, spoon-making, blacksmithing, ironsmithing, and entertainment (music). Generally, Roma found more acceptance in places where their occupational niches were needed, and local groups sought to protect their control over these occupations by refusing to establish wider kinship and marriage ties with Roma in other areas, especially those from different subgroups. Often, the names they assumed described a characteristic trade or occupation, religious affiliation, or other geographical or historical reference. Today, many Serbian Roma still identify themselves by their traditional occupations, even though such occupations no longer exist. It is highly likely that Roma divisions into small groups and subgroups throughout Europe occurred due to pressure for higher mobility in the face of competition for resources and territory, further compounded by oppressive non-Roma legislation and maltreatment, as well as the inclination towards segregation in Roma culture itself.

Roma cultures include a number of mechanisms to prevent non-Roma from meddling in their world. Many Roma place emphasis on the distinction between non-Roma and Roma, that is, *gadje* and *non-gadje*. In the past, Roma law, an oral legal tradition possessing internal concepts of pollution and cleanliness, although applied to varying extent by different Roma groups, prescribed a variety of behaviors in all aspects of social interaction with non-Roma. Roma culture was centered on the concept of *marime* – a set of directives that designated non-Roma as ritually unclean and polluting - which firmly curtailed interactions with outsiders (Weyrauch, 2001). As non-Roma were seen as unclean and polluting and interactions with them were to be avoided, the Roma intentionally also distanced themselves socially from non-Roma (Hancock, 1987; Sutherland, 1975). One of the most important elements in traditional Roma culture was the *kris*. The term referred both to Roma law and to the assembly of elders who imposed it. The law included an elaborate code of morality and family law, with special emphasis on marriage regulations regarding both the Roma and non-Roma. In the past, for a Roma to marry an outsider could mean immediate and permanent exclusion from the community (Sutherland, 1975).

3.3 Marriage and Reproductive Strategies

In most countries, the Roma have remain a separate and distinctive ethnic group. Roma success in retaining their group identity has been due to not participating in one very important way: marriage. For centuries, the Roma marriage pattern has stayed the same: endogamous (toward non-Roma as well as toward other Roma groups), early unions/marriages, an emphasis on girls' virginity, and encouragement of reproduction for all females (Čvorović, 2004). In the past, the function of Roma ethnic endogamy was to preserve and maintain the adaptive traits like reproductive and subsistence strategies, access to resources, and child-rearing practice. In this way, consistently applied endogamy has also functioned as an isolating mechanism by enhancing ethnic identity and reproductive isolation of the Roma population (van den Berghe, 1979).

Today, even for Roma groups with fading or weak traditional practices, most groups restrict their interaction with non-Roma to economic transactions and brief encounters with officials or institutional representatives such as welfare or hospital staff (Čvorović, 2014).

The Roma marriage and reproductive pattern stands out in sharp contrast to their non-Roma host populations. Despite the Roma groups seeming heterogeneous, a common reproductive pattern is observed across all European countries: compared to non-Roma women, Roma women have earlier age at marriage and first reproduction, longer reproductive periods, higher fertility and shorter gestation and birth spacing periods (Szabó et al., 2021; Kamburova et al., 2019; Aisa et al., 2017; Sprocha, 2017).

Roma succeed in achieving their higher fertility in comparison to non-Roma primarily through marriage, this being central to the social and reproductive life of most Roma groups—not just to the "traditional" groups, but also to many "assimilated" parts of Roma populations (Grigore, 2007). Early, pronatalist and patrilocal unions followed by adolescent maternity, with an average of around four children per woman, are typical for most Roma groups. A recent systematic review on European Roma reproductive behavior found that average pregnancy per Roma woman is 3.82, while the average number of live births is slightly lower at 3.33 (Ekezie et al., 2023). Roma total fertility rates vary by country: according to UNICEF MICS 6 reports per country in 2018–2019, in Serbia it was 3.5 children per woman, in Kosovo, it was 3.7, while studies have found that throughout Europe, Roma fertility tends to be way above the majority population average in all birth cohorts and in every country (Szabó et al., 2021). For instance, Roma fertility rates in Serbia and Kosovo resemble a small fraction of countries—mostly located in sub-Saharan Africa— that still have a total fertility rate in excess of 3.0 children per woman (Casterline & El-Zeini, 2022). In contrast, a substantial decline in fertility has taken place in all European countries, particularly the previous communist countries, which together now form one of the regions with the lowest fertility in the world, with total fertility rates (TFRs) ranging between 1.1 and 1.5 children per woman in 2022 (Fihel & Okólski, 2019; Eurostat, 2024).

Traditionally, Roma girls often enter marriage and motherhood as teenagers. Child marriages were historically customary, with a still- present high incidence in low-income countries, especially sub-Saharan Africa and South Asia, and among Roma groups. Legally, child marriage (first marriage before 18 years of age) in Roma communities is still considered as a large-scale problem: child marriage is recognized worldwide as a violation of human and children rights, in particular when the marriage occurs without the free and full consent of both spouses (Joamets & Sogomonjan, 2020). Girl child marriage and subsequent reproduction may involve health risks for both mothers and children, as there is an inherent biological risk associated with young maternal age and reproductive outcomes (Gurven et al., 2016). Additionally, studies have found associations, though not necessarily causal, between girls marrying before 18 years of age and poor educational outcomes (Schaffnit & Lawson, 2021). However, the perceived risks associated with young maternal age may be mitigated by adjusting for maternal, socio-economic and demographic confounding variables. Despite these costs, there may well be fitness benefits associated with early reproduction, such as having a longer reproductive period and higher fertility (Liu & Lummaa, 2011).

3.3 Marriage and Reproductive Strategies

Official available data gathered by United Nations Population Fund show that child marriage is particularly widespread among the Roma: 44% of Roma girls in Serbia, in age groups 13–17 and 15–19, were married or in a union in 2011, with economic factors being one of the most likely driver, in terms of the perceived financial burden for girls in the family and also bride price (UNFPA, 2013). Early marriage is followed by early reproduction: throughout Eastern Europe, adolescent birth rates are significantly higher among Roma than in the overall populations. According to the United Nations Population Fund data, the adolescent birth rate among Serbian Roma is 158 (number of adolescent births per 1000 women 15–19 years), being more than six times the national average of 23.9, and higher than the rate in many of the least developed countries (UNFPA, 2013).

Roma women start reproducing at an optimum age: representative national data show that Roma women start reproduction at an average age of 18 and continue having children in their most fertile years (Čvorović, 2022a, 2022b, 2022c). In many traditional societies, childbirth usually follows soon after marriage, and studies have suggested that the optimal maternal age for first reproduction in traditional societies is 18 years (Liu & Lummaa, 2011). Thus, Roma women are no exception. Roma women attain high fertility at the beginning of their reproductive years, and stop reproducing at least a decade before menopause (Čvorović & Coe, 2017). Regardless of the possible unmet need for contraception, this clearly implies that Roma couples must make a deliberate decision to stop reproducing after the desired number of children is reached. According to data from North Macedonia, the most widely used method of contraception among the Roma is withdrawal, practiced by one in three married Roma women, with the next most popular method being the male condom, while unwanted pregnancies are usually managed through abortions (Toshevska et al., 2018). In 2012, for example, 26% of North Macedonian Roma women used no contraception, resulting in a high percentage - 34% - of the total number of abortions in North Macedonia in contrast against 10% for North Macedonian women.

Census data and official reports suggest that the basic characteristic of the demographic development of the Roma populations is a high natural increase of population, caused by high birth rates and relatively low mortality rates, primarily due to Roma young age structures (Čvorović, 2014). As a consequence of this reproductive pattern, and due to the combination of lower-than-average life expectancy and higher-than-average fertility rates, Roma are a very young population, experiencing a relative increase in size. Thus, it is estimated that in EU countries, 36% of the Roma population is under the age of 15, compared to 16% of the total European population, while the average age of Roma is 25 years compared to 40 years in the EU (EPHA, 2018). Additionally, studies and census data show that as a whole, the Roma female population is characterized by high participation in the total birth rate in the countries in which they reside. At the same time, the level of mortality among Roma children is 2 to 6 times greater than in the rest of the population (Čvorović, 2014).

In addition to early marriage and reproduction, Roma differ from the non-Roma in marriage type: the Roma s mostly practice traditional parentally arranged marriages of their adolescent children, confirmed by the kinship system (Pamporov, 2007). These arranged unions are negotiated by the families involved, and choice of marriageable partner is traditionally limited in an effort to enhance kinship and group solidarity (Čvorović, 2011). The arranged marriages are often accompanied by a custom of bride price, as "payment about [for] the honor of the bride" (Pamporov, 2007:472). Among practicing Roma groups, bride price is regarded as a prestigious custom which signifies the family' higher status within the local hierarchy. Young virgin girls from respectable families are sought after, while the amount of bride price varies; some Roma groups pride themselves for having the priciest girls, for whom several thousands of euros might be paid (Čvorović & Coe, 2019).

According to recent estimates, almost 40% of Serbian Roma females had their first child before their 18th birthday, 10% became mothers before 16 years of age, and among women 15–49 years of age, 16% had a first child before age 15 (UNICEF Srbija, 2020). In regard to schooling, a national representative study on Serbian Roma and non-Roma found a significant association between early marriage and school enrolment among the non-Roma but not among the Roma (Hotchkiss et al., 2016). Despite maternal early marriage, recent studies found that Serbian Roma children up to 5 years of age bear no negative nutritional consequences, while for Roma mothers, personal sacrifice, e.g., poorer health as an outcome of successful reproduction—seems a necessary element for greater reproductive success (Čvorović, 2022a, 2022b, 2022c; Čvorović & Coe, 2017).

Not all Roma arrange the marriages of their children, allowing instead "love unions" (Čvorović & Coe, 2019). However, even in these cases some restrictions apply, especially in the more traditional areas. Endogamy is still preferred and dating is restricted, while a girl's virginity is presumed, and her reputation remaining of the utmost importance. In both types of marriages, encouragement of fertility represents the norm. Many Roma women, regardless of the type of marriage, face rigid gender roles; after marriage, the couple usually lives with the groom's parents. The bride's role is an unsettled one as her duties include maintaining her own kinship system as well as caring for her in-laws, carrying out household chores and producing grandchildren (Fraser, 1992; Timmerman, 2004).

A recent study on marital happiness and health among Roma males and females (91 men and 113 women) in Serbia revealed no significant differences in regard to happiness or health by type of marriage— whether arranged or free choice (Čvorović & Coe, 2019). The majority of participants, both males and females, approved of arranged marriages, declaring that it represents "a true Roma custom". In this study, the majority of Roma in arranged marriages were Muslims, living in extended families. Compared to their free-choice counterparts, Roma in arranged marriages entered their first marriage earlier, were less likely to divorce, and mostly supported the custom of having their marriage arranged parents and families. Females in arranged marriages also lived in larger households as they lived with more kin, had more children and received more social support and alloparenting than their free-choice counterparts. Males in arranged marriages were healthier and engaged less in risky behaviors (smoking and drinking) than their free-choice equivalents. For Roma women, regardless of marriage type, non-subordinate status within the family was the strongest predictor of good health, but the same also held for Roma males: all healthy (happily married) Roma men were alike in that they thought they had subordinate wives.

The findings of the above study underscore the significant impact of what are known to be important selection criteria in societies with arranged marriages. Here, health, in addition to family alliances, stands out as one of the most important of these selection criteria (Stephens, 1963). In general, young people with undesirable behaviors and characteristics (e.g., hard drug use, obesity, short stature) have lower marriage rates than their healthier counterparts (Goldman, 2001). The available data on arranged marriages point out that the mate selection process could be the main factor in creating large differences in life span. In cultures with traditional arranged marriages, unhealthy individuals cannot get married, which leads to the married population having a greater number of healthy individuals (Ikeda et al., 2007). For example, in South Asian countries like India, a diagnosis of diabetes can hinder a young female's marriage prospects, as families preferentially arrange marriages to "healthy" individuals without impediments to bearing children (Goenka et al., 2004). Among the Roma, bride price when combined with arranged marriages serves also as a form of social selection—socially/economically successful Roma males choose fitter Roma females for marriage and this process of assortative mating may in turn create gradients in their offspring (Čvorović, 2019). Besides allowing for "screening" the financial resources and abilities of the future in laws (Apostolou, 2008), bride price also serves to differentiate among Roma groups, while the preferred endogamy further socially separates not only one Roma group from another but from the non-Roma (Čvorović & Coe, 2019).

For many Roma women, having children in marriage is the only socially endorsed route for achieving status (Čvorović & Coe, 2019). Higher maternal status comes with increased age, and it is often equated with motherhood: Roma often address older women as "mother" even if they are not directly related (Čvorović, 2010). Within a Roma family, higher status may afford mothers more power in the decision-making around the child's wellbeing, for example, diet and activities.

3.4 Childbirth and Child Rearming Practices

Many cultures have rich traditions about child birthing: where, how, with whom, and even when a woman gives birth, are increasingly culturally determined. Throughout human history, the childbearing years carried a great risk of mortality for women, with a significant part of that risk being associated with childbirth (Rosenberg & Trevathan, 2018). The period of gestation and the act of childbirth are critical times in the woman's life cycle, when selection operates strongly on the biology of both the mother and her infant (Trevathan, 2017). Cultural adaptations to these risks include attendants of many kinds, including relatives, experienced midwives and obstetricians, who all provide a range of services from emotional support to surgical delivery.

In the past, Roma had elaborate traditions and taboos connected with pregnancy, childbirth and the post-natal period. These traditions varied in degree from group to group and from country to country. However, the significance of many traditional laws has lessened with time, or disappeared altogether.

For example, among Romanian Roma, menstruating and pregnant women, and women 6 weeks up to 2 months after delivery, were considered impure (Grigore, 2007). Numerous taboos determined what she could and could not do. During pregnancy, women were forbidden to perform hard work, e.g. fetching water, and were showered with attention: all their wishes were tended to in order to avoid miscarriage. Among the Serbian Roma, special care was afforded as a means of protection from evil spirits and misfortune, including numerous food taboos to ensure the health of the pregnant woman her unborn child (Vukanović, 1983). Home birth was a rule, and the birth of a child, especially the first, and if it was a boy, was the time of great celebration in traditional Roma communities. In general, childbirth improved a woman's status in society. Even among the contemporary Roma groups, a woman's highest value is her reproductive capacity. If she bears many children, she is respected and rated well; if, on the other hand, she does not produce babies, she may be shunned and returned to her parents (Čvorović, 2004).

Old customs further dictated that, after delivery, for a period of up to 6 weeks, or until the christening, a woman could not leave the house, fetch water, kneed bread, attend to guests or her husband's meals, take care of her father-in-law, or go into her in-laws' room (Grigore, 2007). Only married women who wanted to become pregnant were allowed to visit the new mother and her baby, so as to encourage their own fertility. Thus, a new mother was supposed to limit her activities to caring for her baby (breastfeeding, changing diapers, bathing), with the prohibitions designed to protect postpartum women from difficult tasks, and allow time for rest and childcare.

Early infant care was also regulated by various taboos. In the first 6 weeks after birth, parents or relatives were not allowed to kiss the baby, out of fear of evil spirits. In first year of life, cutting a baby's hair was not allowed; similarly, nail-clipping with a pair of scissors. However, breastfeeding was encouraged early on, while rites protecting a newborn's sleep were numerous.

Nowadays, most pregnant Roma women do not follow any special taboos or prohibitions and childbirth largely occurs in hospital settings: For example, in a recent survey, 99% of mothers in a sample of 2652 Serbian Roma women had a hospital birth (Čvorović, 2022a, 2022b, 2022c). However, in some Serbian rural areas, such as in the remote Roma settlement in northern Vojvodina, many Roma women still opt for a home birth: giving birth at home is regarded among Roma women as something "just natural" (Coe & Čvorović, 2017:9). During home births, women in labor are usually helped by their mothers-in-law, or a female neighbor, while professional help is sought only when something seems off. Some of these Roma women take great pride in home delivery of healthy children and the fact that they did it all by themselves, i.e., without the help of Serbian doctors or nurses, whom they very much distrust. Traditional taboos surrounding pregnancy and child care are now largely forgotten, and, today, there are no special cultural or health recommendations. Furthermore, the majority of Roma women do not alter their diet during pregnancy eat whatever is available, and many continue to smoke and perform their usual day-to-day activities.

3.5 Parenting Practices

Actual Roma parenting practices are largely unknown. There is a general lack of studies, likely as a result of restricted access of non-Roma to the Roma world. Available studies mainly tend to emphasize "traditional Roma child socialization processes", even though most of the traditions are no longer followed, or became altered in contact with majority populations.

Limited studies on the quality of parenting behavior and parenting styles among the Roma have generally found that Roma mothers, in comparison to non-Roma mothers, tend to use more harsh discipline practices (verbal, physical, and psychological control) and less stimulation in interaction with children (Van Laer et al., 2024; Çiçekler et al., 2013; Penderi & Petrogiannis, 2011). Roma overprotective mothering and rigid discipline for children tends to be correlated with lower education, higher degree of poverty, and a number of poverty-related stresses and worries.

Traditional Roma parenting practices have been well described. Traditional Roma child upbringing has been called "community education" (Smith, 1997). This refers to the segregation of the Roma in general: Roma children grow up in an almost exclusively Roma social environment where children are born, raised and live amongst their extended families (Čvorović & Coe, 2019; Engebrigtsen, 2016). Some Roma may live in a nuclear family (parents and their children) within one household; however, quite often excessively many relatives reside in one household. Roma mothers are the primary caretakers of their children with limited support from fathers, but in most families they are assisted by helpers at the nest, i.e., close or distant relatives (Čvorović, 2022a, 2022b, 2022c). Thus, typically, Roma children grow up surrounded by many allomothers—siblings, aunts, grandmothers and other close and distant kin. Infants and toddlers tend to be carried around by their mothers most of the time, while older children are frequently nearby. Children participate in their extended family' day-to-day activities and learn by watching, listening and imitating older kin in whatever they are doing. In a typical rural Roma settlement, adult Roma frequently engage with children in playing games, storytelling, joking and teasing (Čvorović, 2010).

In the past, child labor was an important part of the family's subsistence, thus it was important that a child learn work skills required for the particular traditional occupations and contribute to the family economy. Roma children would accompany family members on jobs such as flower selling, tarmacking, scrap metal collecting, begging, or fortune-telling (Christianakis, 2010). Even today with traditional occupations no longer in use, Roma children engage in child labor and work in the streets, with the level of poverty directly determining the frequency of child labor (Bogetić & Jugović, 2018).

There are differing expectations with regard to gender. Roma girls are expected to assume certain responsibilities from a relatively early age, such as help with their younger siblings, or around the house. Unlike the girls, boys may be frequently left unattended to play in groups or engage in sports such as football. At puberty, boys acquire more rights and even fewer obligations than girls (Smith, 1997).

Storytelling was practiced by many Roma groups in the past (Čvorović, 2010). Traditional stories served as a source of knowledge and information on the history of their ancestors, proper kin behavior, economic life, relationships with other peoples, and many other aspects of the everyday world. In the past, these stories were retold over many generations, and in many cases repeated, with few alterations from one telling to the next. They were told to children and teenagers to influence their behavior in specific ways. For instance, for the Serbian Roma, telling and listening to stories helped to preserve and enforce patterns of behavior which promoted group success, such as endogamous marriage and respect for traditional occupations. In this sense, traditional storytelling was a parental mode of influencing the behavior, especially social behavior, of children and potentially even distant descendants. Many stories focus on kin relationships and describe the rules and conventions of how people within a certain kin category ought to behave towards one another. Much of the behavior encouraged by the stories includes forms of kin obligations relating to various significant life events or phases, such as marriage and dying. Some stories and poems describe Roma childcare, expressing in a poetic way the practicality of Roma life philosophy: there will always be some things in their immediate environment that they can use to fulfill existing needs without expending much effort on their part.

In some Roma communities, storytelling practices persist to a certain extent, while in many others the stories are forgotten. Many of the older Roma grew up with traditional stories, learning their way through life from these stories. Older generations of Roma often complain that the youngsters, children and adolescents, do not care and do not know about "the old ways", and that the traditions will die with them: "…The way we are, if they [the younger generation] don't learn [the traditional stories], it's goodbye [to Gypsy ways] (Čvorović, 2010:46).

In other traditional Roma groups, however, like the Njamci subgroup in Mačva, Western Serbia, the traditional stories are still told almost every day, especially to young children and teenagers, forming an important part of their education. In this settlement, many of the children do not attend the local school regularly; even when they do, most drop out in their early teens and get married. For many older Roma, traditional stories are regarded as the only true "education". in addition to observing and copying the everyday lifestyle of the older members of their extended family. Both the young and old Roma enjoy the storytelling; usually, the stories are told by grandparents or older members of the family. The stories are usually told in their full extent - even lascivious parts are described to young children, since, only then are the stories "true" and serve their purpose.

3.6 Formal Education of Roma Children

Formal education is a fundamental component of parental investment, and believed to improve a child's wellbeing and success worldwide (Hedges et al., 2016). Parental investment can increase child's reproductive success by improving connected spheres such as economic success and social standing. Worldwide, as populations undergo demographic and economic transitions, formal schooling is replacing the more traditional forms of learning as an important feature of capital attainment.

For the Roma, the increasing need for literacy and pressure to conform to mainstream social norms, especially in regard to formal education, have created many conflicts. Throughout Europe, Roma parents rarely invest in their children's formal education. Schooling may be costly for parents, directly through spending on school tuition and supplies, but also indirectly, as it reduces children's ability to contribute to household economics (Liddell et al., 2003). Thus, Roma generally have poor school attendance, and for those children who do enroll, few make any progress at school (Čvorović, 2019). Large numbers of European Roma can neither read nor write: the share of Roma between the ages of 16 and 24 who say that they cannot read or write is 35% (FRA, 2014). Even in cases where schooling is provided in their own language, Romani, many fail to complete even a basic education (Mag, 2012).

To try mitigate this, over the past couple of decades governments in Central and South-Eastern Europe have introduced strategies aimed at improving the Roma situation in several areas, including children's education and inclusion; however with little effect. Typically, encouraged by various incentives, Roma children may start pre-and primary school, but rarely succeed in finishing elementary education. Data from Eastern Europe show that Roma boys spend on average 6.71 years in formal education, while girls tend to spend on average even less: around 5.66 years (Selander & Walter, 2020).

In Central and Eastern Europe, children are tested at the age of five or six or seven for entry into primary school. As a result of these tests, a disproportionate high number of Roma children are assigned to special classes or placed in special schools where simplified curricula are used (Bennett, 2012). For instance, in Serbia, the enrolment rate for Roma children in special schools is 36 times higher than the rest of the population (Čekic Marković, 2016).

At the same time, available census data reveal that 15% of Roma older than 10 years are illiterate; 21.2% of female Roma are illiterate, with only 33.3% having finished elementary school. These figures, however, may be an overestimation since the data were self-reported. For those who reported as having finished elementary school, 17% of Roma females and 24% of Roma males could not read a simple statement (Čvorović, 2019). Among rural Roma, female illiteracy rates are even more disturbing: in some areas, some women never attend school and thus lack basic reading skills, while for those who attended school, the average number of years spent there is 3 (Coe & Čvorović, 2017). As a reflection of multigenerational transmission of educational inequality, Roma children may rarely attend school even though there are elementary schools in the settlements where they live.

Findings from the MICS6 in Kosovo, Montenegro, North Macedonia and Serbia, conducted from 2018 to 2020, reveal that children in Roma settlements typically lag behind in education and learning. Compared to national averages, Roma children are less likely to attend school, more likely to be over-age thus facing higher risk of dropout, less likely to complete primary and secondary education, and have a lower chance of acquiring basic skills across education levels (UNICEF, 2024).

In Roma settlements in all countries socio-economic status was found to be negatively associated with risk of being out of school. In Kosovo, for example, the risk of school non-attendance is higher for girls, children with functional difficulties, and those not living with both parents.

Multi-dimensional factors, including poverty, financial ability of the parents and child labor, may explain the Roma deficit in formal education. Additionally, many tend to blame the language barrier for this situation. However, in this regard, a large proportion of East European Roma (at least 80 percent in Hungary, for instance) speak no Romani at all (Barany, 1998). In Serbia, the census shows that approximately half of the Roma use Romani as their native language, while the other half use Serbian and other languages (Statistical office of the republic of Serbia 2022).

Roma school absenteeism may further be explained by the impact of cultural practices, such as the early ages of marriage and early childbearing of Roma females, but also the low value placed on education and professional success among the Roma in general. Among Roma women aged 20–49 in the Western Balkans region, those who married before age 18 have lower educational achievement compared with those who did not experience child marriage (Robayo-Abril & Millán, 2019). However, data from Serbia do not confirm this finding: a recent nationally representative household survey found Roma girls in Serbia to be at very high risk of being married before age 18, in contrast to the general population; however, the study failed to find any significance in the association between early marriage and school enrolment among the Serbian Roma (Hotchkiss et al., 2016). Furthermore, empirical evidence points to lower educational expectations and aspirations in some Roma families, which tend to limit the children's chance of schooling (UNICEF, 2024). This is usually explained by the low socioeconomic status of Roma parents: educated parents with steady jobs are more likely to be aware of the importance of formal education and invest accordingly. For instance, in the Western Balkans, Roma parents are significantly less likely to expect their child to get tertiary education compared to non-Roma parents (Robayo-Abril & Millán, 2019). And, just like their parents, Roma children have lower educational aspirations than non-Roma children (Dimitrova et al., 2018).

A study on mother-child interaction and maternal child stimulation among the Serbian Roma found that mothers showed limited involvement in their child's learning and development: of 584 Roma mothers, only 14% engaged in book reading, whereas the majority (60%) engaged in storytelling, singing songs (74%), playing with the child (86%), taking the child outside (77%), with only 16% counting or drawing with the child (Čvorović & Vojinović, 2020). Maternal level of basic literacy was low: only 36% of mothers were literate. Many Roma children are deprived of books and toys, while stimulating activities, such as reading books or teaching children about letters and numbers, require not only actual books but also basic literacy and numeracy skills, which many Roma women do not possess.

Somewhat counterintuitively, however, research from Romania has found that children from families with a relatively good income gained through a traditional Roma profession, tend to abandon school after the eighth grade, whereas children from families with low income tend to continue with secondary education (Popovici, 2008). Thus, the intention to be economically successful from an early age influences some Roma children to opt for a traditional occupation rather than a school education, despite their parents' preferment of mainstream schooling.

A possible further factor contributing to the unfavorable educational situation of Roma children relates to their culture (Bafekr, 1999). Thus, Roma absenteeism from school may be partially explained by breaking of contact as a cultural means of overcoming a difficult situation. The feeling is that the material learned in school is not congruent with the values of Roma culture, especially at the cognitive and semantic levels. Within a typical Roma family, verbal communication is characterized by the absence of abstract or subtle concepts (Mag, 2012). At school, the Roma child will have difficulty in understanding these abstract concepts, which in many cases do not appear to have any connection with their life. This difficulty is especially important in the acquisition of reading and writing, with little stimulation and support given at home for the subjects taught in school. As an outcome of these contrasting cultural values, there exists a communication gap, where neither party understands the other. Consequently, not only are Roma parents afraid that their children will be changed by foreign influences, they also fail to understand or accept the importance of school as an institution (Smith, 1997). Formal school thus becomes merely the place for learning to read and write, if at all – as soon as the children learn the basics, they leave (Čvorović, 2014). In fact, this breaking of social contact is a feature of Roma culture practiced frequently by both adults and children. Since the Roma then are unable to categorize new objects or events, they turn away from them as a specific cultural method of overcoming conflict in addition to the deliberate rejection of the other culture (Bafekr, 1999).

3.7 Why Roma Have High Fertility

Many studies have been conducted to explain the reasons leading to the higher fertility and mortality rates of the Roma, and several theories were put forward as to the possible association between the Roma's way of life and their demography. Roma reproductive behavior is usually perceived as worsening their inability to integrate (Kaneva & Popescu, 2014). The Roma high birth and mortality rates and shorter life expectancy are usually regarded as the result of their poverty, low level of education and socioeconomic status, associated with poor judgment about future difficulties caused by having a large number of children and inadequate health care.

Similar explanations stress Roma women's non-use of contraception, poor reproductive knowledge or lack of decision-making in respect of their reproductive behavior (Čvorović, 2014).

Others argue that because the Roma have limited access to modern medical devices, health care and family planning, they are much less able to control their fertility than other Europeans. In addition, since the majority of Roma have little schooling or vocational skills, many of them are unemployed and they do not feel the need to sacrifice reproduction for "cultural goals" as much as a European with higher socioeconomic status (Bereczkei et al., 2000).

A recent study on Roma fertility in the European Union established a connection between maternal nativity and high levels of adolescent fertility (Kamburova et al., 2019). The study showed that the increasing trend in Roma early childbirth corresponded to the increased share of Roma population within countries: the average adolescent live birth rate in countries with highest proportion of Roma was 5.6 times higher compared with the average in countries with the lowest proportion of Roma population. Another study analyzed Roma fertility in four neighboring countries in Central and Eastern Europe with a large Roma minority (Hungary, Slovakia, Romania and Serbia), and found significantly higher fertility of Roma women compared to ethnic majority populations, with education as a modifying factor (Szabó et al., 2021). The degree of assimilation may also play a role in Roma fertility: women in segregated settlements in Serbia tend to have higher fertility than women living in closer proximity to the majority (Battaglia et al., 2021). Other suggested that Roma reproductive behavior and fertility form the core of their cultural expression, serving as a form of resistance or 'weapon of the poor', against discrimination and life challenges (Gamella, 2018).

A study on the Roma in Hungary suggested that the main motivation behind the Roma high fertility is manipulation of the welfare system: Roma families benefit more from welfare benefits through having many children (Durst, 2001). In more affluent European countries, a large proportion of Roma live - and reproduce - on social assistance exclusively (Castañeda, 2015). For instance, for many Roma mothers in Serbia, government-provided cash benefits are the only guaranteed source of income; the Serbian welfare state guarantees the Roma benefits in health care, schooling, and social assistance incentives, mitigating the hardships to at least a certain extent (Čvorović, 2024). These child cash benefits compensate partially at least for the additional costs of an extra child and increase household spending on inputs. Thus, Roma are achieving a successful reproductive strategy "on welfare", which may help to maintain fertility, feed the children, and balance the costs of health and nutrition that mothers would otherwise face.

There are, however, alternative hypotheses to explain Roma increased reproductive success, derived from evolutionary theory. Several studies based on life history theory have attempted to explain the adaptive character of Roma behaviors. Thus, it has been suggested that Roma populations in the studied areas (Hungary and Serbia) exhibit more "fast-selected" traits that are associated with high reproductive rates, reduced parental investment, and relatively short intergeneration times than surrounding non-Roma populations (Bereczkei et al., 2000; Čvorović, 2004). From the life history perspective, this difference is attributable to the different socio-economic environments faced by Roma and non-Roma populations, but also as a result of a combination of genetic and cultural factors. In these studies, neither low education or low occupational status were found to be the main cause of high Roma fertility. A further hypothesis suggested to account for the difference in fertility and higher fertility rates among the Roma is their more extensive kinship networks (Bereczkei, 1998). Extended kinship cooperation has been shown to be evolutionarily successful, and within traditional settings, a major influence for the survival and preservation of populations, thus accounting for greater reproductive success (Limb et al., 2014; van Den Berghe, 1979). Generally, traditional Roma have many more close and distant kin than non-Roma: they keep closer contact with one another, and spend more time helping relatives with direct child-rearing activities than non-Roma, who lack such kinship support as a means to decrease the costs of childrearing and increase chances of investing in another offspring. This was shown in a recent study where decreased kin support among Serbian Roma resulted in decline of reproductive success (Čvorović & Vojinović, 2020).

Another line of explanation focuses on the status of women, which may be of a particular importance in fertility behaviors, determined more by religious and other cultural values, than by socioeconomic development per se (Knodel & Van de Walle, 1979). Among the Roma groups in more traditional settings, the female role is subordinate, marriages are typically arranged by parents and/or kinship group at an early age to ensure virginity and chastity, and high fertility serves as a social and gender obligation (Čvorović, 2014). In the past, this Roma traditional marriage system ensured that every male obtained a wife at the beginning of her reproductive years-- who else would marry him – while the girls' obligatory virginity affirmed paternal confidence. The role of the parents and kinship group can thus be seen as the key factor in decision-making in the area of reproduction and the means by which individuals can promote their interests within kinship groups.

Yet a further explanation is that the Roma came to identify with a model of large family that has a high value as a norm in their culture. Children born to a large circle of kinship network will learn to identify with the model that encourages a great number of children, thus a demand for high fertility may remain strong through generations (Bereczkei et al., 2000:294).

Thus, the above evolutionary- and culturally based explanations suggest the most probable reasons for the high fertility seen among the Roma. However, there are still other factors that may account for the success of Roma groups in maintaining successful reproduction.

Evolutionary theory has suggested that the way humans behave today can be understood by considering which behaviors increased the relative survival and reproduction of our ancestors (Michalski & Shackelford, 2010). In certain ancestral environments, engaging in particular types of behaviors increased ancestral humans' chances to out-survive and out-reproduce those less successful. Thus, while the offspring of these ancestors had a chance of inheriting the genetic features responsible for successful development, regardless of the genes involved, all offspring might also have inherited certain successful, learned patterns of behavior, i.e., traditions. Therefore, in response to similar cues, both inheritances may have resulted in reproductive success. This implies that when we study the Roma and their traditions, including reproductive behavior, we are actually studying adaptations and broad traits that were presumably successful in the past (Steadman & Palmer, 2015; Čvorović, 2014). A notable example is religion: given that religion tends tended to be traditional (i.e., vertically inherited from parents to offspring, see Steadman & Palmer, 2015), different religions may have encouraged different traditional reproductive strategies and life histories (Čvorović, 2011). Worldwide, religiosity–fertility links are a near–universal characteristic of today's cultures (Kaufmann, 2010). More specifically, individuals who incline to have dogmatic and traditional religious beliefs, out-reproduce those with more secular worldviews. Demography appears to be important for the historical rise and decline of religions as, more than for most other cultural traits, religion is transmitted within families (Steadman & Palmer, 2015). This is especially seen with the Roma where, throughout the Balkans, the main division among the various Roma tribes/groups has always been along the line of tribal and religious affiliation, i.e., Islam versus Christianity (Marushiakova & Popov, 2001). Thus, from the above research, a considerable fitness differential by religion exists between the various Serbian Roma groups: Muslim groups tend to be reproductively more successful, with reduced investment allocation per child than their Christian counterparts, even after controlling for education and socioeconomic status.

3.8 Cost of Reproduction for Roma Women

Everywhere, Roma out-reproduce non-Roma. However, a successful reproductive strategy is not without cost (Čvorović & Coe, 2017). Life history predicts that the energy invested in reproduction is traded off against investments in maintenance and survival. Thus, having more offspring is associated with the aging process, which potentially shapes other life-history traits (Alonso-Alvarez et al., 2017). From an evolutionary perspective, this cost has to result in a lower contribution to the gene pool of the next generation, as a consequence of reduced longevity and reduced reproductive success. Individual health is not the anticipated outcome of selection, apart from its contribution to reproductive success: When health and reproductive success conflict, selection will favor reproduction at the expense of health (Nesse, 2001).

It remains unclear as to whether or not a (an evolutionary, long-term) cost of reproduction definitely exists among humans. Recent studies seem to confirm Williams' theory: that aging may be a side effect of natural selection's impact on fertility (Long & Zhang, 2023). A recent study by Long and Zhang (2023) found that the genetic variations associated with fertility, such as number of children, are also associated with shorter life span: mutations that increased fertility could cause harm in later life, and over many generations, these mutations could create a burden that would eventually lead to death.

In regard to short-term cost, as the direct costs of reproduction—pregnancy, breast-feeding and childcare—require energy, energetic costs are an essential feature of reproduction (Jasienska, 2017). Pregnancy and lactation also involve many physiological changes, including decreased the functioning of the maternal immune system and increased levels of oxidative stress. The metabolic demands associated with these changes can lead to women experiencing significant physiological costs associated with the reproductive effort and are thus at risk as a result of the negative consequences of these trade-offs (Kirkwood & Rose, 1991). The trade-offs are more critical in resource-poor environments. For instance, lifetime parity was found to shorten maternal lifespan in some, although not all, energetically constrained environments (Hurt et al., 2006). Studies of modern populations have reported a U-shaped effect, whereby nulliparous and women with more than four children experience highest mortality. These results may, however, be confounded by differences in phenotypic quality: healthy women may have both high fertility and a long life, thus any unfavorable effect of parity on longevity could be masked by unobserved health characteristics (Sear, 2007). Nonetheless, even if total reproduction is not consistently associated with maternal depletion, the timing and intensity of reproduction can still produce somatic costs that can affect different aspects of maternal health and fitness (Gurven et al., 2016).

3.8.1 Roma Women's Health

A recent systematic review of Gypsy, Roma and Traveller (GRT) women reproductive outcomes suggests that GRT women and their children experience more negative outcomes than non- GRT populations (Ekezie et al., 2023). The review included various populations such as English, Scottish and Welsh Gypsies, Scottish and Irish Travellers, and Roma from Central and Eastern Europe. The studies under review were conducted in 13 European countries: Croatia, Czech Republic, Hungary, Ireland, Kosovo, Macedonia, Romania, Serbia, Slovakia, Spain, Turkey, and the UK. According to the review, these studies reported a lower level of prenatal care utilization by GRT women, a shorter gestation period, higher fertility (an average of 4 children per woman), and higher child mortality and pre-term births, compared with the majority populations. Being a GRT was also noted as an important predictor of lower mean birth weight and low birth weight.

According to European Public Health Alliance report (EPHA, 2018), Roma women tend to have much shorter lives than non-Roma women. For example, in the Czech Republic, Roma life expectancy is around 10–15 years less than the majority population; this figure being generally accepted for the whole Roma population in Europe. In European Union, figures for life expectancy from birth are 81.0 to 83.6 years for all women and 78.2 years for all men, while 64 years for Roma men and 70 years for Roma women. Similar figures have been found in Croatia, Greece, Hungary, Italy, North Macedonia, Portugal, Romania, Serbia and Spain (FRA, 2022).

A study from Serbia addressed the potential costs of reproduction and the effects this may have on health among Roma women (Čvorović & Coe, 2017). The study, conducted in a sample of 486 Roma women, measured the effect of all forms of reproductive investment, e.g. the timing, reproductive intensity, reproductive effort, and investment after birth. The study findings appeared to be consistent with simple trade-off models that suggest inverse relationships between reproductive effort and health, while evolutionary, long-term costs were not observed. In contrast, Roma women in poor health contributed more to the gene pool of the next generation than their healthy Roma counterparts. Thus, the short-term costs of reproductive investment after birth (duration of breastfeeding, number of surviving children and higher BMI (body mass index) all contributed to poor health. Consequently, personal sacrifice—breastfeeding and childcare, even though poor health is an outcome—seems crucial for greater reproductive success, i.e., leaving more descendants.

In another study, it was found in Romanian Roma women living in Serbia, who frequently engaged in risky behaviors, nevertheless appeared to be at lower risk for ovarian and breast cancer (Coe & Čvorović, 2017). Traditional Roma share similar marriage and reproductive characteristics with Mormons and Seventh Day Adventists, and may therefore be at lower-than-average risk due to these shared characteristics, which include early age at marriage and first pregnancy, multiparity, breastfeeding, and relatively early menopause. Taken together, these behaviors can be combined into what may be referred to as "protected time", characterized by periods of anovulation, during which the woman is not exposed to hormones associated with increased cancer risk.

Roma women's lives are characterized by repeated pregnancies, intensive breastfeeding and many dependent children. These, combined with deficient prenatal care, poor diet, and caffeine, alcohol and tobacco consumption during pregnancy may all contribute to their impaired health (Šupínová et al., 2020). In turn, the costs of maximizing reproduction, in addition to other costs borne by mothers, may be intergenerational, i.e., also borne by the offspring (Coall & Chisholm, 2003). That is, parents tend to balance costs and benefits of investment by taking decisions that maximize fitness, and when they decrease investment in a particular offspring, the costs fall on the development of the child, while parents lose only potential future benefits (Alonso-Alvarez & Velando, 2012; Nettle, 2010).

3.8.2 Child Outcomes

Across Europe, the poor health of adult Roma is well documented, but there is only limited data on the health of Roma children (Sárváry et al., 2019).

3.8.2.1 Infant Mortality

Studies and reports have consistently found that Roma children have higher mortality than infants and children of non-Roma, usually attributed to poverty and inadequate living conditions (EPHA, 2018). Overall, hygiene in Roma settlements tends to be poor, little attention is paid to health, and there is resistance to child immunization programs (Čvorović, 2014). In addition to causes created by poverty, there are behavioral and cultural causes—lack of proper childcare and investment, which contribute to the high mortality. In Roma culture, the father and other caregivers are valuable, but mothers tend to be the most important care-givers so that their behavioral characteristics are without doubt the most important for child health. Among the general Roma population, a certain level of infant mortality is "expected", and, for some children, there may be an under-investment in care, feeding, and response to illnesses. Many Roma seem to be aware of high risks that may affect their infants and children. And while some Roma parents openly joke on their own account about their untroubled attitudes towards children—when they fail to take measures to prevent child death or accidents, some joke that they will make another one instead—others do their best to rationalize child losses. For example, in some remote Serbian Roma villages, mothers with many children often may not remember the cause of death of the deceased children nor all the names of the living children or their year of birth. When asked why they bore so many children, they usually respond by a saying "One for Death, one for me" (Čvorović, 2010: 48).

Data from Bulgaria, Bosnia and Herzegovina and Spain show the infant mortality rate of Roma to be consistently three to four times higher than other populations. Mortality also tends to be higher for Roma infants (under 1 year) than older children (Ekezie et al., 2023). The majority of the causes of infant mortality are prematurity, developmental and congenital anomalies, newborn cerebral haemorrhage, chronic lung and heart disease, infections, and abnormalities (Bereczkei et al., 2000).

In Slovakia, data show that, while both fertility and infant mortality of Roma are in slow decline, both population parameters are still much higher, by approximately 3-times, than for non-Roma mothers (Koval' et al., 2012). Slovakian Roma mothers tend to have low interest in providing healthcare to their children, which includes low immunization and poor healthcare education.

Due to their lack of basic healthcare education, many Roma mothers are unable to provide even the simplest preventive care, e.g. mucus suction, application of drops, oral medication administration, fever treatment, etc. An additional problem could be that Slovakian Roma have the highest inbreeding coefficient (level of mating between blood relatives) in Europe, resulting in a high incidence of developmental congenital defects (Ferák et al., 1987; Koval' et al., 2012). A recent study found that Roma children living in segregated settlements suffer more often from infectious and chronic diseases, injuries, poisoning and burns than children from the majority population, and make up the majority of hospitalized children (Filakovska Bobakova & Dankulincova Veselska, 2024).

In some Serbian Roma groups, the loss of infants is so common that almost every woman grows up with the certain knowledge that she will lose children (Čvorović,

2011). Official reports point out that in the general Serbian Roma population one half of children die in the first and second years of their lives, with the majority of these (fifty-two per cent) dying of an unknown cause (Oxfam and Belgrade Institute for Health Protection, 2003: 15).

A common theme in Serbian Roma folklore is losing one's child to the harmful action of local witches, used to justify unexplained child and infant deaths without blaming the mother (Čvorović, 2013). Some Roma groups, like the Kalderashi (cauldron makers) in western Serbia, have conjured elaborate narratives that explain the loss of infants. These narratives are told exclusively by women who have lost at least one infant to "the deadly doings of witches", where they describe the actual event of losing one's child to the action of local witches. These stories are endorsed by husbands and the community despite the belief that a witch which harms children is only encountered by women, sometimes during their pregnancy, but most of the time after a child has been born. The (usually silent) approval of the audience, and the acceptance of the mother's claims that her child was killed by a local witch, takes away any responsibility from the mother. These narratives are a combination of facts, exaggeration, and fiction, using false emphasis, loaded descriptions, and the introduction of a supernatural being, carefully cast as guilty. The narratives thus tread a line between the truth and lying, allowing for a mislead or distraction from a real investigation into how the children lost their lives (Čvorović, 2013:218). These stories have become so established within the Roma communities, just like other Roma stories, literally "as is" – as traditional folklore that no one seriously disapproves or opposes. Still, a few that have dared to dismiss the stories have alleged that at least one of the mothers, who had lost several children, was herself responsible for their deaths. In this Kalderashi village, ten per cent of the infants who died were twins. All the mothers who had lost their twins claimed that "witches" were to blame for death of their babies. However, without birth and death certificates, Roma witches and alleged dead children exist only in narratives. Nonetheless, such cultural beliefs on the causes of infant death provide equal weight to both actual and supernatural agents (Levine, 1987). Thus, when a child dies, the death may be attributed as much to supernatural forces beyond human control as to illness or parental neglect.

3.8.2.2 Child Nutrition

Studies assessing Roma nutritional status are limited, especially for children (Llanaj et al., 2020). Generally, Roma children in Central and Eastern Europe have a high prevalence of undernutrition compared to children from other populations, usually explained by socio-economic gradients (Janevic et al., 2010; UNICEF, 2015).

A study from North Macedonia found that anthropometric parameters of nutritional status of Roma children are significantly different from those of non-Roma children, with the health risk mostly related to underweight (Spiroski et al., 2011). In Serbia, the prevalence of stunting, wasting, and underweight was 20.1%, 4.3%, and 8.0%, respectively (Janevic et al., 2010); another study found the prevalence of stunting to be 19%, and wasting 9% (Čvorović, 2022a, 2022b, 2022c).

Research in Serbia found that Roma children tend to have a significantly greater occurrence of comorbidity, malnutrition, skin diseases, and anemia than non-Roma; in addition, the length of hospitalization, number of laboratory tests performed and number of drugs prescribed is significantly higher for Roma children compared to non-Roma children (Djurovic et al., 2014).

To date, only one study from Serbia has addressed the effect of unwantedness on children's nutritional status. In a sample of 130 children aged 0–24 months, it was found that children born with low birth weight (lower maternal investment in utero) face a significant deficit in terms of their nutritional outcomes, measured by HAZ and WAZ, while the effect was aggravated for height if the child was unwanted (Čvorović, 2023).

3.8.2.3 Sibship Size

In addition to social determinants of health, Roma children face additional challenges as a result of growing up with many siblings (Čvorović, 2024). In most environments, parental resources are limited and parents face a trade-off in number of children and allocation of investment per child (quantity-quality trade-off) (Lawson & Mace, 2008). Evolutionary life history theory predicates that siblings in large families compete for limited parental resources (quantity-quality trade-off effects) (Kramer et al., 2016).

Early childhood growth (height and body size) is an important proxy for offspring quality (health and fitness), for a trade-off between offspring number and quality, or between number and size of offspring, and therefore children's growth is expected to be negatively associated with family size (Walker et al., 2008). Growing up in large families, with many siblings, may especially be harmful for the later borns, as parents tend to invest more in offspring who have a greater likelihood of contributing to parental fitness, which, are often older children (Hertwig et al., 2002). Thus, the negative effects of competition between offspring (quantity-quality trade-off effects) most often occur under conditions of resource scarcity and high fertility (Gibson & Lawson, 2011).

Among humans, research on trade-offs between family size (quantity) and child quality has provided mixed results, where several studies have found a negative effect of family size on growth, while others have not (Lawson & Mace, 2008). A recent study on 1096 Serbian Roma children aged 0–59 months found that only children were taller and heavier than those with three and four or more siblings, indicating that growing up in a small family is beneficial for Roma children, at least in regard to their physical growth (Čvorović, 2024). The study also found that older children tend to be taller and heavier than their younger counterparts, reflecting maternal favoritism of older children: older offspring are valued much more highly than younger ones as the reproductive value of offspring tends to increase with higher age.

3.8.2.4 Weight at Birth

Another health consideration regarding Roma infants, likely associated with Roma reproductive strategy, is low birthweight. Numerous studies have suggested that Roma ethnicity is independently associated with lower birthweight among at-term newborns, and that the association remains even after controlling for known risk factors (Balázs et al., 2013; Stanković et al., 2016; Čvorović, 2004; Bereczkei et al., 2000). Generally, Roma women tend to give birth to shorter and lighter infants, with higher rates of low birthweight, on average being more than double that of non-Roma women. As low birth weight carries significant health risks for children, it may explain the disparity in mortality rates between Roma and non-Roma children.

Potential environmental and social determinants of lower birthweight of Roma children are well known, these being exacerbated by poverty, low socioeconomic status and inadequate prenatal health care utilization. However, adult Roma nutritional status shows that they are well-fed despite their low socioeconomic position, while among females, more than one third are overweight and one tenth are obese (Gallagher et al., 2009; Čvorović & Coe, 2017). The high incidence of low birth weight among the Roma does not therefore have to be a result of social disadvantage, but may rather be a reflection of human biological diversity in response to particular environmental cues (Čvorović, 2014).

Height is an important determinant of several reproductive outcomes (Emanuel et al., 2004). Maternal height may reflect intergenerational linkages in health because adult height proxies childhood circumstances, i.e., it reflects growth, nutrition and social environment in earlier life (Silventoinen, 2003). Thus, previous studies have found that shorter maternal height is a risk factor for offspring outcomes in developing countries (Stulp & Barrett, 2016), but the results appear inconsistent in non-Western populations (Arendt et al., 2018). When resources are limited, mothers with small body size may experience higher offspring survival compared to mothers with bigger body size, as small body size may reflect possible adaptive responses to poor environmental conditions (Bernasovská et al., 1998; Durankova et al., 2013; Gluckman et al., 2007). In other words, short maternal height may have been selected for as a result of an advantage of an earlier growth cessation and enhanced reproduction, where low birth weight may be considered a part of an adaptive behavioral complex for increasing reproduction (Walker et al., 2008). The constraints on fetal size can be interpreted in life history terms as means by which a mother limits her investment in an offspring in expectation of subsequent pregnancies (Pike, 2005).

Compared to average Europeans, Roma tend to have lighter weight at birth, lower height for both males and females, a lighter/build, smaller muscles, and a weaker physical constitution (Gallagher et al., 2009; Čvorović, 2004; Stanković et al., 2016). Research among Serbian Roma found that Roma mothers of short height (1st quartile) and higher parity were more likely to have lower birthweight infants than women of tall or medium height (Čvorović, 2018). Small body size is a response to disease and malnutrition and may be a life-history consequence of relatively faster ontogeny in high-mortality environments (Migliano et al., 2007).

3.8 Cost of Reproduction for Roma Women

Shorter women thus may have less room for fetal development and reduced protein and energy stores, resulting in poorer birth outcomes, including low birthweight infants (Addo et al., 2013). Life history theory predicts that parental investment during pregnancy will differ according to the mother's early-life circumstances and reproductive strategy (Pike, 2005). Disadvantaged early life may increase fecundity and fertility as means to allocate resources in current reproduction in a high-risk environment (Lawson & Borgerhoff Mulder, 2016). This trade-off between offspring number and size assumes optimal allocation of parental resources to reproduction that maximizes parent's genetic representation expression in future generations (Walker et al., 2008).

Population-specific growth references may serve as a more biologically accurate assessment of within-population child growth (Kramer et al., 2016), however, no specific growth references have yet been produced for the Roma, despite their Indian origins (Čvorović, 2022a, 2022b, 2022c). Studies from Indian and South Asian populations living in Britain show considerable similarities with the Roma population measures (Kandraju et al., 2012; Stanković et al., 2016). Indian children are usually smaller for all anthropological parameters wherever they are born, regardless of socioeconomic variables (Bernasovská et al., 1998). Indian infants weighting 2500 g are better off when compared with the European infants of the same weight, In light of the average low birth weight of full-term Roma infants, several studies proposed that the specific limit birth weight of 2250 g shouldbe used for Roma infants (Bernasovská et al., 1998). Around 10 percent of full-term Roma infants have low birth weight according to WHO criteria, i.e., under 2500 g. Reducing the limit to 2250 g would result in just 2.03 percent of Roma newborns with low birth weight. This percentage corresponds to the percentage of non-Roma infants with the birth weight below 2500 g. A Prague study of full-term newborns produced comparable results. In addition, full term Roma infants with birth weight under 2500 g, but more than 2250 g, present themselves mostly as the full-term mature infants (Bernasovská et al., 1998: 134). Therefore, given the same medical care, Roma infants are better able to adapt to their environment than non-Roma infants, which are more frequently born premature. Today, the "small baby" is well known as a "thrifty phenotype" (Wells, 2007). The thrifty phenotype represents a short-term adaptive response resulting in reduced investment in some organs to protect other organs. In the low birth-weight infant, the thrifty phenotype manifests as a "survival" phenotype (Gluckman et al., 2007). Additionally, populations with lighter babies do not necessarily have worse mortality: low weight babies in high-risk populations usually have lower mortality than low weight babies in better off populations (Wilcox, 2001). Among the Serbian Roma, for instance, children tend not to succumb to nutrition-based mortality risks typical of marginalized populations, but rather most of the infant and child mortality is due to deaths resulting from neglect, domestic violence, or other unknown or unreported causes (Čvorović & Coe, 2017).

Until now, only one study addressed Roma maternal responses (differential investment) in regard to birthweight: among Serbian Roma, this research found both compensatory and reinforcing maternal behavior in response to low birth weight, depending on the type of investment (Čvorović & Vojinović, 2020). While other studies have emphasized the significance and importance of children in Roma culture (Engebrigtsen, 2016), very little is known about the Roma actual childrearing practices and whether differential parental investment might be responsible for the variation in children's health outcomes.

However, it was generally found in earlier studies that Roma children, experience poorer outcomes in development and nutrition than non-Roma children, affecting some children more than others (UNICEF, 2015). Thus, there may exist some health differentials among Roma children in themselves, suggesting that some of these children may be especially vulnerable (Janevic et al., 2010).

3.8.2.5 Child Development and Stress

Recent research from Slovakia indicate that Roma children tend to be exposed to a much higher levels of stress than their non-Roma counterparts (Filakovska Bobakova et al., 2024). The results suggest that living in poor Roma settlements may affect the mental health of children as early as in the first years of life. In Romania and Bulgaria, Roma children have significantly higher odds than non-Roma children of internalizing disorder, phobias, separation anxiety disorder, generalized anxiety disorder, major depressive disorder, externalizing disorder, oppositional defiant disorder, conduct disorder, emotional problems, peer-relational problems, and lack of prosocial behavior. (Lee et al., 2014). A study that estimated the occurrence of disability and significant cognitive delay among Roma and non-Roma children in Kosovo, Montenegro, the Republic of North Macedonia, and Serbia, found that disability and cognitive delay are significantly more prevalent among Roma children than non-Roma children, which may be a result of social determinants of health (Emerson & Llewellyn, 2022).

Worldwide, the association of poverty with parenting practices and its effects on early childhood development is well documented across various countries. In low-resource settings, maternal investment may be a good indicator of child development, as it may buffer against the effects of poverty and stimulate child development. Among 1075 Serbian Roma children aged 36 to 59 months, increasing maternal investment was found to be positively associated with overall Early Child Development scale scores and with higher scores in each of the individual developmental domains (physical, learning/cognition, literacy/numeracy and socio-emotional domains), except socio-emotional (Čvorović, 2019). In this sample, the majority of Roma mothers engaged in "non-instrumental" teaching practices (playing, singing, and storytelling), while notably few engaged in book reading or name counting. Both types of activities were found to be beneficial to children's development and education, but it was the extent of maternal investment in child well-being, regardless of activity type, that was critical. The findings of this study indicate that in a limited parental literacy context, mother-child interactions, regardless of type of activity, may buffer against the detrimental effects of poverty and thus stimulate child development.

3.8.2.6 Roma Child Abandonment

Child abandonment is among the least-investigated consequences of Roma fertility control strategy, partially because direct abandonment records are not publicly available to scholars. Nevertheless, scarce data suggest that throughout Europe, Roma children are several times more likely to end up in institutional care and foster care (Romea, 2012). In Central and Eastern Europe especially, Roma children predominate in homes and shelters for abandoned children, while many are disabled (Bulgaria Helsinki Committee, 2011). According to the research conducted in 2010 by the Bulgarian Helsinki Committee and the European Roma Rights Centre, Roma children make up 82.5% of the population of children's homes in Slovakia, 65.9% in Hungary, 63% in Bulgaria, 40.6% in the Czech Republic, and 28% in Romania. The percentage of abandoned Roma children is extremely high considering that the overall Roma population in these countries, at the time of the survey, was only between three and ten percent. According to the most recent five-country report (2020), not much has changed for the Roma children: in Bulgaria, Czech Republic, Romania, Slovakia, and Moldova, Roma children remain overrepresented in institutional care (ERRC, 2021). Based on the report, data also indicate that over recent years, the number of children left without adequate parental care due to migration has increased in Moldova, Bulgaria and Romania. Social work interventions, such as when children are placed in the care of the state by local welfare agencies, occur most frequently in cases related to poverty with consequent inadequate childcare, parental neglect and absence, health concerns, and family tragedies. In addition, data suggest that many Roma families abandon, i.e., give up, their children by choice to institutions. Both for cases of parental child abandonment and forcible removal from families, poverty related issues, including the migration of the parents in search of employment, poor housing conditions, but also lack of effective family planning among Roma women, appear to be the main reasons for the overrepresentation of Roma children in institutional care systems (D'arcy & Brodie, 2015). Thus, in Bulgaria, Roma children born to women with poor education, early marriage and reproduction, and high fertility, divorced, low-paid, and of unknown occupation, are at highest risk of being abandoned. Once in care, Roma children's chances of being adopted or placed in foster care are slim, while mothers tend to lose contact with their children even though they retain parental rights (Bulgaria Helsinki Committee, 2011). Although cross-country data is limited, the existing evidence suggests that Roma and all other children living in institutionalized care are at heightened risk of trafficking and child sexual exploitation (D'arcy and Brodie, 2015).

References

Addo, O. Y., Stein, A. D., Fall, C. H., Gigante, D. P., Guntupalli, A. M., Horta, B. L., et al. (2013). Maternal height and child growth patterns. *The Journal of Pediatrics, 163*(2), 549–554. https://doi.org/10.1016/j.jpeds.2013.02.002

Aisa, R., Andaluz, J., & Larramona, G. (2017). Fertility patterns in the Roma population of Spain. *Review of Economics of the Household, 15*, 115–133. https://doi.org/10.1007/s11150-015-9289-6

Alonso-Alvarez, C., & Velando, A. (2012). Benefits and costs of parental care. In N. J. Royle, P. T. Smiseth, & M. Kölliker (Eds.), *The evolution of parental care* (pp. 40–61). Oxford University Press.

Alonso-Alvarez, C., Canelo, T., & Romero-Haro, A. Á. (2017). The oxidative cost of reproduction: Theoretical questions and alternative mechanisms. *Bioscience, 67*(3), 258–270. https://doi.org/10.1093/biosci/biw176

Apostolou, M. (2008). Bridewealth and brideservice as instruments of parental choice. *Journal of Social, Evolutionary, and Cultural Psychology, 2*(3), 89. https://doi.org/10.1037/h0099352

Arendt, E., Singh, N. S., & Campbell, O. M. (2018). Effect of maternal height on caesarean section and neonatal mortality rates in sub-Saharan Africa: An analysis of 34 national datasets. *PLoS One, 13*(2), e0192167. https://doi.org/10.1371/journal.pone.0192167

Bafekr, S. (1999). Schools and their undocumented polish and "Romany Gypsy" pupils. *International Journal of Educational Research, 31*(4), 295–302. https://doi.org/10.1016/S0883-0355(99)00007-5

Balázs, P., Rákóczi, I., Grenczer, A., & Foley, K. L. (2013). Risk factors of preterm birth and low birth weight babies among Roma and non-Roma mothers: A population-based study. *The European Journal of Public Health, 23*(3), 480–485. https://doi.org/10.1093/eurpub/cks089

Barany, Z. D. (1998). Orphans of transition: Gypsies in Eastern Europe. *Journal of Democracy, 9*(3), 142–156. https://doi.org/10.1353/jod.1998.0038

Barany, Z. (2002). *The east European gypsies: Regime change, marginality, and Ethnopolitics*. Cambridge University Press.

Battaglia, M., Chabé-Ferret, B., & Lebedinski, L. (2021). Segregation, fertility, and son preference: The case of the Roma in Serbia. *Journal of Demographic Economics, 87*(2), 233–260. https://doi.org/10.1017/dem.2020.8

Bennett, J. (2012). *Roma early childhood inclusion*. Open Society Foundations.

Bereczkei, T. (1998). Kinship network, direct childcare, and fertility among Hungarians and gypsies. *Evolution and Human Behavior, 19*(5), 283–298. https://doi.org/10.1016/S1090-5138(98)00027-0

Bereczkei, T., Hofer, A., & Ivan, Z. (2000). Low birth weight, maternal birth-spacing decisions, and future reproduction. *Human Nature, 11*(2), 183–205. https://doi.org/10.1007/s12110-000-1018-y

Bernasovská, J., Bernasovský, I., & Pačin, J. (1998). Anthropometric studies of Romany (Gypsy) newborns in East Slovakia delivered within 1991-1992. *Journal of Human Ecology, 9*(2), 131–135.

Bogetić, D., & Jugović, A. (2018). Risk factors for work on the street in Roma children population in Serbia. *Socijalna misao, 25*(1), 23–39.

Bulgaria Helsinki Committee. (2011). Abandoned Roma children fill Europe's orphanages: study. https://www.bghelsinki.org/en/news/abandoned-roma-children-fill-europes-orphanages-study. Accessed September 2024.

Castañeda, H. (2015). European mobilities or poverty migration? Discourses on Roma in Germany. *International Migration, 53*(3), 87–99. https://doi.org/10.1111/imig.12166

Casterline, J. B., & El-Zeini, L. O. (2022). Multiple perspectives on recent trends in unwanted fertility in low-and middle-income countries. *Demography, 59*(1), 371–388. https://doi.org/10.1215/00703370-9644472

References

Çiçekler, C. Y., Orçan, M., & Aral, N. (2013). Child-rearing attitudes of Roma and non-Roma mothers and analysis of receptive language levels of their children. *International Journal of Social Sciences and Education, 2*(2), 50–60.

Coall, D. A., & Chisholm, J. S. (2003). Evolutionary perspectives on pregnancy: Maternal age at menarche and infant birth weight. *Social Science and Medicine, 57*(10), 1771–1781. https://doi.org/10.1016/S0277-9536(03)00022-4

Crețan, R., & Turnock, D. (2008). Romania's Roma population: From marginality to social integration. *Scottish Geographical Journal, 124*(4), 274–299. https://doi.org/10.1080/14702540802596608

Christianakis, M. (2010). Lessons for life: Roma children, communal practices, and the global marketplace. *Penn GSE Perspectives on Urban Education, 8*(1), 11–18.

Coe, K., & Čvorović, J. (2017). The health of Romanian Gypsy women in Serbia. *Health Care for Women International, 38*(4), 409–422. https://doi.org/10.1080/07399332.2017.1292278

Crowe, D.M. (1996). *A history of the Gypsies of Eastern Europe and Russia.* St. Martin's Griffin.

Crowe, D. M. (2000). Muslim Roma in the Balkans. *Nationalities Papers, 28*(1), 93–128. https://doi.org/10.1080/00905990050002470

Čekic Marković. J. (2016). Analiza primene afirmativnih mera u oblasti obrazovanja roma i romkinja i preporuke za unapređenje mera (Analyses of Roma affirmative measures in education and recommendations). Tim za socijalno uključivanje i smanjenje siromaštva Vlada Republike Srbije.

Čvorović, J. (2004). Sexual and reproductive strategies among Serbian Gypsies. *Population and Environment, 25*(3), 217–242. https://doi.org/10.1007/s11111-004-4485-y

Čvorović, J. (2010). *Roast chicken and other Gypsy stories.* Peter Lang GmbH.

Čvorović, J. (2011). The differential impact of religion on life history and reproductive strategy: Muslim and orthodox gypsies in Serbia. *Mankind Quarterly, 51*(3), 330–348. https://doi.org/10.46469/mq.2011.51.3.5

Čvorović, J. (2013). Serbian Gypsy witch narratives: 'Wherever Gypsies Go, There the Witches Are, We Know!'. *Folklore, 124*(2), 214–225. https://doi.org/10.1080/0015587X.2013.798535

Čvorović, J. (2014). *The Roma: A Balkan underclass.* Ulster Institute for Social Research.

Čvorović, J. (2018). Influence of maternal height on children's health status and mortality: A cross-sectional study in poor Roma communities in rural Serbia. *Homo, 69*(6), 357–363. https://doi.org/10.1016/j.jchb.2018.11.004

Čvorović, J. (2019). Self-rated health and teenage pregnancies in Roma women: Increasing height is associated with better health outcomes. *Journal of Biosocial Science, 51*(3), 444–456. https://doi.org/10.1017/S0021932018000196

Čvorović, J. (2022a). Maternal age at marriage and child nutritional status and development: Evidence from Serbian Roma communities. *Public Health Nutrition, 25*(5), 1183–1193. https://doi.org/10.1017/S1368980022000544

Čvorović, J. (2022b). Paternal investment, stepfather presence and early child development and growth among Serbian Roma. *Evolutionary Human Sciences, 4*, e15. https://doi.org/10.1017/ehs.2022.14

Čvorović, J. (2022c). Stunting, maternal investment, and early child development in Serbian Roma children aged 36–59 months. *Bulletin of the Institute of Ethnography SASA, 70*(3), 175–191. https://doi.org/10.2298/GEI2203175C

Čvorović, J. (2023). Do unwanted children face growth penalties in resource poor environments? Evidence from Roma Settlements in Serbia. *Journal of biosocial science, 55*(4), 697–707.

Čvorović, J. (2024). The impact of welfare on maternal investment and sibling competition: Evidence from Serbian Roma communities. *Journal of Biosocial Science, 56*(3), 560–573. https://doi.org/10.1017/S0021932023000184

Čvorović, J., & Coe, K. (2017). Reproductive investment and health costs in Roma women. *International Journal of Environmental Research and Public Health, 14*(11), 1337. https://doi.org/10.3390/ijerph14111337

Čvorović, J., & Coe, K. (2019). Happy marriages are all alike: Marriage and self-rated health among Serbian Roma. *Bulletin of the Institute of Ethnography SASA, 67*(2), 341–359. https://doi.org/10.2298/GEI181031001C
Čvorović, J., & Vojinović, Ž. (2020). The effect of social assistance on kin relationships: Evidence from Roma communities. *Biodemography and Social Biology, 65*(1), 16–30. https://doi.org/10.1080/19485565.2019.1681256
D'arcy, K., & Brodie, I. (2015). Roma children and young people in Bulgaria: Patterns of risk and effective protection in relation to child sexual exploitation. *Social Inclusion, 3*(49), 1–9. http://hdl.handle.net/10547/559601
Dimitrova, R., Johnson, D. J., & van de Vijver, F. J. (2018). Ethnic socialization, ethnic identity, life satisfaction and school achievement of Roma ethnic minority youth. *Journal of Adolescence, 62*, 175–183. https://doi.org/10.1016/j.adolescence.2017.06.003
Djurovic, D., Prcic, S., Milojkovic, M., Konstantinidis, G., & Tamburlini, G. (2014). The health status of Roma children—a medical or social issue? *European Review for Medical and Pharmacological Sciences, 18*(8).
Durankova, S., Carnogu, J. R., Bernasovska, J., Boronova, I., & Bernasovsky, I. B. (2013). Birth weight of Romany and non–Romany newborns depending on the age of mother from Kežmarok District. *New Trends In the Biological and ecological Research*, 83–87. http://www.unipo.sk/public/media/16067/Zbornik%20-%20New%20Trends%20in%20Biological%20-%20nahlad.pdf
Durst, J. (2001). "Nekem ez az élet, a gyerekek". Gyermekvállalási szokások változása egy kisfalusi cigány közösségben' ["This is my life, the children". Changes in child-bearing habits in a rural Roma community']. *Századvég, 3*, 71–92.
Ekezie, W., Hopwood, E., Czyznikowska, B., Weidman, S., Mackintosh, N., & Curtis, F. (2023). Perinatal health outcomes of women from Gypsy, Roma and Traveller communities: A systematic review. *Midwifery*, 103910. https://doi.org/10.1016/j.midw.2023.103910
Emanuel, I., Kimpo, C., & Moceri, V. (2004). The association of grandmaternal and maternal factors with maternal adult stature. *International Journal of Epidemiology, 33*(6), 1243–1248. https://doi.org/10.1093/ije/dyh268
Emerson, E., & Llewellyn, G. (2022). The prevalence of disability among Roma and non-Roma children in four West Balkan countries. *Disability and Health Journal, 15*(4), 101338. https://doi.org/10.1016/j.dhjo.2022.101338
Engebrigtsen, A. I. (2016). Lost between protective regimes: Roma in the Norwegian state. In M. Seeberg & E. Goździak (Eds.), *Contested childhoods: Growing up in Migrancy* (IMISCOE research series). Springer. https://doi.org/10.1007/978-3-319-44610-3_5
Ena, G. F., Aizpurua-Iraola, J., Font-Porterias, N., Calafell, F., & Comas, D. (2022). Population genetics of the European Roma—a review. *Genes, 13*(11), 2068. https://doi.org/10.3390/genes13112068
EPHA. (2018). Roma Health and Early Childhood Development Study. https://epha.org/wp-content/uploads/2019/02/closing-the-life-expectancy-gap-of-roma-in-europe-study.pdf. Accessed June 2024.
ERRC. (2021). "Blighted Lives: Romani Children in State Care", The European Roma Rights Centre Brussels. https://www.errc.org/reports%2D%2Dsubmissions/blighted-lives-romani-children-in-state-care. Accessed June 2024.
Eurostat. (2024). How many children were born in the EU in 2022? https://ec.europa.eu/eurostat/web/products-eurostat-news/w/ddn-20240307-1#:~:text=The%20total%20fertility%20rate%20in,fertility%20published%20by%20Eurostat%20today. Accessed June 2024.
Ferák, V., Siváková, D., & Sieglová, Z. (1987). Slovenskí Cigáni (Rómovia)–populácia s najvyšším koeficientom inbrídingu v Európe. *Bratislavské Lekárske Listy, 87*, 168–175.
Fihel, A., & Okólski, M. (2019). Population decline in the post-communist countries of the European Union. *Population Societies, 567*(6), 1–4. https://shs.cairn.info/journal-population-and-societies-2019-6-page-1?lang=en

References

Filakovska Bobakova, D., & Dankulincova Veselska, Z. (2024). Early childhood in marginalized Roma communities: Health risks and health outcomes. *International Journal of Public Health, 69*, 1606784. https://doi.org/10.3389/ijph.2024.1606784

Filakovska Bobakova, D., Chovan, S., & Van Laer, S. (2024). Perceived stress of mothers, harsh discipline, and early childhood mental health: Insights from a cross-sectional study in marginalized Roma communities. *International Journal of Public Health, 69*, 1606721.

FRA. (2014). Roma Survey – Data in Focus Education: The Situation of Roma in 11 EU Member States. European Union Agency for Fundamental Rights, Publications Office of the European Union, Luxembourg. URL: https://fra.europa.eu/en/publication/2014/education-situationroma-11-eu-member-states

FRA. (2022). Roma in 10 European countries https://fra.europa.eu/sites/default/files/fra_uploads/fra-2022-roma-survey-2021-main-results2_en.pdf. Accessed June 2024.

Fraser, A. M. (1992). *The Gypsies*. Blackwell.

Gallagher, A., Čvorović, J., & Štrkalj, G. (2009). Body mass index in Serbian Roma. *Homo, 60*(6), 567–578. https://doi.org/10.1016/j.jchb.2009.10.002

Gamella, J. F. (2018). Marriage, gender and transnational migrations in fertility transitions of Romanian Roma women. Intersections. *East European Journal of Society and Politics, 4*(2), 57–85.

Gibson, M. A., & Lawson, D. W. (2011). "Modernization" increases parental investment and sibling resource competition: Evidence from a rural development initiative in Ethiopia. *Evolution and Human Behavior, 32*(2), 97–105. https://doi.org/10.1016/j.evolhumbehav.2010.10.002

Ginio, E. (2004). Neither Muslims nor Zimmis: The Gypsies (Roma) in the Ottoman State. *Romani Studies, 14*(2), 117–144.

Gluckman, P. D., Hanson, M. A., & Beedle, A. S. (2007). Early life events and their consequences for later disease: A life history and evolutionary perspective. *American Journal of Human Biology, 19*(1), 1–19. https://doi.org/10.1002/ajhb.20590

Goenka, N., Dobson, L., Patel, V., & O'Hare, P. (2004). Cultural barriers to diabetes care in south Asians: Arranged marriage–arranged complications? *Practical Diabetes International, 21*(4), 154–156. https://doi.org/10.1002/pdi.624

Goldman, N. (2001). Social inequalities in health. *Annals of the New York Academy of Sciences, 954*(1), 118–139. https://doi.org/10.1111/j.1749-6632.2001.tb02750.x

Grigore, D. (2007). Family and health in the traditional Rromani culture. In S. McKelvey, J. Ray, & P. Riseborough (Eds.), *Introduction to Roma culture: Exploring cultural diversity for family doctors*. JSI Research and Training Institute.

Gurven, M., Costa, M., Trumble, B., Stieglitz, J., Beheim, B., Eid Rodriguez, D., et al. (2016). Health costs of reproduction are minimal despite high fertility, mortality and subsistence lifestyle. *Scientific Reports, 6*(1), 30056. https://doi.org/10.1038/srep30056

Hancock, I. (1987). *The pariah syndrome: An account of Gypsy slavery*. Karoma Publishers.

Hedges, S., Mulder, M. B., James, S., & Lawson, D. W. (2016). Sending children to school: Rural livelihoods and parental investment in education in northern Tanzania. *Evolution and Human Behavior, 37*(2), 142–151. https://doi.org/10.1016/j.evolhumbehav.2015.10.001

Hertwig, R., Davis, J. N., & Sulloway, F. J. (2002). Parental investment: How an equity motive can produce inequality. *Psychological bulletin, 128*(5), 728.

Hotchkiss, D. R., Godha, D., Gage, A. J., & Cappa, C. (2016). Risk factors associated with the practice of child marriage among Roma girls in Serbia. *BMC International Health and Human Rights, 16*, 1–10. https://doi.org/10.1186/s12914-016-0081-3

Hurt, L. S., Ronsmans, C., & Thomas, S. L. (2006). The effect of number of births on women's mortality: Systematic review of the evidence for women who have completed their childbearing. *Population Studies, 60*(1), 55–71. https://doi.org/10.1080/00324720500436011

Ikeda, A., Iso, H., Toyoshima, H., et al. (2007). Marital status and mortality among Japanese men and women: The Japan collaborative cohort study. *BMC Public Health, 7*, 73. https://doi.org/10.1186/1471-2458-7-73

Janevic, T., Petrovic, O., Bjelic, I., & Kubera, A. (2010). Risk factors for childhood malnutrition in Roma settlements in Serbia. *BMC Public Health, 10*, 1–8. https://doi.org/10.1186/1471-2458-10-509

Jasienska, G. (2017). Costs of reproduction, health, and life span in women. In G. Jasienska, D. Sherry, & D. Holmes (Eds.), *The arc of life: Evolution and health across the life course* (pp. 159–176). Springer.

Joamets, K., & Sogomonjan, M. (2020). Influence of forced child marriage and domestic violence on mental health and well-being. Conflict of traditions and rights of Roma children. *International and Comparative Law Review, 20*(1), 58–76. https://doi.org/10.2478/iclr-2020-0003

Kamburova, M., Georgieva, S., Tsanova, D., & Stoyanova, E. (2019). Roma origin as a factor for high level of adolescent fertility and abortion rate in European Union. *European Journal of Public Health, 29*(Supplement_4), ckz186-660. https://doi.org/10.1093/eurpub/ckz186.660

Kandraju, H., Agrawal, S., Geetha, K., Sujatha, L., Subramanian, S., & Murki, S. (2012). Gestational age-specific centile charts for anthropometry at birth for South Indian infants. *Indian Pediatrics, 49*, 199–202.

Kaufmann, E. (2010). *Shall the religious inherit the earth?: Demography and politics in the twenty-first century*. Profile Books.

Kalaydjieva, L., Calafell, F., Jobling, M. A., Angelicheva, D., de Knijff, P., Rosser, Z. H., Hurles, M. E., Underhill, P., Tournev, I., Marushiakova, E., & Popov, V. (2001). Patterns of inter- and intra-group genetic diversity in the Vlax Roma as revealed by Y chromosome and mitochondrial DNA lineages. *European Journal of Human Genetics, 9*(2), 97–104. https://doi.org/10.1038/sj.ejhg.5200597

Kaneva, N., & Popescu, D. (2014). "We are Romanian, not Roma": Nation branding and postsocialist discourses of alterity. *Communication, Culture and Critique, 7*(4), 506–523. https://doi.org/10.1111/cccr.12064

Kirkwood, T. B., & Rose, M. R. (1991). Evolution of senescence: Late survival sacrificed for reproduction. *Philosophical Transactions of the Royal Society of London. Series B: Biological Sciences, 332*(1262), 15–24. https://doi.org/10.1098/rstb.1991.0028

Knodel, J., & Van de Walle, E. (1979). Lessons from the past: Policy implications of historical fertility studies. *Population and Development Review*, 217–245.

Koval', J., Mrosková, S., & Schlosserová, A. (2012). Natality and infant mortality in Roma children in the Prešov region. *Medycyna Środowiskowa-Environmental Medicine, 15*(2), 92–101.

Kramer, K. L., Veile, A., & Otárola-Castillo, E. (2016). Sibling competition and growth tradeoffs. Biological vs. statistical significance. *PLoS One, 11*(3), e0150126. https://doi.org/10.1371/journal.pone.0150126

Ladányi, J., & Szelényi, I. (2002). The nature and social determinants of Roma poverty. *Review of Sociology, 8*(2), 75–96.

Lauwagie, B. N. (1979). Ethnic boundaries in modern states: Romano Lavo-Lil revisited. *American Journal of Sociology, 85*(2), 310–337. https://doi.org/10.1086/227012

Lawson, D. W., & Mace, R. (2008). Sibling configuration and childhood growth in contemporary British families. *International Journal of Epidemiology, 37*(6), 1408–1421. https://doi.org/10.1093/ije/dyn116

Lawson, D. W., & Borgerhoff Mulder, M. (2016). The offspring quantity–quality trade-off and human fertility variation. *Philosophical Transactions of the Royal Society B: Biological Sciences, 371*(1692), 20150145. https://doi.org/10.1098/rstb.2015.0145

Lee, E. J., Keyes, K., Bitfoi, A., Mihova, Z., Pez, O., Yoon, E., & Masfety, V. K. (2014). Mental health disparities between Roma and non-Roma children in Romania and Bulgaria. *BMC Psychiatry, 14*, 1–7. https://doi.org/10.1186/s12888-014-0297-5

Levine, N. E. (1987). Differential child care in three Tibetan communities: Beyond son preference. *Population and Development Review*, 281–304. https://doi.org/10.2307/1973194

Liddell, C., Barrett, L., & Henzi, P. (2003). Parental investment in schooling: Evidence from a subsistence farming community in South Africa. *International Journal of Psychology, 38*(1), 54–63. https://doi.org/10.1080/00207590244000232

References

Limb, G. E., Shafer, K., & Sandoval, K. (2014). The impact of kin support on urban American Indian families. *Child and Family Social Work, 19*(4), 432–442. https://doi.org/10.1111/cfs.12041

Liu, J., & Lummaa, V. (2011). Age at first reproduction and probability of reproductive failure in women. *Evolution and Human Behavior, 32*(6), 433–443. https://doi.org/10.1016/j.evolhumbehav.2010.10.007

Llanaj, E., Vincze, F., Kósa, Z., Sándor, J., Diószegi, J., & Ádány, R. (2020). Dietary profile and nutritional status of the Roma population living in segregated colonies in Northeast Hungary. *Nutrients, 12*(9), 2836. https://doi.org/10.3390/nu12092836

Long, E., & Zhang, J. (2023). Evidence for the role of selection for reproductively advantageous alleles in human aging. *Science Advances, 9*(49), eadh4990. https://doi.org/10.1126/sciadv.adh4990

Mag, A. G. (2012). Education of the Roma/Gypsy children in Romania. *Educazione Democratica. Rivista di pedagogia politica, 4*, 73–78.

Marushiakova, E., & Popov, V. (2001). *Gypsies in the Ottoman Empire*. University of Hertfordshire Press.

Mendizabal, I., Valente, C., Gusmão, A., Alves, C., Gomes, V., Goios, A., et al. (2011). Reconstructing the Indian origin and dispersal of the European Roma: A maternal genetic perspective. *PLoS One, 6*(1), e15988. https://doi.org/10.1371/journal.pone.0015988

Michalski, R. L., & Shackelford, T. K. (2010). Evolutionary personality psychology: Reconciling human nature and individual differences. *Personality and Individual Differences, 48*(5), 509–516. https://doi.org/10.1016/j.paid.2009.10.027

Migliano, A. B., Vinicius, L., & Lahr, M. M. (2007). Life history trade-offs explain the evolution of human pygmies. *Proceedings of the National Academy of Sciences, 104*(51), 20216–20219. https://doi.org/10.1073/pnas.0708024105

Nesse, R. M. (2001). On the difficulty of defining disease: A Darwinian perspective. *Medicine, Health Care and Philosophy, 4*, 37–46. https://doi.org/10.1023/A:1009938513897

Nettle, D. (2010). Dying young and living fast: Variation in life history across English neighborhoods. *Behavioral Ecology, 21*(2), 387–395. https://doi.org/10.1093/beheco/arp202

Oakley, J. (1983). *The traveler-Gypsies*. Cambridge University Press.

Pamporov, A. (2007). Sold like a donkey? Bride-price among the Bulgarian Roma. *Journal of the Royal Anthropological Institute, 13*, 471–476. http://www.jstor.org/stable/4622960

Oxfam. (2003). *The Roma from Belgrade settlements*. Oxfam, GB.

Penderi, E., & Petrogiannis, K. (2011). Parental ethnotheories and customs of childrearing in two Roma urban communities in Greece: Examining the developmental niche of the 6-year-old child. *Journal of Social, Evolutionary, and Cultural Psychology, 5*(1), 32. https://doi.org/10.1037/h0099276

Pike, I. L. (2005). Maternal stress and fetal responses: Evolutionary perspectives on preterm delivery. *American Journal of Human Biology, 17*(1), 55–65. https://doi.org/10.1002/ajhb.20093

Popovici, S. (2008). The influences of family factors on the choice of having a secondary education among the Romani children: A survey of family influences among Romani children at the eighth grade in Romania (Master's thesis). https://www.duo.uio.no/bitstream/handle/10852/31986/1/StefanxPopovici.pdf.

Ringold, D., Orenstein, M. A., & Wilkens, E. (2005). *Roma in an expanding Europe: Breaking the poverty cycle*. World Bank Publications. http://siteresources.worldbank.org/EXTROMA/Resources/roma_in_expanding_europe.pdf. Accessed Jun 2024

Robayo-Abril, M., & Millán, N. 2019. Breaking the cycle of Roma exclusion in the Western Balkan. The World Bank. https://documents1.worldbank.org/curated/fr/642861552321695392/pdf/Breaking-the-Cycle-of-Roma-Exclusion-in-the-Western-Balkans.pdf. Accessed June 2024.

Romea, C.Z. (2012). Romani children predominate in east European homes for abandoned children. https://romea.cz/en/world/romani-children-predominate-in-east-european-homes-for-abandoned-children. Accessed June 2024.

Rosenberg, K. R., & Trevathan, W. R. (2018). Evolutionary perspectives on cesarean section. *Evolution, Medicine, and Public Health, 2018*(1), 67–81. https://doi.org/10.1093/emph/eoy006

Sárváry, A., Kósa, Z., Jávorné, R. E., Gyulai, A., Takács, P., Sándor, J., et al. (2019). Socioeconomic status, health related behaviour, and self-rated health of children living in Roma settlements in Hungary. *Central European Journal of Public Health, 27*(1), 24–31. https://doi.org/10.21101/cejph.a4726

Schaffnit, S. B., & Lawson, D. W. (2021). Married too young? The behavioral ecology of 'child marriage'. *Social Sciences, 10*(5), 161. https://doi.org/10.3390/socsci10050161

Sear, R. (2007). The impact of reproduction on Gambian women: Does controlling for phenotypic quality reveal costs of reproduction? *American Journal of Physical Anthropology: The Official Publication of the American Association of Physical Anthropologists, 132*(4), 632–641. https://doi.org/10.1002/ajpa.20558

Selander, M., & Walter, E. (2020). Lack of educational opportunities for the Roma people in Eastern Europe. *Ballard Brief, 2020*(3), 2. https://scholarsarchive.byu.edu/ballardbrief/vol2020/iss3/2

Silventoinen, K. (2003). Determinants of variation in adult body height. *Journal of Biosocial Science, 35*(2), 263–285. https://doi.org/10.1017/S0021932003002633

Smith, T. (1997). Recognizing difference: The Romani 'Gypsy' child socialization and education process. *British Journal of Sociology of Education, 18*(2), 243–256. https://doi.org/10.1080/0142569970180207

Spiroski, I., Dimitrovska, Z., Gjorgjev, D., Mikik, V., Efremova-Stefanoska, V., Naunova-Spiroska, D., & Kendrovski, V. (2011). Nutritional status and growth parameters of school-age Roma children in the Republic of Macedonia. *Central European Journal of Public Health, 19*(2), 102–107. http://hdl.handle.net/20.500.12188/7471

Sprocha, B. (2017). The Roma population in Slovakia and the cohort fertility of Roma women according to the 2011 population and housing census. *Demografie, 59*(2), 118–131.

Stanković, S., Živić, S., Ignjatović, A., Stojanović, M., Bogdanović, D., Novak, S., et al. (2016). Comparison of weight and length at birth of non-Roma and Roma newborn in Serbia. *International Journal of Public Health, 61*, 69–73. https://doi.org/10.1007/s00038-015-0736-1

Steadman, L. B., & Palmer, C. T. (2015). *Supernatural and natural selection: Religion and evolutionary success*. Routledge.

Stephens, W. N. (1963). *The family in cross-cultural perspective*. Holt, Rinehart and Winston.

Stulp, G., & Barrett, L. (2016). Evolutionary perspectives on human height variation. *Biological Reviews, 91*(1), 206–234. https://doi.org/10.1111/brv.12165

Šupínová, M., Sonkolyová, G., & Klement, C. (2020). Reproductive health of Roma women in Slovakia. *Central European Journal of Public Health, 28*(2), 143–148. https://doi.org/10.21101/cejph.a5817

Sutherland, A. (1975). Gypsies, the hidden Americans. *Society, 12*(2), 27–33. https://doi.org/10.1007/BF02701827

Szabó, L., Kiss, I., Šprocha, B., & Spéder, Z. (2021). Fertility of Roma minorities in central and Eastern Europe. *Comparative Population Studies, 46*. https://doi.org/10.12765/CPoS-2021-14

Timmerman, J. (2004). When her feet touch the ground: Conflict between the Roma familistic custom of arranged juvenile marriage and enforcement of international human rights treaties. *Journal of Transnational Law and Policy, 13*(2), 475–497. https://ir.law.fsu.edu/jtlp/vol13/iss2/5

Toshevska, B. A., Madjevikj, M., Ljakoska, M., & Sokoloski, P. (2018). The reproductive behaviour of the female population in the only Roma governed community in Europe. *Human Geographies: Journal of Studies and Research in Human Geography, 12*(2). https://doi.org/10.5719/hgeo.2018.122.2

Trevathan, W. R. (2017). *Human birth: An evolutionary perspective*. Routledge.

Van Baar, H. (2021). The production of irregular citizenship through mobile governmentalities: Racism against Roma at the security-mobility nexus. *Mobilities, 16*(5), 809–823. https://doi.org/10.1080/17450101.2021.1902241

Van den Berghe, P. L. (1979). *Human family systems: An evolutionary view*. Elsevier Press.

References

Van Laer, S., Fiľakovská Bobáková, D., Kolarcik, P., Engel, O., Madarasová Gecková, A., Reijneveld, S. A., & de Kroon, M. L. (2024). Parenting by mothers from marginalized communities and the role of socioeconomic disadvantage: Insights from marginalized Roma communities in Slovakia. *Frontiers in Psychology, 15*, 1362179. https://doi.org/10.3389/fpsyg.2024.1362179

Vukanović, T. P. (1983). *Romi (cigani) u Jugoslaviji (Roma-Gypsies in Yugoslavia)*. Nova Jugoslavija.

UNFPA. (2013), Adolescent pregnancy in Eastern Europe and Central Asia. https://eeca.unfpa.org/sites/default/files/pub-pdf/Adolescent_pregnancy_in_Eastern-Europe_and_Central_Asia_0.pdf.

UNICEF Srbija. (2020). *Srbija—Istraživanje višestrukih pokazatelja (Serbia—MICS)*. UNICEF.

UNICEF. (2015). Early childhood development. The analysis of Multiple Indicator Cluster Survey data. https://www.unicef.org/serbia/media/1201/file/MICS%20ECD.pdf.

UNICEF Regional Office for Europe and Central Asia. (2024). Breaking barriers: An analytical report on Roma children and women in Kosovo (UNSCR 1244), Montenegro, North Macedonia and Serbia. UNICEF, Geneva.

Walker, R. S., Gurven, M., Burger, O., & Hamilton, M. J. (2008). The trade-off between number and size of offspring in humans and other primates. *Proceedings of the Royal Society B: Biological Sciences, 275*(1636), 827–834. https://doi.org/10.1098/rspb.2007.1511

Wells, J. C. K. (2007). The thrifty phenotype as an adaptive maternal effect. *Biological Reviews, 82*(1), 143–172. https://doi.org/10.1111/j.1469-185X.2006.00007.x

Wilcox, A. J. (2001). On the importance—and the unimportance—of birthweight. *International Journal of Epidemiology, 30*(6), 1233–1241. https://doi.org/10.1093/ije/30.6.1233

Weyrauch, W. O. (Ed.). (2001). *Gypsy law: Romani legal traditions and culture*. University of California Press.

Chapter 4
The Roma in the Successor States of Former Yugoslavia

The Roma have been settled in the Balkans for centuries, with the first recorded mention in the thirteenth century. The former Yugoslavia had one of the largest Roma populations in Eastern Europe, with an estimated 850.000 in the 1980s. The policy of the Yugoslav socialist government was to assimilate Roma, thus considerable efforts were made to help them to improve their economic, social and cultural lot. In the early 1980s, the Yugoslav Roma were recognized as a national minority and given an equal constitutional standing with other minorities. The Roma seemingly became assimilated, as they mostly adopted the culture, language, and religion of the majority populations in the areas where they lived. However, their position in the Yugoslav federation was more a case of somewhere between: not completely included into the working class but not completely excluded. Following the collapse of the former Yugoslavia and transition to a market economy, the Roma have been greatly affected by disadvantages and difficulties. In the successor states of the former Yugoslavia, with their failing economies, widespread unemployment and uncertain social safety nets, the largely unskilled and poorly educated Roma are unable to compete with other populations. Presently, in all the successor states of the former Yugoslavia, the situation of the Roma is more-or-less the same: the Roma population is significantly younger than the non-Roma majorities, and they suffer from higher infant and child mortality and lack of education and skills.

4.1 The Roma in the Western Balkans

The Roma have been settled in the Balkans for centuries, with the first recorded mention in North Macedonia in 1289 (Latham, 1999). The largest Roma populations before World War II lived in Serbia and North Macedonia. During World War

II, many Roma died in concentration camps. About 80,000 Roma perished throughout the Yugoslav territory during World War II.

The former Yugoslavia had one of the largest Roma populations in Eastern Europe, with an estimated 850.000 in 1981 (Čvorović, 2014). The strategy of the Yugoslav socialist government was to assimilate the Roma, with efforts made to help them to improve their economic, social and cultural lot. Many different institutions and policies were created by the Yugoslav government, to ensure equal access to all its citizens across ethnic lines, including its Roma citizens. In the early 1980s, the Yugoslav Roma were acknowledged as a national minority and were given equal constitutional standing with other minorities. Among other undertakings, Romani language was introduced in a number of primary schools, particularly in Kosovo. This multicultural policy was aggressively pushed, and the former Yugoslavia has been praised for treating its Roma more proficiently than any other East European state (Fraser, 1992). Thus, the Roma had become seemingly more assimilated, as they mostly adopted the culture, language and religion of the majority populations in the areas where they lived (Čvorović, 2014). However, their standings in the Yugoslav federation was somewhere in-between: not completely included into the working class but not completely excluded (Sardelić, 2013). In fact, all Roma benefited from the communist regime, which, amongst other things, had helped them to preserve their way of life and reproduction (Čvorović, 2004). Roma have thus maintained their own traditions in regard to residence pattern, marriage, and fertility. Restrained in marriage with outsiders and even with different Roma groups, endogamy preserved their ethnic distinctiveness. As a result, throughout the region, many Roma do not consider themselves as members of a single cohesive group but instead identify only with their subgroup. These subgroups are often divided by language used, while religion depends on location and circumstances, often serving as nationalism (Čvorović, 2004). Since their arrival in the Balkans, the main division between various Roma groups was in their religious affiliation, with the two main religions being Islam and Christianity. In turn, cultural traditions encouraged divisions into groups based on descent alone, with the group remaining the primary social unit.

The plight of the Roma in the former Yugoslavia was not without setbacks. Throughout all periods, and regardless of which Yugoslav republic, Roma school absenteeism and high drop-out rates have remained consistently high, while the socialist policies in the former Yugoslavia created a welfare dependency for many Roma (Čvorović & Vojinović, 2020). Although protected to some extent by socialist regime, the disadvantages and difficulties that came with the collapse of the former Yugoslavia and transition to a market economy have hit the Roma hard. In the successor states of the former Yugoslavia, with failing economies, widespread unemployment, and uncertain social safety nets, the largely unskilled and poorly educated Roma are unable to compete with other populations.

At present, in all the successor states of the former Yugoslavia, the situation of the Roma is much the same. There are no reliable data for the Roma in the Western Balkans; however, available estimates suggest that the share of Roma in national populations is between 1.7 percent in Bosnia and Herzegovina and 9.6 percent in North Macedonia, or between 700.000 and 1.360.000 individuals in the region

(Robayo-Abril & Millán, 2019). Census data collect only ethnic self-identification; however, there is likely a case of significant underreporting by Roma individuals.

According to a recent World Bank report, and in contrast to the general population in most of the Western Balkan countries, Roma are a particularly young population, with relatively high fertility rates and accelerating/ population growth (Robayo-Abril & Millán, 2019). Various surveys across all Balkan countries reveal that the Roma populations are significantly younger than the non-Roma majorities, even when compared to other groups with lower socioeconomic status than the general population. Even the youngest countries in the region, Albania and Kosovo, are dissimilar to the Roma age pyramid: for instance, data from 2020 show that Kosovo, with a median age of 29, and the region's youngest population, has a fertility rate just under the replacement level (2.0), which has been falling for years. Among the Roma, there is a large proportion of children and only a small share of elderly people. Often, Roma live in slums or informal settlements and experience severe overcrowding.

Additionally, Roma suffer from lack of education and skills, despite National Action Plans for Roma Inclusion by governments to raise Roma education and living standards. According to the World Bank report (2019), literacy rates among the general population (both males and females, aged 15 and above) are at or close to 100 percent. However, in Albania and Montenegro, self-reported literacy among Roma females aged 15–64 is only 58 percent. Roma rarely finish elementary school, with a large gender gap: in Bosnia and Herzegovina, Kosovo and North Macedonia, females aged 18–21 are significantly less likely than males to have completed compulsory schooling. Among older cohorts, tertiary (higher education) completion is almost nonexistent. Both Roma boys and girls tend to drop out of school early, girls earlier than boys, with the underlying mechanisms being different. For Roma girls, the reasons behind early drop-out include early/child marriage, virginity protection before marriage, and helping out with household chores, while for males, the main reason is the desire to start working.

Despite the desire to join labor force being the main reason behind school dropouts, unemployment is especially high among Roma in all countries. In Albania and in Bosnia and Herzegovina, over 50 percent of economically active working-age Roma are unemployed, while the share of formally employed Roma ranges from only 13 percent of working-age Roma in Kosovo to 22 percent in North Macedonia (Robayo-Abril & Millán, 2019). Formal employment for the Roma mostly involves working in public utilities (city sanitation units), rarely as industrial workers/ in industry, and for females, custodian work. The large majority of Roma, however, are engaged in informal work, such as trading in open-air markets, bin diving, or the collection of recyclables (informal recycling), cleaning jobs, working on construction sites, etc. Across countries, Roma face a deepening dependence on state benefits and services (Čvorović, 2014). Substantial reliance on welfare benefits/cash transfers and other types of monetary assistance may have contributed to the low labor force participation rates and high unemployment among the Roma. Bosnia and Herzegovina, Kosovo, and Montenegro show especially bleak employment outcomes for the Roma.

4.2 Country Reports

4.2.1 North Macedonia

The first presence of the Roma in North Macedonia dates back to the thirteenth century. Numerous folktales describe the Roma origins in North Macedonia (see more in Čvorović, 2014). One such Macedonian Roma folk tale traces their roots back to Alexander the Great, as he was "one of their own bloods" (Crowe, 2000:113).

Census data show increasing numbers of Roma in North Macedonia: at the beginning of the twentieth century, there were around 8.500 Roma; in 1912, more than 12.000. There is little information on the Macedonian Roma during the interwar period. After the formation of communist Yugoslavia, most of the former Yugoslavian Roma lived in North Macedonia. From 1948, their number progressively increased, due to high fertility (Toshevska et al., 2018). According to the most recent census (2021), there were 46.433 Roma, or 2.53% of the population. However, owing to a combination of civil registration issues and the Roma identifying as members of other ethnic groups, this number may be an underestimation of actual Roma population size: according to unofficial estimates by non-governmental organizations (NGOs), the Roma make up closer to 6% of the total population. Another estimate has put the number of Roma at 197.000, or around 10% of the population (Robayo-Abril & Millán, 2019).

The majority of Roma are Muslims, with a Christian Roma minority belonging to the Eastern Orthodox Church. Approximately 80 percent of the Roma in North Macedonia speak Romani as their first language, while the rest, especially the younger generation, and speak Turkish, Albanian or Macedonian as their first language.

The North Macedonian Roma have been the most drastically affected by the Macedonian transition from socialism to neoliberal capitalism, with the biggest challenges seen in the provision of education, healthcare, housing and employment. Most Roma partake in low-skilled jobs in the informal sector, with majority living in cities, mostly in Skopje, the capital. The Roma population is sedentary, with settlements separated from the majority. The Roma settlements are often poor, lacking in basic infrastructure, and have overcrowded households with limited access to heating, electricity, water, and improved sanitation (Hoelscher, 2007). As a result of poor education and lack of skills, poverty and unemployment rates among the Roma are much higher than for non-Roma. Illiteracy is still common - data show that 76.6 percent of the Roma women between 15 and 24 years are literate. Amongst the poorest quintile of the Roma population, the literacy rates may be over 50 percent (UNICEF, 2012). Many are dependent on social welfare to survive.

In the past, Roma groups were known by their occupational designations while other differences arose from religious and linguistic lines. The relationship between Muslim and Christian religious groups is marked by mutual distrust and a lack of respect. In the opinion of Muslim Roma, Orthodox Christian Roma are not true Roma (Čvorović, 2014).

All cities and towns in Macedonia have Roma settlements of some kind, most of which face problems typically associated with poverty. The majority of the North Macedonian Roma live in the cities, with only around 5 percent residing in rural areas (Trbojevik & Bogoevska 2011). Most dwell in large *mahalas*, in slums or unplanned settlements that lack asphalt roads or access to water, electricity or sewage disposal. The majority live on social support and in the "grey" economy. Almost 85 percent of the country's Roma live in the Shuto Orizari settlement. This settlement is the first to be run by the Roma themselves; it has a Roma mayor, and Roma dominate in the local council. In general, Roma communities in North Macedonia have the highest concentration of young people, and are the fastest growing ethnic community in the country.

A recent study from the settlement in Shuto Orizari found that reproduction and infant mortality of the Roma tend to be twice the state average or any other ethnic group (Toshevska et al., 2018). Another study, on women's autonomy found that Roma women in North Macedonia have an unemployment rate over 80 percent, with close to 30 percent having had no schooling at all, while almost 40 percent of last-born children were reported as unwanted (Stojanovski et al., 2017). In such Roma settlements child marriages are common: 45.1 percent of women aged 20 to 24 years old married before the age of 18, compared to 7.5 percent in the general population, while 15.5 percent of Roma women were first married (or in a union) before the age of 15 (Spirkovska, 2020).

The most recent data regarding the situation of children come from UNICEF Multiple Indicator Cluster Surveys (MICS), conducted in Roma settlements in 2011 (round 4) and 2018–2019 (round 6) (UNICEF North Macedonia, 2012, 2020b). The key survey findings are that most children living in Roma settlements in North Macedonia– 89 percent of Roma children under 5 years of age living in the poorest households and 96 percent from the richest households (UNICEF, 2024) - are covered by health insurance. The majority of children (89 percent) live in households with access to water piped into the dwelling.

In regard to early childbearing, young Roma women, especially those with poor education and living in household poverty, had higher rates of childbirth: 19 percent of Roma women aged 15–19 had a live birth or were pregnant at the time of the surveys. The use of modern methods of contraception tended to be low. Most women received at least one antenatal care visit from skilled health personnel during their pregnancy, with 62 percent having received eight or more visits. The majority of women gave birth in a hospital. Most Roma newborns in North Macedonia (99 percent) received postnatal health checks within 2 days of birth. Also, the majority (57 percent) of Roma children living in Roma settlements in North Macedonia were fully immunized in accordance with the national schedules, although some children were less likely to receive some of the basic vaccines on time (based on MICS 6 round data). In children aged 0–59, stunting prevalence was 12 percent, wasting - 4 percent, while there were 6 percent of underweight children. In addition, 6 percent of children were classified overweight. Only around 15 percent of Roma children had three or more children's books in their homes.

For the older children, the risk of dropping out from elementary education is high; children tend to drop out school at 10 or 11 years of age, while for younger children (2–4 years), parental engagement in learning and stimulating activities is 88 percent. Furthermore, for children attending elementary school grades 2–3, the minimum proficiency in reading, and mathematics is low, at half the rate of the national population.

In addition, children's experience of violent discipline by parents (physical or psychological) is high: 82 percent of children aged 1–14 experienced some form of violent disciplining methods, with more than 70 percent of Roma children up to the 18 years in receipt of social benefits (child cash payments).

4.2.2 Kosovo

The Republic of Kosovo is inhabited by a majority ethnic Albanian Muslim population. An Ottoman census from 1520 recorded small numbers of Roma living in Priština and other areas of Kosovo (Čvorović, 2014). Kosovo Roma communities continued to increase in size over the next several centuries. Most Roma in Kosovo are Muslim, with some in the past identifying as Turks or Albanians. The present population comprises Kosovo Roma, Kosovo Ashkali and Kosovo Egyptians (OSCE, 2020). The two latter groups present themselves as separate entities, whereas scholars consider the Egyptians and Ashkali to be separate subgroups of the larger Roma community (Marushiakova et al., 2001). Nevertheless, the creation and separation of these groups was supported by international and local authorities, corresponding to their own political and national interests. Before the Kosovo war, the Egyptians and Ashkali declared themselves mostly as Albanians. With the escalation of conflict between, on the one side, Serbia and North Macedonia, and on the other, ethnic Albanians, the Albanian speaking Roma emerged as two separate groups. The Serbian and Macedonian officials supported the creation and separation of these two groups. Thus, today, Egyptian and Ashkali communities are recognized as Albanian-speaking Muslim ethnic cultural minorities, while all three entities are known as RAE (Roma, Ashkali, Egyptians) (Fazliu, 2017).

The process of publicly establishing a new identity of the Egyptians came to the surface during the 1990s (Čvorović, 2014). As early as 1981, some Roma had tried to claim "Egyptian" as a new ethnic status on the national census. Then, in 1990, some Macedonian Roma founded an Egyptian Association of Citizens in Ohrid (Crowe, 2000). A parallel Roma organization was soon established in Kosovo. Shortly afterwards, a national Yugoslav Egyptian Association, led by a Macedonian Albanian, claimed membership of 15.000. In the 1991 census for the former Yugoslavia, the Egyptians were noted for the first time, with a membership of around 6.355. In fact, the "Egyptians" in different regions in the Balkans were known under various names: Jedjupci, Gjupci, Egjup, Adjupci, or Jevg, for example

(Vukanović, 1983). These various appellations were also used for Muslim Roma ethnic groups in Serbia, Kosovo, Macedonia, and Montenegro. In Montenegro, for example, while in Kosovo they are also known as Kovači (Blacksmiths) or Ashkali (charcoal-burners), these names being connected to their traditional occupations in the Balkans. Following the Kosovo war, after the former Yugoslavia broke apart and the territory was handed over to ethnic Albanians, a new minority emerged: the Ashkali. In the past, the name "Ashkali" was used for the Roma in southern Serbia and Kosovo who were Muslim Roma, who had gradually lost their Romani language and adopted the language and customs of the Albanian minority (Vukanović, 1983:138). Their traditional occupations included blacksmithing and coppersmithing. Today, most Roma from Kosovo consider the Ashkali and the Egyptians to be Albanian-speaking Roma (Visoka, 2008). According to the Egyptians, the Ashkali are pure Egyptians who deliberately hid their identity, and the word *ashkali* comes from an Albanian word for charcoal (Marushiakova et al., 2001). Yet, following the Egyptian example, the Ashkali launched a separate political organization through which they declared their separate ethnic identity. They claim that there are around 200,000 Ashkali in Serbia, the majority of whom were displaced from Kosovo after the war. The Ashkali in Serbia explicitly maintain that they are neither Roma nor Albanians but a native people from Kosovo having their own language which only resembles Albanian. The Kosovo Ashkali, on the other hand, state that they came from Egypt; some of them call themselves Hashkali. They claim that this is the name that was given to them by the Kosovo Roma. Today, they live mostly in Albanian villages, in their own *mahallas,* and follow mainly Albanian customs (Cocozzelli, 2008).

The best official estimates from the late 1990s indicate that between 100,000 and 150,000 Roma, Ashkali, and Egyptians lived in Kosovo, just fewer than ten percent of the overall population (Crowe, 2000). At the political level, the Kosovo Albanian leadership in the 1990s paid only limited attention to the Roma and other minorities. The Yugoslav authorities, on the other hand, provided direct support to the Roma and the new communities in Kosovo. In some schools in Kosovo, it was possible to study Romani, which was not the case in Serbia proper. Thus, the Roma in Kosovo benefited from an extensive Romani-language media network (European Roma Rights Center, 2011). Many Roma, Ashkali, and Egyptians could also profit economically when Albanian workers were fired from their jobs. Though mostly Serbs received their positions, in some cases Roma, Ashkali, and Egyptians, jobless for many years, were chosen to fill the vacant positions. Nevertheless, years later, Kosovo Roma were also fired from their jobs when Serbian refugees from the wars in Croatia and Bosnia were settled in Kosovo by the Serbian Government (Latham, 1999).

In 1998, increasing numbers of Roma, Ashkali, and Egyptians began to leave Kosovo out of fear of armed conflict, attacks from Serbs, threats of expulsion by ethnic Albanians, and arson attacks targeting Romani houses (Crowe, 2000). According to some sources, more than 100,000 Roma, Ashkali, and Egyptians left the province prior to and during the conflict, and after the NATO intervention

(European Roma Rights Center, 2011). As many as 50,000 Roma, Ashkali, and Egyptians found refuge in Serbia, tens of thousands more tried to reach Western Europe, and thousands took refuge in Montenegro, Macedonia, and Bosnia and Herzegovina. According to a November 1999 UNHCR figure, there may have been as few as 11,000 Roma in Kosovo at that point. Other estimates indicate that about 30,000 Roma, Ashkali, and Egyptians were still living in Kosovo by the end of 2002.

At the present time, there is a lack of accurate data on the Roma population presence in Kosovo (OSCE, 2020). The RAE in Kosovo are not a homogeneous population but composed of several sub-communities differentiated by settlement model, culture, religion, legal status, language and period of migration. According to the most recent census in 2011, the number of Roma, Ashkali, and Egyptians living in Kosovo, was estimated as: 8.824 Roma, 15.436 Ashkali and 11.524 Egyptians (Kosovo Center for Gender Studies, 2018). Another estimate puts the number of Roma, Ashkali, and Egyptians at 37.500 or 2.1% of the population (Robayo-Abril & Millán, 2019).

The majority of the Kosovo Roma population are Muslims. The circumstances of the Roma, Ashkali, and Egyptians in Kosovo are similar to that in other countries: they face discrimination, are not fully integrated into the education system or labor market, have difficulties accessing essential services such as healthcare, and live partly segregated from other ethnic groups. Many receive social help either from Pristina or Belgrade. All three populations have poor education, low levels of basic literacy, poor standards of living, many families in acute poverty, little or no employment prospects, poor health and housing conditions, and limited access to public services. Living conditions for many RAE in Kosovo are thus extremely inadequate, lacking even the most basic infrastructure.

Life in the RAE communities is predominantly based on tradition and customary law. Fertility is high, the average number of children being 3.7, with 17 percent having a first child before 18 years of age. Both consanguineous and arranged marriages are equally common: parents marry their daughters at the age of 15 or 16, followed by first childbirth before adulthood (Kosovo Center for Gender Studies, 2018). Around 10 percent of Roma, Ashkali and Egyptian women aged 15–19 have already given birth, while 17 percent of aged 20–24 years have had a live birth before age 18.

According to a report from 2015, under-age marriages are arranged by parents and families involved, with 42% of the couples not knowing each other until the wedding day, while bride price is common, usually between 400–4000 euros (Centar za romske inicijative, 2015).

According to MICS 6 (UNICEF, 2020a), the share of RAE under 18 years of age is 43%, which makes them a very young population. The rates of infant and child mortality, illness, and disabilities are much higher than the majority population (Kosovo Center for Gender Studies, 2018). For children aged 0–59 months, the incidence of stunting is 15%, wasting - 3 percent, and underweight - 7.1 percent. The percentage of children under age 5 who have three or more children's books is

4%. The percentage of children under age 18 living in the households that received any type of social transfers is 68% (UNICEF, 2020a).

School attendance is low, especially among women and girls. RAE girls generally spend very little time in school: 38.3 percent of women and girls are illiterate while the majority have unfinished primary school. RAE girls are expected to take on caring roles from the age of about 11. Many live in extended families, with the oldest male usually being head of the household. The majority live according to strict patriarchal rules, with clearly defined gender roles. From early on, females are brought up with the knowledge that men make all decisions, including ones concerning future marriages.

4.2.3 Bosnia and Herzegovina

The Roma have been living in the territory of Bosnia and Herzegovina since the mid-fourteenth century. One of the earliest sources dates to 1574, when Turkish sultan Selim III issued a law regulating Roma miners residing in Bosnia, near Banja Luka (Čvorović, 2014). The law specified the Roma position and brought tax exemptions for the Roma miners (Vukanović, 1983). A recent genetic study suggests that the paternal gene pool of the Roma in Bosnia and Herzegovina might be the result of an early separation from the proto-Roma population and the subsequent gene flow, as well as the isolation of Roma populations in some areas (Halilović et al., 2022).

In the past, Roma groups made firm distinctions between themselves. There were a couple of main groups: the White Roma and Black Roma, both Muslims. The White Roma were members of the non-Vlach or Ottoman group of southern Slavic Roma who spoke in a dialect known as Arlija, which included a few traces of Romani ((Djordjević, 1924). The Black Roma were known as Čergaši, from the Turkish word *čergi*, meaning a "tent"; they referred to themselves as Turks. Another group were the Karavlax Roma (Black Vlachs or Black Romanians). The majority were spoon-makers, who migrated from Wallachia and Moldavia into Bosnia and Vojvodina (present day Serbia) to escape the hardships of enslavement. They were called "Serbs" by the local population, or the Serbian Roma (Serbian *Cigani*), since they were Orthodox Christians. In the early nineteenth century, one source estimates there were around 30.000 Roma in Bosnia and Herzegovina, though others put this figure as low as 8.000 (Latham, 1999).

There is a lack of information on Bosnian Roma during the nineteenth century, other than accounts of nomadic Roma traveling and performing as bear trainers throughout the area. Nomadism was an important part of the Roma lifestyle throughout Bosnia, although, at that time, some tribes had already adopted a semi-sedentary lifestyle (Crowe, 2000). Overall, the Roma in Bosnia occupied the bottom of socioeconomic ladder, with their status unaltered after Bosnia and Herzegovina became part of the Kingdom of the Serbs, Croats, and Slovenes after World War I. In the later period, after the formation of the socialist Yugoslavia, a census from 1948 showed only 422 Roma in Bosnia and Herzegovina, out of the total Yugoslav Roma population of 72.651 (Vukanović, 1983). In the 1953 census, 2.297 declared themselves as Roma (out of 84.713 Roma in all of the former Yugoslavia). These figures grossly underestimated the true Roma number owing to the fact that some Roma also declared as members of other ethnicities; usually as "Yugoslavs"; only 31.674 Roma chose Romani as their mother tongue in the 1961 census. In spite of this "Yugoslavism", the circumstances of the Roma remained unaltered: the majority of children were illiterate, and few adults had the minimum educational skills necessary to compete successfully in the workplace (Crowe, 2000). Many engaged in trade, selling goods in markets while other small nomadic groups traveled around Bosnia and Herzegovina. The ultimate break-up of the former Yugoslavia, and the ensuing wars, inflicted a devastating effect on Roma communities in Bosnia and Herzegovina (Kahanec & Yuksel, 2010).

At present, the exact number of Roma in Bosnia and Herzegovina is unknown. Bosnia and Herzegovina conducted its first census in 2013. According to the official estimates, around 13.000 Roma live in Bosnia and Herzegovina, that is, 3.6% of total population of the country. However, the research conducted by various civil society organizations estimates the true Roma number between 40,000 and 75,000. International estimates also differ from the aforementioned figures (Roma Integration, 2020).

The Roma ethnic group in Bosnia and Herzegovina is generally the largest, most neglected and most vulnerable population in the country, experiencing enduring chronic, multidimensional poverty. The literature about human trafficking in Bosnia and Herzegovina show that Roma children are routinely mentioned being most at risk of being trafficked. A recent report on child trafficking in Bosnia and Herzegovina found that Roma children trafficking manifests as forced begging and forced work in the street (Dottridge et al., 2021). Additionally, there are reports that children have also been trafficked out of Bosnia and Herzegovina to engage in criminal activities in other countries (for instance, France). In the 1990s, child sexual exploitation was the most frequently reported form of exploitation of trafficked children in Bosnia and Herzegovina. There are several root causes of Roma children's vulnerability to trafficking. Generally, mass poverty and unemployment frequently cause Roma families to resort to survival strategies that include depending on income generated by children, which in turn requires them to drop out of school. Having few social ties with non-Roma, and lacking in basic documents such as birth registration, residence registration and identity cards, contribute to Roma social exclusion, encouraging further isolation and self-reliance.

Studies addressing the Roma in Bosnia and Herzegovina are limited. The only new study on Roma women assessed unmet health needs in the two biggest Roma communities - in the Republic of Srpska and in Bosnia and Herzegovina (Stojisavljević et al., 2020). The study found that 94.0% of women had health insurance, a health ID card, and were registered with a family doctor. Despite good coverage, unmet health needs were sizeable due to various family and background characteristics: being divorced, widowed or unemployed were associated with higher odds of having unmet health needs.

Almost all information about Roma in Bosnia and Herzegovina comes from the UNICEF Multiple Indicator Survey, conducted in 2011 and 2012 for the first time, which included data on health, nutrition, education, child protection and other indicators related to the lives of Bosnian Roma (UNICEF, 2013). The survey was based on a representative sample of 1791 households, with a response rate of 86 percent. In these households, 1380 women and 1456 men aged 15–49 were interviewed and questionnaires completed for 748 children under age five. The survey revealed a considerable gap between the Roma and the majority populations, and reflected Roma poorer housing conditions, low education, high unemployment rates and non-utilization of healthcare, whereas Roma women were in a particularly difficult situation. The survey reported a high infant and children mortality rate (in the report, the infant mortality rate was the probability of dying before the first birthday; the under-five mortality rate was the probability of dying before the fifth birthday). The infant mortality rate for Roma children was estimated at 24 per one thousand live births, while the under-five mortality rate was 27 per one thousand live births. Low birth weight (less than 2500 g) was also high: almost all Roma children born in the 2 years preceding the survey were weighed at birth (96 percent), with fourteen percent of them weighing below 2500 g. Compared to non-Roma, Roma children are three times more likely to live in poverty, five times more likely to be malnourished, and twice as likely to be lagging behind in growth. Thus, 21 percent of Roma children are of short stature, with eight percent seriously lagging behind in growth.

Immunization of the Roma children was low: this was only four percent in children aged 18–29 months, with thirteen percent not having received any of the recommended vaccinations.

The survey also noted that small Roma children are often left without adequate care. For instance, during the week prior to the survey's interviews, seven percent of children aged 0–59 months were without adequate care. Five percent of children were left alone at home, while four percent were left in the care of other children under 10 years of age. Inadequate care was more common amongst children whose mothers had no formal education (seven percent), while children mothers who had received secondary or higher education were not left without adequate care. Also, children in the poorest 60 percent of the population (nine percent) were more often left without adequate care than children in the richest 40 percent of the population (two percent).

Roma elementary school enrollment is lower by one third than among the non-Roma population, and the rate of immunization is only four percent compared to 68 percent among the majority of the population. Additionally, more than half of Roma children aged between two and 14 years were exposed to some form of psychological or physical punishment by their parents or other adult members of their households.

Among the Roma, higher fertility and early childbearing are common. According to the above survey, the adolescent birth rate was 145 births per 1000 women aged 15–19 for the one-year period preceding the survey, while the Total Fertility Rate was 3.2 births per woman. More than a quarter of women aged 15–19 had a live birth (27 percent), with three percent having had a live birth before age fifteen, while nearly one-third aged 20-24 (31 percent) had a live birth before age eighteen. Early marriage is also common. Fifteen percent of women aged 15-49 were married before age fifteen, with the highest percentage of these women having had no formal education and belonging to the poorest wealth quintile. Three percent of Roma women aged 15-19 as well as five percent of women aged 20-24, were married to a man 10 years older or more. Polygyny is also present, albeit in small numbers: a very small percentage of Roma women and men aged 15-49 were living with a husband who had more than one wife/partner. Furthermore, Roma women have less education, are more likely to be unemployed, financially dependent, exposed to domestic violence, and subject to more frequent discrimination than Roma males.

A study in Bosnia and Herzegovina from 2007 found that physical punishment of children is more frequent in Roma families (23.7 percent) than in non-Roma families (11.4 percent). The study also claimed that, in Bosnia, domestic violence is accepted amongst the Roma people, and its most severe impact is on children who in turn suffer both emotionally and physically (Nikšić and Kurspahić-Mujcić, 2007). The most recent study addressed the widespread practice of early marriage and obligatory virginity at marriage for Roma girls (Bošnjak and Acton, 2013). Interviews were conducted with 35 Roma adolescents and women from Serbia and Bosnia, eighteen of whom had lived in Germany as migrants for a long period. The results showed that, compared with their host societies, the practice of early marriage remains common in many Roma communities.

4.2.4 Montenegro

According to early sources, presence of the Roma in Montenegro can be traced back to the early sixteenth century; they are mentioned in 1508 as engaged in construction, repairs and other building labor (Vukanović, 1983). In later centuries, the majority of Roma migrated towards the coast; coastal towns were centers of trade and various business activities, and here the Roma found much more favorable living conditions (Vukadinović, 2001). There are two main Roma groups in Montenegro: the nomads (Čergari) and the Roma Blacksmiths. The Nomads were present in Montenegro only temporarily and mostly as seasonal workers, whereas the Blacksmiths were permanently settled in the Montenegrin territory. Before adoption of the constitution in 1905, the Roma in Montenegro were protected by tribal and unwritten laws, and fulfilled the needs of the local economies. After 1945, and especially in the period from 1981 to 1991, the Roma Montenegro population doubled – their numbers in the whole population according to the official demographic statistics rose from 0.25 percent to 0.54 percent. Thus, according to the 1991 Population Census, in Montenegro there were 3282 Roma or 0.54 percent of the overall population, but in 2011 this number was estimated to have increased to more than 12,000. (Statistical Office Montenegro, 2011). At the same time, many

Roma declared themselves as members of other national groups, most often Muslim or Montenegrin.

Most of the Roma who today, are permanently settled in Montenegro, migrated from Kosovo (63 percent), while smaller numbers came from central Serbia (23 percent), Bosnia and Herzegovina (6.3 percent) and Macedonia (5.8 percent) (Zahova, 2013). A very small number also arrived from Slovenia, Croatia, Vojvodina, and elsewhere abroad. The current best estimate is that around 21,000 Roma live in Montenegro. Of these, 12 percent are Orthodox Christians and 82 percent Muslims. After the Kosovo war, around 43,000 Roma came to Montenegro either as refugees or displaced persons. At the same time, many left for other European countries in the search of a more favorable place of residence.

Previous wars in the former Yugoslavia territory had seen a smaller Roma exodus to Montenegro: then, only fifteen Roma families from Croatia and 1000 Roma from Bosnia found refuge in Montenegro (Vukadinović, 2001). Those that came from Kosovo were ratified by the Montenegrin state as the RAE population (Roma, Ashkali, Egyptian), but they, later on, with the independence of Montenegro in 2006, became refugees. Today, according to the census conducted by the Montenegrin National Census Institute, as part of a project supported by the National Council of Roma and Egyptians in Montenegro, the RAE refugee population is estimated to be 4285 people (of whom 2733 are Roma, 1441 Egyptians, and the remainder - Ashkali) (Zahova, 2013).

The 2009 UNHCR report points out that the RAE populations are among the poorest and most vulnerable minority groups in Montenegro (UNHCR, 2009). Chronic and inter-generational poverty is the greatest problem for most of the RAE families– unemployment rates are extremely high and RAE families are nearly five times more likely to be poor than average Montenegrin families. At the same time, as in other countries, RAE are a young population, but have shorter life expectancy. They usually live in large households - average of 6 members - and are disadvantaged and marginalized in all spheres of life, including housing, education, health protection, nutrition, labor, and cultural and political life. Illiteracy is a further area of concern, as approximately 80% of RAE are illiterate.

According to a recent UNDP report (2019), the situation has not changed much in the past decade: there is still a wide disparity between the RAE populations and the others in regard to human capabilities and material well-being, especially for young people. For instance, only 18 percent of Roma aged 18–24 are in employment, education or training, compared to 63 percent of their non-Roma neighbors, bringing with this life-long implications such as blocking of further opportunities. Early marriage is common, amongst the highest in the Western Balkans after Albania and Serbia. Forty-one percent of Roma women aged 20–49 years in Montenegro were reported to have married before age 18, compared to 8 percent of same age non-Roma women. Material status does not impact age at first marriage: young women from the middle and fourth quintiles enter into marriage before age 18 in 37% and 36% of cases, respectively. Additionally, marriage occurs before age

18 in 27% of young women from the poorest families and in 26% of the wealthiest families. Among Roma who marry before age 18, just 54% are literate.

The age structure of the Montenegrin Roma is similar to other countries: 59 percent are 19 years or younger, and 16.7 percent are younger than 29. School attendance for school-aged children is low: children from Roma settlements who do not complete primary school are most often boys, belonging to families of poor material status. According to statements from mothers/ guardians in the Roma population, almost every third child (31%) of age 5–17 has functional difficulties in at least one learning domain. However, it has also been found that family wealth status does not necessarily influence children's difficulties: indeed, a higher percentage of children from wealthier families have functional difficulties compared to their peers from poorer families (UNDP, 2019). Children from wealthier families account for 37% of cases of functional difficulties, while the percentage for the poorest population is 30%.

Recent MICS data (UNICEF Montenegro, 2019) have shown that 38 percent of Roma women and 33 percent of men are functionally illiterate (unable to read a simple short statement about everyday life). The percentage of women aged 20–24 years who have had a live birth before age 18 is 36 percent. The prevalence of underweight in children under 5 years is 8 percent, stunting - 20 percent, and wasting - 3.2 percent.

4.2.5 Serbia

The first mention of the Roma in Serbia is in 1467: a public record documented five Roma blacksmiths living in the Resava fortress in eastern Serbia (Čvorović, 2014; Vukanović, 1983). According to census from 1522, there were 17,191 Roma houses, out of which 10,294 or 59.9 percent were Christians at the territory of Serbia. Roma were first recorded in Belgrade in 1536. In Serbia, as in other South-Slavic countries areas then under Turkish rule, the Roma were a separate ethnic group: they lived apart in *mahalas*, towns, or isolated villages, with some tax benefits for Muslim Roma. In 1866, the percentage of the Roma population in Serbia was estimated at around 2.1 percent (Djordjević, 1924). Records from 1867 show that Roma were living in and on the outskirts of Belgrade. A 1921 census recorded 16,674 Roma in northern Serbia, 14,489 in southern Serbia (including Kosovo and Macedonia), and 3756 in Vojvodina.

In past times, the Roma lived in extended families, engaging in traditional occupations, making them part of the economy, benefiting both themselves and the Serbs. Traditional Roma occupations included crafts such as trough-making, basket-making, spoon-making, blacksmithing, ironsmithing and entertainment (music). Although contributing to the agriculturally based Serbian economy, they were despised by the Serbian peasantry; craftsmen in general were isolated and occupied the lowest status in society (Djordjević, 1932). In time, Roma artisanal products became much valued, especially in Serbian lowland areas where they could make a living by selling their crafts. However, in general, despite their contempt for the Roma, the Serbian peasantry displayed a tolerant attitude towards them. In everyday encounters, the Roma were called craftsmen; blacksmiths were especially in demand, and there were often cases where these craftsmen were given land in a village in exchange for their services. In 1884, by an order of Serbian law, all Roma were compelled to settle down, and their nomadic life mostly ceased.

In time, some intermarriage occurred between the Roma and Serbs, especially in places where Roma became fully assimilated into the local culture. The incidence of intermarriage, however, was low, and to this day, the Roma have remained a separate ethnic group. There are today, however, few Roma subgroups in Serbia – some have lost the Romani language and Serbian is now their mother tongue. There are also different forms of Romani, depending on which Roma group they belong to. Interaction between the different groups is limited, and the dialect of Romani spoken is an important means of distinguishing between groups (Čvorović, 2004).

Serbian peasantry has long recognized the distinction between Muslim and Christian Roma (Čvorović, 2011). For example, many Serbs used to call the Muslim Roma - *Cigani* (equivalent to Gypsy) -, while Orthodox Roma were called Đorgovci (by their ancestor Đorgo or Jorgo, a common Romanian male name) (Djordjević, 1932). Further, the majority of Serbian Roma are Muslims, while the Romanian-derived Karavlax Roma groups only follow Orthodox Christianity. These divisions between the Serbian Roma have had a long history. Ever since the different Roma tribes came to Serbia in the fourteenth and fifteenth centuries, the main division between them has been their religious affiliation. All the Roma who came from the south, via Turkey, to Serbia were Muslims; only those who came from Romania were Orthodox (Djordjević, 1932). A large proportion of Roma arrived with the Turkish army, and these Roma are known as Turkish/Muslim Gypsies (Serbian Cigani--Gurbeti, Horahane, or White Gypsies, Čergari, Ashkali, etc.). These groups lived mostly in cities, in *mahalas*, or *cigan-mala*, where they are usually found even today. Their traditional occupations included ironsmithing and cattle and horse-trading (including horse stealing, called *dzambasluk*).

The majority of Orthodox Roma came later, about two centuries ago, from Romania (Djordjević, 1932; Čvorović, 2004). From approximately 1370, all Romanian Roma were enslaved, converted to Orthodoxy, and divided into several groups: slaves of the crown, monastery slaves, field slaves, etc. (Hancock, 1987). Most were forbidden to speak their Roma language. In the eighteenth century, the Romanian Roma began to move into Serbia in order to escape the slavery and political instability, especially in Wallachia and Moldavia, which were also under the Ottoman rule (Crowe, 1999). In Serbia, they were called Karavlax Roma (or "black Romanians", from the Turkish). From Serbian state archives, they were first mentioned in around 1833 (Djordjević, 1932: 99). In Serbia, all Romanian Roma are currently Orthodox. Today, a large proportion of these Orthodox Roma live in the Serbian rural areas, and do not marry or mix with other Roma groups (Čvorović, 2010).

Little information is available for the period between the two world wars; two censuses were performed but without ethnic breakdown. A survey conducted in 1929 noted more than 20,000 Roma in some Belgrade slums (Knežević, 2013). Just before the breakup of Yugoslavia in 1991, Serbian official censuses estimated the number of Roma as 140,237, then as 108,193 in 2002. The 2011 census recorded 147,604 Roma in Serbia, and the 2022 census - 131.936 (Statistical Yearbook for Serbia, 2013, 2024). However, domestic and international sources estimate Serbia's Roma population to be 300,000–460,000, which would mean that the Roma are the largest minority in Serbia.

In Serbia, a particular characteristic of the Roma is so-called "ethnic mimicry" or "favored identity", by which the Roma declare themselves members of the majority community. Many Roma refer to themselves as to "smoked Serbs", or just Serbs. Sometimes they call the Serbs "Whites" and refer to themselves as "Blacks", implying that the only difference between them is the skin color (Čvorović, 2010).

For the most part, the Roma in Serbia live in poverty, reside in sub-standard housing, often in segregated communities, and are poorly educated, resulting in high unemployment. To combat this, the Serbian government has introduced strategies aimed at improving the Roma's situation in areas such as education, housing and access to social assistance. However, the lives of many Roma remain unaltered, with entire parts remaining poor, uneducated and unemployed, particularly for females (Čvorović, 2020). According to the latest census with ethnic breakdown, data from 2011 show that 15% of Roma older than 10 years are illiterate, while 21.2% of female Roma are illiterate, with only 33.3% having finished elementary school (Radovanović & Knežević, 2014). In the early 2000s, numerous affirmative measures were introduced to improve Roma education. These included entry facilitation into the education system allowing children from vulnerable groups to enroll in school without proof of residency or health certificate. Despite these equity measures, Roma school absenteeism and high drop-out rates persist (Čvorović, 2020).

Additionally, through the social protection system, Serbian Roma enjoy the right to reduction in costs for electricity, water and other utilities (Čvorović, 2024). In 2011, new regulations were introduced to facilitate access to financial social assistance (cash transfers) as the most important state measure against poverty and social exclusion, and the number of Roma clients has rapidly increased. It is estimated that the percentage of Roma welfare recipients is almost four times higher than among the general population in Serbia (Čvorović & Vojinović, 2020).

Yet, at the same time, the unemployment rate of the Serbian Roma is estimated at 50.8% - more than triple that of the general population. For Roma, unemployment is often long-term, with as many as 67% of unemployed Roma never having held a job. The majority of those who work are engaged in the informal sector (the black market or underground economy), with minimal job security and benefits, which, along with avoidance of taxes and regulations, leads in turn to an absence of any official data on Roma average income (Marković, 2020).

In Serbia, the Roma population shows a significant time delay in demographic transition. Thus, Roma demographics differ greatly from the non-Roma population, being a young population with higher fertility, earlier onset of reproduction, longer reproductive period, and high infant and child mortality (Čvorović, 2014). In regard to marriage practices, a lot of Roma live in informal unions arranged by parents and kin groups, and often accompanied by the custom of bride price – usually a significant sum of money and/or gifts, given by the groom's parents to the bride's household. According to available data, the average number of children per woman is 3.5 (UNICEF Serbian Roma Settlements, 2020c). A large number of births is common: per 2011 census data, more than one-fifth (22%) of Roma women gave birth to five or more children, compared to only 2.2% of non-Roma women (Radovanović & Knežević, 2014). At the same time, however, the more assimilated Roma, living in mixed settlements, may show a different pattern: recent study found that on average, the more integrated Roma have significantly fewer children than the general Roma population, which is attributable to their greater exposure to the majority Serbian culture (Battaglia et al., 2021).

According to UNICEF reports, rates of low birthweight have been increasing among the Serbian Roma, while estimates for infant and under 5 years old child mortality rates are running three and four times higher than for non-Roma (UNICEF, 2014). Compared to non-Roma children, Roma children are at higher risk of poor nutrition and developmental underachievement, which may negatively influence later life outcomes, leading further to an intergenerational cycle of poverty and poor development (UNICEF, 2015).

References

Battaglia, M., Chabé-Ferret, B., & Lebedinski, L. (2021). Segregation, fertility, and son preference: The case of the Roma in Serbia. *Journal of Demographic Economics, 87*(2), 233–260. https://doi.org/10.1017/dem.2020.8

Cocozzelli, F. (2008). Small minorities in a divided polity: Turks, Bosniaks, Muslim Slavs and Roms, Ashkalis and Egyptians in post-conflict Kosovo. *Ethnopolitics, 7*(2–3), 287–306. https://doi.org/10.1080/17449050802307528

Crowe, D. M. (1999). The gypsies of Romania since 1990. *Nationalities Papers, 27*(1), 57–67.

Crowe, D. M. (2000). Muslim Roma in the Balkans. *Nationalities Papers, 28*(1), 93–128. https://doi.org/10.1080/00905990050002470

Čvorović, J. (2004). Sexual and reproductive strategies among Serbian Gypsies. *Population and Environment, 25*(3), 217–242. https://doi.org/10.1007/s11111-004-4485-y

Čvorović, J. (2010). *Roast chicken and other Gypsy stories*. Peter Lang GmbH.

Čvorović, J. (2011). The differential impact of religion on life history and reproductive strategy: Muslim and orthodox gypsies in Serbia. *Mankind Quarterly, 51*(3), 330–348. https://doi.org/10.46469/mq.2011.51.3.5

Čvorović, J. (2014). *The Roma: A Balkan underclass*. Ulster Institute for Social Research.

Čvorović, J. (2020). Stature and education among Roma women: Taller stature is associated with better educational and economic outcomes. *Journal of Biosocial Science, 52*(2), 260–271. https://doi.org/10.1017/S0021932019000427

Čvorović, J. (2024). The impact of welfare on maternal investment and sibling competition: Evidence from Serbian Roma communities. *Journal of Biosocial Science, 56*(3), 560–573. https://doi.org/10.1017/S0021932023000184

Čvorović, J., & Vojinović, Ž. (2020). The effect of social assistance on kin relationships: Evidence from Roma communities. *Biodemography and Social Biology, 65*(1), 16–30. https://doi.org/10.1080/19485565.2019.1681256

Djordjević, T. R. (1924). *Iz Srbije Kneza Miloša. Stanovništvo—naselja*. Geca Kon.

Djordjević, T. R. (1932). *Naš narodni život i običaji*. Knjiga VI. Beograd.

Dottridge, M., Ninković, O. L., Sax, H., & Vujović, S. (2021). The phenomenon of child trafficking in Bosnia and Herzegovina. Council of Europe. https://www.researchgate.net/profile/Srdan-Vujovic/publication/353958105_THE_PHENOMENON_OF_CHILD_TRAFFICKING_IN_BOSNIA_AND_HERZEGOVINA/links/611c0c341e95fe241adba749/THE-PHENOMENON-OF-CHILD-TRAFFICKING-IN-BOSNIA-AND-HERZEGOVINA.pdf.

European Roma Rights Center. (2011). *Abandoned minority: Roma rights history in Kosovo.* European Roma Rights Centre. http://www.errc.org/cms/upload/file/abandoned-minority-roma-rights-history-in-kosovo-dec-2011.pdf. Accessed September 2024.

Fazliu, E. (2017). Minority political representation: Roma, Ashkali and Egyptians. https://kosovotwopointzero.com/en/minority-political-representation-roma-ashkali-egyptians/. Accessed July 2024.

Fraser, A. M. (1992). *The Gypsies.* Blackwell.

Halilović, E., Ahmić, A., Kalajdžić, A., Ismailović, A., Čakar, J., Lasić, L., et al. (2022). Paternal genetic structure of the Bosnian-Herzegovinian Roma: AY-chromosomal STR study. *American Journal of Human Biology, 34*(6), e23719. https://doi.org/10.1002/ajhb.23719

Hancock, I. (1987). *The pariah syndrome: An account of Gypsy slavery.* Karoma Publishers.

Hoelscher, P. (2007). Romani Children in South East Europe - the challenge of overcoming centuries of distrust and discrimination. https://www.reyn.eu/wp-content/uploads/2017/11/Romani-Children-in-SEE.Overcoming-Centuries-of-Distrust.pdf. Accessed June 2024.

Kahanec, M., & Yuksel, M. (2010). *Intergenerational transfer of human capital under post-war distress: The displaced and the Roma in the former Yugoslavia* (Vol. 8, pp. 415–443). Emerald Group Publishing Limited. http://www.econstor.eu/bitstream/10419/44188/1/643916415.pdf.

Knežević, A. (2013). Demographic characteristics of Roma population in Belgrade. *Revista Română de Geografie Politică, 15*(1), 43–55.

Latham, J. (1999). Roma of the former Yugoslavia. *Nationalities Papers, 27*(2), 205–226. https://doi.org/10.1080/009059999109037

Marković, J. (2020). *Availability of local support services and measures for Roma children.* Social Inclusion and Poverty Reduction Unit of the Republic of Serbia.

Marushiakova, E., Heuss, H., Boev, I., Rychlik, J., Ragaru, N., Zemon, R., Popov, V., & Friedman, V. (2001). *Identity formation among minorities in the Balkans: The cases of Roms, Egyptians and Ashkali in Kosovo.* Minority Studies Society "Studii Romani". https://home.uchicago.edu/vfriedm/Articles/Edit008Friedman01.pdf.

OSCE. (2020). Overview of Roma, Ashkali and Egyptian communities in Kosovo. https://www.osce.org/files/f/documents/6/7/443587_1.pdf. Accessed October 2024.

Radovanović, S., & Knežević, A. (2014). *Romi u Srbiji (Roma in Serbia, census).* Republički zavod za statistiku, Beograd.

Robayo-Abril, M., & Millán, N. (2019). Breaking the cycle of Roma exclusion in the Western Balkan. The World Bank. https://documents1.worldbank.org/curated/fr/642861552321695392/pdf/Breaking-the-Cycle-of-Roma-Exclusion-in-the-Western-Balkans.pdf. Accessed June 2024.

Roma Integration. (2020). Annual report. https://www.rcc.int/romaintegration2020/participants/2/bosnia-and-herzegovina. Accessed June 2024.

Sardelić, J. (2013). Romani minorities on the margins of post-Yugoslav citizenship regimes. *CITSEE Working Paper Series, 31,* 1–33. http://www.citsee.ed.ac.uk/working_papers/files/CITSEE_WORKING_PAPER_2013-31a.pdf.

Spirkovska, I. (2020). Escaping child marriage in North Macedonia: 'Once you leave your mark, others can follow'. https://eeca.unfpa.org/en/news/escaping-child-marriage-north-macedonia-once-you-leave-your-mark-others-can-follow. Accessed June 2024.

Stojanovski, K., Janevic, T., Kasapinov, B., Stamenkovic, Z., & Jankovic, J. (2017). An assessment of Romani women's autonomy and timing of pregnancy in Serbia and Macedonia. *Maternal and Child Health Journal, 21,* 1814–1820. https://doi.org/10.1007/s10995-017-2292-1

References

Stojisavljević, S., Grabez, M., & Stojanovski, K. (2020). Unmet health needs of Roma women in the two biggest Roma communities in the Republic of Srpska, Bosnia and Herzegovina. *Frontiers in Public Health, 8*, 30. https://doi.org/10.3389/fpubh.2020.00030

Toshevska, B. A., Madjevikj, M., Ljakoska, M., & Sokoloski, P. (2018). The reproductive behaviour of the female population in the only Roma governed community in Europe. *Human Geographies: Journal of Studies & Research in Human Geography, 12*(2).

Trbojevik, S., & Bogoevska, N. (2011). Migracija, socialna izključenost in vprašanja identitete makedonskih Romov. Dve Domovini. (34). https://ojs.zrc-sazu.si/twohomelands/article/view/10992

UNDP (2019). *Labour Market Inclusion of Persons from Roma, Ashkali and Egyptian communities in Kosovo.* https://www.undp.org/sites/g/files/zskgke326/files/migration/ks/Labor-Market-Inclusion-of-persons-from-Roma-Ashkali-and-Egyptian-community.pdf

UNHCR (2009). *Social inclusion of Roma, Ashkali and Egyptians in South-Eastern Europe.* https://www.unhcr.org/sites/default/files/legacy-pdf/4b75652e9.pdf

UNICEF. (2012). *Severna Macedonia—Istraživanje višestrukih pokazatelja (North Macedonia—MICS).* UNICEF.

UNICEF. (2013). *Bosnia and Herzegovina Roma survey 2011–2012.* UNICEF.

UNICEF. (2014). *Srbija—Istraživanje višestrukih pokazatelja (Serbia—MICS).* UNICEF.

UNICEF. (2015). Early childhood development. The analysis of Multiple Indicator Cluster Survey data. https://www.unicef.org/serbia/media/1201/file/MICS%20ECD.pdf.

UNICEF. (2019). *2018 Montenegro multiple indicator cluster survey and 2018 Montenegro Roma settlements multiple indicator cluster survey, survey findings report.* MONSTAT and UNICEF.

UNICEF. (2020a). *Kosovo multiple indicator cluster survey and 2019–2020 Roma, Ashkali and Egyptian communities multiple indicator cluster survey, survey findings report.* Kosovo Agency of Statistics and UNICEF.

UNICEF. (2020b). *Severna Macedonia—Istraživanje višestrukih pokazatelja (North Macedonia—MICS).* UNICEF.

UNICEF. (2020c). *Srbija—Istraživanje višestrukih pokazatelja (Serbia—MICS).* UNICEF.

UNICEF (Regional Office for Europe and Central Asia). (2024). Breaking barriers: An analytical report on Roma children and women in Kosovo (UNSCR 1244), Montenegro, North Macedonia and Serbia. UNICEF, Geneva.

Visoka, G. (2008). Political parties and minority participation: Case of Roma, Ashkalia and Egyptians in Kosovo. http://doras.dcu.ie/17127/1/Political_Parties_and_Minority_Participation-_Case_of_Roma,_Ashkalia_and_Egyptians_in_Kosovo.pdf. Accessed June 2024.

Vukadinović, S. (2001). The status of the Gypsies in Montenegro. *FACTA UNIVERSITATIS-Series Philosophy, Sociology, Psychology and History, 8*, 517–525.

Vukanović, T. P. (1983). *Romi (cigani) u Jugoslaviji (Roma-Gypsies in Yugoslavia).* Nova Jugoslavija.

Zahova, S. (2013). Gypsies/Roma in Montenegro: Group identity and the role of language. In V. Romani (Ed.), *Papers from the annual meeting of the Gypsy lore society, Graz 2011* (pp. 81–96). Grazer Romani Publikationen.

Chapter 5
Parental Care in High-Risk Fertility Settings: Roma Nationally Representative Data from UNICEF MICSs Surveys

The only available nationally representative data on the Roma populations in the Western Balkans come from UNICEF MICS surveys. The surveys estimated conditions of women and their children (aged 0–59 months), and collected data on basic parenting practices (direct child care), allomaternal support child anthropometrics, and also unwanted childbearing among Roma mothers for all live births for the two-year period prior to the surveys (for children aged 0–24 months). Evidence of bias in parental investment in early childhood from traditional societies is scanty/limited: the cross-national data addressing the effects of key child and maternal characteristics that may be associated with biased parental investment is limited. From a Life History perspective, it is expected that a higher reproductive value of a child should correspond to higher levels of any measure of investment. Child outcomes such as weight at birth, height, and nutritional outcomes are often used as estimates of investment made by parents. These inferences may be especially relevant for children coming from the most disadvantaged backgrounds, which may be at increased risk of nutritional deprivation. To assess the associations between parental investment, unwanted births and child nutritional outcomes, as well as country similarities and differences in parenting, data were retrieved from MICS rounds 4, 5 and 6 for Roma settlements in Bosnia-Herzegovina, Kosovo, North Macedonia, Montenegro and Serbia.

5.1 Background to the Research Questions

For the Roma, to date, based on extensive and comparable cross-country data, there is no evidence of the effects of key factors on reproductive and parental investment. Data about Roma reproductive strategies and child outcomes as proxies of parental investment have been reported for individual countries, focusing mainly on differences in Roma maternal reproductive behavior and child health outcomes compared with non-Roma, while within Roma differences have been mostly overlooked. The studies and reports often lack sufficient information about the Roma parenting practices, including their effect on child nutritional status. With regard to Roma children, there is a lack of studies not only on current nutritional and growth status but also on health differentials among Roma children themselves.

In light of the widespread presence of the Roma population in different European countries, especially in the Western Balkans, and particular interest in child health outcomes, assessing Roma parenting practices across different countries is essential for supporting the children and understanding how Roma mothers make reproductive and parenting decisions.

A common, distinctive feature of the otherwise heterogenous European Roma population is their pronatalist, endogamous tradition evidenced by the encouragement of early marriages for all females, and high fertility rates. Consequently, many Roma females exhibit early marriage, early onset of reproduction, and continuous reproductive activity throughout their most fertile years, resulting in relatively high fertility but also infant and child mortality rates. Nevertheless, previous studies on Roma reproductive strategies have suggested that, in certain settings, the children bear no negative consequences for maternal early marriage and rather that it is the bias in maternal investment likely being the main contributor to health disparities observed in the children (Čvorović, 2022b). At the same time, very little is known about unwanted childbearing among the general Roma population: the effects of unwanted childbearing resulting in a live birth (child wantedness) on a child health outcomes have not been extensively studied (Čvorović, 2020). In general, research on unwanted children remains limited: there are a limited number of studies investigating the relationship between parental investment, unwanted births and child nutritional outcomes, while direct comparisons of unwanted with unwanted children in regard to child outcomes has rarely being conducted, especially in traditional, high-fertility populations (Hall et al., 2017; Kost & Lindberg, 2015; Costa et al., 2018). For instance, among mothers living in cultures with traditionally encouraged fertility, cultural pressure and gender expectations may frequently result in unwanted births being rationalized as to include "the excess" births, and thus it may appear that even children who were wanted suffer from reduced parental investment (Čvorović, 2020; Costa et al., 2018). In turn, under poor conditions, a mismatch between desired fertility and parental behavior may be associated with reduced child investment or complete disinvestment: for example, high mortality among the very young children may in part reflect mother's reactions to unwanted births (Čvorović, 2013; Knodel & Van de Walle, 1979).

The only available nationally representative data on the Roma populations in the Western Balkans comes from UNICEF MICS surveys. These surveys estimated the condition of women and their children (0–59 months) and collected data on basic parenting practices (direct child care), allomaternal support, and child anthropometry, and also on unwanted childbearing among Roma mothers for all live births 2 years prior to the surveys (for children aged 0–24 months). The surveys were cross-sectional and retrospectively reported on pregnancy intention: Roma mothers of young children were asked to think back in time and remember whether they wanted a child at that particular moment, or not.

Evidence for bias in parental investment in early childhood from traditional societies is scarce: cross-national data addressing the effects of key child and maternal characteristics, which might be associated with biased parental investment, is limited (Abufhele et al., 2017; Uggla & Mace, 2016). From the Life History perspective, it is expected that a higher reproductive value of a child should correspond to higher levels of any measure of investment. Child outcomes such as weight at birth, height, and nutritional outcomes are often used as estimates of investment made by parents.

The above implications may be especially relevant for children coming from the most disadvantaged backgrounds, which are at increased risk of nutritional deprivation. To assess the associations between parental investment, unwanted births and child nutritional outcomes, along with-country similarities and differences in parenting, data were obtained from MICS 4, 5 and 6 rounds for Roma settlements in Bosnia-Herzegovina, Kosovo, North Macedonia, Montenegro and Serbia.

5.2 Material and Methods

5.2.1 Study Design and Sample

The analyses were performed as a secondary data examination of the MICS 4, 5 and 6, for the Balkan Roma settlements, public use data sets, conducted in the period 2011–2013 and 2018–2020. The surveys were designed by UNICEF to collect analogous data on key indicators on the health and well-being of Roma women and their children. The analyses cover Roma settlement representative probabilistic samples in Bosnia-Herzegovina, Kosovo, North Macedonia, Montenegro and Serbia.

The Multiple Indicator Cluster Surveys (MICS) program is the largest household survey program on children and women worldwide. The MICS was developed by UNICEF to assist countries in filling data gaps on children's and women's health statuses. MICS was officially launched in 1994 in South Asia with 28 indicators, and now includes over 300 surveys in 112 countries, with 237 distinct indicators. Some MICS surveys cover a specific population group in a country, such as the Roma population in the Balkans. All MICS are publicly available data sources that can be used to examine nutritional status by health, demographic, and geographic variables for a nationally representative sample of women and children worldwide. Response rates in MICS are usually high, around 90–95% at the household level and child level, and slightly lower – around 90% - at the women's level. Children aged 0–59 months (under 5 years of age) are a key population for many MICS indicators.

The MICS questionnaire is made up of three core segments. A household module was administered to a head of the household, to gather basic information regarding the age and sex of all household members. All women between ages 15 and 49 reported in the household module were suitable for individual interview. Mothers or caretakers of children aged less than 5 at the date of the survey were asked also to complete a child health segment and provide information on several domains of child development and parental engagement. Roma mothers provided information on their children's age, gender, birth order, care and feeding practices, and parental stimulating caregiving practices. The Child health segment also included an anthropometric section which involved recording height and weight of each child using standard measuring boards and electronic scales. Weight at birth and whether the child was wanted were reported for children aged 0–24 months. Weight at birth was obtained from health cards, health facilities and mothers' recall.

The sample included 5229 Roma mothers, aged 15–49, in a marriage or with partners in unregistered unions, and their 7602 children, aged 0–59 months. As weight at birth and child wantedness were available only for children aged 0–24 months, the sample was divided into younger children aged 0–24 months (N = 2857), and older children aged 25–59 (N = 4745) months.

Statistical analyses were conducted in SPSS 22.0.

5.2.2 Measures of Parental Investment

For the Roma children aged 0–24 months, weight at birth, maternal parity and child growth and nutritional outcomes were used as proxies of investment made by parents. According to Life History Theory, if a woman's reproductive efforts, either over the entire lifetime or only early in her reproductive years, are biased toward increasing number of offspring, there will be a trade-off reflected in the size of offspring i.e., she should produce smaller offspring, corresponding to lower parenting effort and thus lower offspring quality (Promislow & Harvey, 1990). Evolutionary studies have used birthweight as a simple proxy for maternal investment in utero, with the rationale that low weight at birth, a well-known risk factor for increased infant morbidity and mortality, represents the trade-off between current and future reproduction (Wells, 2018). Under environmental risk and poor resource conditions, reproducing at a younger age may be evolutionary adaptive: early reproduction tends to maximize offspring quantity, accompanied by reduced offspring quality, of which low weight at birth may be the major part (Coall & Chisholm, 2003). Thus, rather than pathological, low weight at birth can be regarded as part of an adaptive response to environmental risk and uncertainty.

Maternal parity reflects a fundamental trade-off between number and size of offspring, influencing the differentials in parental investment across and within species (Walker et al., 2008). Parity may also affect variation in the offspring, as individuals born to mothers of different parity experience different prenatal environments that may influence growth, health, and survival (Skjærvø & Røskaft, 2013). Among mammals, including humans, parity influences on birth weight are well documented: lower birth weight is observed among low-parity offspring, in comparison to high-parity offspring (Fessler et al., 2005).

In addition, a number of studies show that high parity births are more closely associated with higher child mortality than low parity births. This is usually explained by biological factors, such as advanced maternal age, maternal depletion syndrome, sociological factors regarding access and poor utilization of health services for high parity births, or a result of reduced parental investment and competition between siblings for limited resources (Sonneveldt et al., 2013).

For the younger children there was no data on paternal involvement with the children.

5.2.3 Child Outcome Variables: Growth and Nutritional Status for Children Aged 0–24 Months

Early-life conditions and childhood growth and development play an important role in later life outcomes, especially in human capital formation (Abufhele et al., 2017). Additionally, early-life growth is a key fitness-related trait: adult height serves as an indicator of growth, nutrition and social environment in early life, while short stature is frequently associated with reduced reproductive success, though being short may be disadvantageous in one environment but advantageous in another (Silventoinen, 2003; Gluckman et al., 2007).

No population specific references describing the physical development of Roma children currently exist. In the absence of local standards, the WHO has recommended the use of international growth charts, where this is computed as the number of SD below or above the median of the international reference population. These measures reflect child health both in the long and short term. Children whose measurements fall below −2 z-scores of the reference population median are considered undernourished, i.e., a deficit in HAZ-stunting (a child is short for his/her age), WAZ or under-weight (a child can be either thin or short for his/her age), a combination of chronic and acute malnutrition, and WHZ-wasting (a child is thin for his/her height but not necessarily short) or acute malnutrition, with consequences including long-term developmental risks, and increased risk of morbidity and mortality (de Onis & Branca, 2016).

However, numerous studies have shown that nutritional outcome measures tend to be positively correlated with health and development among children throughout the measures' range, without cut-off effect at −2 SD or any other cut-point (Sudfeld et al., 2015). Accordingly, Roma child's health is also quantified through measures of individual children height-for-age z-score (HAZ), weight-for-age z score (WAZ) and weight-for- height z-score (WHZ), for children aged 0–24 months.

5.2.4 Maternal Direct Care

For the older Roma children (aged 25–59 months), direct childcare was used as a proxy for parental and allomaternal investment. Direct child care refers to the quantity of mother-child, father-child and allomother-child interaction. Roma women were asked to report on whether mothers, fathers, and/or other household members older than 18 were engaged in any of the following 6 activities with their children over the past 3 days: reading books or looking at picture books; telling stories to the child; counting or drawing with the child; singing songs/lullabies; taking the child outside the home into a yard or park; and playing with the child. A summary score of parental and allomaternal direct care (the quantity of engagement) was created, ranging from 0 (no maternal/paternal/allomother engagement in any stimulation activity) to 6 (engagement in all stimulation activities over the past 3 days). The total number of engagement activities was categorized as 3 groups: low engagement (0–2 activities), moderate engagement (3–4 activities), and high engagement (5–6 activities), similar to how it has been used as a measure of caregiving in other studies (Jeong et al., 2016; Čvorović, 2022b).

The internal consistency of the scales for the sample as a whole (all countries) was at Cronbach $\alpha > 0.7$.

5.2.5 Maternal and Child Variables

To reduce the risk of confounding, additional variables were used in the analyses to account for maternal and child conditions.

Maternal variables included whether a mother ever had a child who later died as a proxy for child mortality, maternal age at the time of the survey, maternal age, age at childbirth of the sample child, maternal literacy skills, and household wealth, based on the MICS wealth index comprising of a list of assets measured at the household level and ordered into five quintiles, the first of which being lowest wealth and maternal parity. Many Roma women are illiterate or functionally illiterate, thus literacy skills were divided into two categories: those who can read a whole sentence - basic literacy skills, or only part of a sentence - functionally illiterate (SD = 0.50).

The child variables were gender, age, birthweight, and whether the child was wanted, assessed by the question if the pregnancy with a particular child was desired at that exact time. Mothers who reported unwanted pregnancies were further asked if they wanted a baby later on (mistimed pregnancy, i.e., mistimed children) or did not want any more children (unwanted children). As with all retrospective reports, the mothers in the MICS surveys may have been disposed to rationalize an unwanted pregnancy as a wanted birth, or they may have shifted their position from "wanted" pregnancy to "unwanted" child if the child characteristics differed from those that what the mother was hoping for (Gipson et al., 2008). However, previous studies have suggested that this is more likely the result of unstable estimates of whether the child was wanted, and not so much bias in a particular direction (Marston & Cleland, 2003). As in previous studies, to mitigate the possible bias in reporting child health outcomes from mistimed (wanted later) and unwanted pregnancies were compared (Nguyen, 2024; Chatterjee & Sennott, 2021).

5.2.6 Statistical Analyses

Descriptive statistics and Chi-square tests with Yates' Correction for Continuity, Fisher, ANOVA, and t-tests were used to detect and describe differences across variables in the sample, including maternal age at childbirth, parity, child wantedness, birthweight, maternal investment (direct care), growth and nutritional differences between children wanted later or not wanted at all, and child's sex.

Repeated Cross-Sectional Analysis were conducted and included country and survey year fixed effects to lessen any confounding through differences in survey methodology or time. Bosnia and Herzegovina was not included as MICS was conducted only once. Hierarchical binomial logistic regressions were performed to assess predictors of Roma children birth weight, stunting, underweight and wasting, separate per for each, for children aged 0–24 months. Birth weight was dichotomized as $0 - \leq 2.5$ kg and $1 - >2.5$ kg, SD = 0.36), while for stunting (SD = 0.38), underweight (SD = 0.30), and wasting (SD = 0.26) as $0 - < -2SD$ and $1 - > -2SD$. For birthweight (≤ 2.5 kg and > 2.5 kg), the predictor variable was whether the child was wanted or not (SD = 0.40), while controlled variables included maternal characteristics: age at childbirth, household index as a proxy for socioeconomic position (SD = 0.50), literacy (SD = 0.50), parity (dichotomized as ≤ 4 and > 4 children, SD = 0.37), child sex (SD = 0.39) and mortality (SD = 0.28). For stunting, underweight and wasting, weight at birth (continuous, in gr) and household wealth index were controlled variables.

To account for children's individual HAZ, WAZ and WHZ scores, hierarchical multiple regressions were separately conducted for each measure (children aged 0–24 months). Weight at birth and household wealth index were controlled variables, while independent variables were maternal characteristics: age, literacy, parity (≤ 4 and > 4 children), child mortality, and child's sex and age in months. Wealth index was dichotomized as 0- first three quintiles and 1- fourth and fifth quintiles. Controlled variables were entered into the model in the first step, followed by the predictor variables in the second step. Only the full models are shown.

For older children, aged 25–59 months, hierarchical binomial logistic regression was performed to assess predictors of maternal high investment. Independent variables were maternal age, parity, and child's age and height (HAZ scores), while maternal literacy skills, socioeconomic status (dichotomous: four and fifth quintile vs first three quintiles) and allomaternal investment were controlled for. Paternal investment/care was not included due to high correlation with maternal direct care.

Although data were collected in both urban and rural areas, the variable "Area" was not a significant predictor in any of the analyses. As there were no data describing paternal investment for the younger group of children (aged 0–24 months), father presence/absence was used instead. As both variables were not significant, they were excluded from the analysis.

Statistical significance was set at $p \leq 0.05$.

An additional measure for significance was created – a proxy for biological significance. There is great variation in population growth trajectories and size, not all of which may have biologically significant fitness outcomes (Stulp & Barrett, 2016). For instance, if a measure estimate is statistically significant but very small, it may have a negligible effect on early childhood health or fitness. In contrast with statistical significance, "biological significance" refers to a significant effect that has an important impact on health, survival, and reproduction (Kramer et al., 2016). In order to estimate biological significance, we need to have knowledge of population-specific growth metrics to compare growth outcomes. However, to date, no specific growth references have been constructed for the Roma, despite the influence of their Indian origin and ethnicity on anthropometric measures (Čvorović, 2022a). When WHO standards appear unfitting or there is absence of established biological significance criteria for a studied population, a common practice for authors is to assign a reasonable-effect size (Kramer et al., 2016). Therefore, in the absence of population specific growth references for the Roma, an alternative proxy for a more biologically relevant measure of within population assessment of children's growth was calculated. Based on previous studies (Čvorović, 2022a; Winking & Koster, 2015), and to allow for comparisons to established standards for evaluating effect sizes, statistically significant results were put into SD units: the coefficient is the estimated SD change in Y associated with a one SD change in X1 (keeping any other X variables in the model, such as X2, X3 etc., constant). Thus, multiplying the beta coefficient by the SD of Y turns this into the change in Y in the original units associated with a 1 SD change in X1. For instance, standard deviations are equivalent to z-scores (1 standard deviation = 1 z-score), as they take on the units of measure of the data that they represent. This can be useful because original units are usually much more meaningful. The measures were applied to all proxies of parental care: child's birthweight, stunting, wasting and underweight, and also maternal direct care. The effects were regarded as significant if they were two or above two standard deviation differences (Winking & Koster, 2015).

5.3 Sample Characteristics by Country

5.3.1 Bosnia and Herzegovina

MICS for Roma settlements in Bosnia and Herzegovina was conducted for the first, and so far, the only time in 2011–2012 (round 5). There were 760 children aged 0–59 months for whom data were available (UNICEF, 2013, 2014a), mostly living

5.3 Sample Characteristics by Country

in the rural areas (90%). MICS round 6 was not conducted in Bosnia and Herzegovina.

The survey estimated the infant mortality rate for Roma children at 24 per 1.000 live births, while the under-five mortality rate was estimated at 27 per 1.000 live births (the estimates refer to 2005).

Early marriage was common: fifteen per cent of women aged 15–49 were married before age 15, with the highest percentage of these women having no formal education in the poorest wealth quintile.

In the year preceding the survey, the total fertility rate (TFR, the average number of children to whom a woman will have given birth by the end of her reproductive years at the currently prevailing fertility rates) was 3.2 births per woman, while the adolescent birth rate was 145 births per 1.000 women. Almost thirty percent of women aged 15–19 already had a live birth, while 4 percent were pregnant with their first child at the time of the survey. Three per cent of women of had a live birth before age 15, while nearly one-third of women aged 20–24 (31 per cent) had a live birth before age 18. For all women, there was a negative correlation between early childbearing and education level.

The majority of Roma women received antenatal care four or more times (62 per cent), and all births by Roma women that occurred in the 2 years preceding the survey were delivered by skilled personnel in public sector health facilities (99 per cent).

Almost all women aged 15–49 were aware of at least one contraceptive method (95 per cent), while one quarter of Roma women (25%) aged 15–49 who were married or in union were using some form of contraception during the survey period, the most common methods being withdrawal (16 per cent) and male condom. Unmet need for contraception was present in three in ten (30%) Roma women aged 15–49 who were currently married or in union, with nineteen per cent wanting to cease reproduction altogether and nine percent wanting to postpone their next birth.

5.3.1.1 Descriptive Statistics and Parental Investment Measures for Roma Children in Bosnia and Herzegovina

There were 722 Roma mothers and 760 children (0–59 months) in the sample. Bosnian Roma children were on average, two and a half years old, and there was an excess of male to female children (53 vs. 47%). Children were on average third born. Average HAZ and WAZ scores were below 0 (−0.59, SD = 1.84, and − 0.28, SD = 1.30, respectively), while only the WHZ score was above 0 (0.09, SD = 1.52). Stunting incidence was 21 percent, 8% of children were wasted, and 9% were underweight. There was no difference in underweight between boys and girls, while boys were more stunted (22% vs 20%) and wasted (8.4% vs 8.3%) than girls.

Roma mothers, on average, were 27 years old, with three children per woman and a range from 1 to 11 children. Birth spacing on average was 22 months. Child mortality was 5%. A small majority of mothers were literate (55%), while 45% were illiterate. The majority of mothers came from households in the poorest quintile (30%), while 14% (the richest) lived in better-off households.

For the children aged 25–59 months (n = 456), maternal direct care was moderate (M = 3.72, SD = 1.87), as well as for allomaternal direct care (M = 3.13, SD = 2.00), while paternal care was low (M = 2.27, SD = 1.47).

The majority of mothers provided high direct care (43%), followed by low (37%), and moderate (20%). In contrast, the majority of Roma fathers provided low direct care (74%), while only 7% provided high direct care. A similar pattern was observed for allomothers, with the majority providing low direct care (51%), while 33% provided high direct care.

296 of the Roma women gave (live) birth 2 years prior to the survey. Thus, there were 304 Roma children aged 0–24 months, with an average age of 12 months. Around 19% of children were unwanted. Birthweight was on average 3 kg, while 15% of children were born with low birthweight (< 2.5 kg). There were more boys than girls (54.6% vs. 45.4%). Average HAZ and WAZ scores were below 0 (−0.30, SD = 2.09, and − 0.35, SD = 1.42, respectively), while WHZ score was 0.24 (SD = 1.71). Around 17% of Roma children were stunted, while 13% were wasted and underweight. Children were on average third born. The majority of children (90%) lived with both biological parents.

Roma mothers were on average 25 years old, while birth spacing was on average 14 months. Half of the Roma mothers were literate (50%), and the majority were from the poorest quintile (30%).

5.3.2 Kosovo

MICS round five (2013–2014) and MICS round 6 (2019–2020) included 1605 children aged 0–59 months. Birthweight and child wantedness were available for 589 children aged 0–24 months, for both surveys.

Child indicators for MICS 5 and 6 showed that neonatal mortality (probability of dying within first month of life) and infant mortality (probability of dying between birth and the first birthday) rates were high for the surveys periods. For MICS 5, neonatal mortality was 29 per 1000 live births, and infant mortality 41 per 1000 live births; for MICS 6, neonatal mortality was 21 per 1000 live births, and infant mortality 26 per 1000 live births. Under-five mortality rates (probability of dying between birth and the fifth birthday) were 49 and 27 per 1000 live births for MICS 5 and 6, respectively (UNICEF Kosovo, 2020a).

For MICS 5, early childbearing (before age 15) was present in 7.3% of women, while more than a third of women had given birth before age 18; for MICS 6, more than sixteen percent of women aged 20–24 years had a live birth before age 18.

5.3 Sample Characteristics by Country

TFR (total fertility rate) for women 15–49 in MICS 5 was 3.7 and in MICS 6–3.6, while adolescent birth rate (15–19 years of age) per 1000 women was 69 and 78 (MICS 5 and 6, respectively). Contraceptive usage rates (percentage of women age 15–49 years married or in union who were using any contraceptive method) for MICS 5 and 6, respectively were 53% and 62.1%, respectively, while those not using any contraceptive method did not use any contraceptive method were 18% and 38% for MICS 5 and 6, respectively. According to the MICS 5 survey, abortions tended to be frequent: overall, 14 percent of women aged 15–49 years had at least one induced abortion; this increased to 37 percent for women aged 45–49 years. Among women who had an abortion, 45 percent had two or three abortions, while 13 percent had four or more abortions.

5.3.2.1 Descriptive Statistics and Parental Investment Measures for Roma Children in Kosovo

Roma children in Kosovo were on average 30 months old and there were more boys than girls (51% vs. 49%). Children were on average third born, and all three anthropometric measures were below 0: average HAZ was −0.83 (SD = 1.19), average WAZ was −0.55 (SD = 1.11), while average WHZ was −0.10 (SD = 1.08). Around 8% of children were underweight, 15% were stunted, and 4% were wasted. More girls than boys were underweight (11% vs 5%), stunted (16% vs 13%) and wasted (5% vs 3%).

Roma mothers were on average 28 years old (range 15–47), the majority illiterate (54.4%) and from the poorest quintile. Parity was on average four children while birth spacing was 2 years.

Maternal direct care was predominantly moderate, while both fathers and allomothers provided low care.

The majority of mothers provided low child direct care (48%), followed by moderate (36%), and high (15% or 57 mothers). Paternal and allomaternal direct care followed the same pattern: 77% of Roma fathers engaged in 0–2 activities with their children (low direct care), 18% engaged in moderate activities, and only 8 fathers (5.4%) engaged in 5–6 activities with their children (high direct care). Allomaternal direct care was mostly low (65%), then moderate (25%), while 18% provided high direct care.

There were 589 children aged 0–24 months. Average age of children was 12 months. Birthweight was on average 3 kg, 13% of children were born with low birth weight and, on average, were third born. There were more males than females (52.3%vs. 47.7%). More than 13% of children were stunted, 10% were underweight, while 5% were wasted.

Around half of children lived with biological parents, while 24% were unwanted.

Roma mothers were 27 years old, with on average three children (range 1–15). Child mortality was 9%, and birth spacing 12 months. Around 38% of mothers were illiterate, and the majority were from the poorest quintile.

5.3.3 North Macedonia

MICS surveys are available for North Macedonia Roma for 2011 (round 4) (UNICEF, 2012) and 2019–2019 (round 6) (UNICEF North Macedonia Roma, 2020b). There were 1186 children aged 0–59 months in both surveys.

For North Macedonia Roma settlements, infant and under-five mortality rate for MICS 4 were respectively 13 and 14 per 1000 live births. Total fertility rate for Roma settlements was not determined in 2011. Adolescent birth rate was 94 per 1000 women aged 15–19 years. 14 percent of Roma women aged 15–19 already had a birth, while 5 percent were pregnant with their first child at the time of the survey. 0.5 percent have had a live birth before age 15. Out of all Roma women aged 20–24, 27 percent had a live birth before age 18.

In MICS 4, over 90 percent of the surveyed Roma women aged 15–49 years had heard of at least one modern contraceptive method, although the majority (63 percent used nil contraception. The majority (64%) of Roma women reported that their demand for contraception was satisfied.

For the three-year period preceding the MICS 6 survey, the total fertility rate was three, while the adolescent birth rate was 114 per 1000 women aged 15–19 years. Percentage of women aged 15–19 years who had a live birth before age 15 was 0.5%, while the percentage of women aged 20–24 years who had a live birth before age 18 was around 30%. The majority of women (67.3%) used some form of contraception, with 6.5 for limiting reproduction and 1.8 for birth spacing, while only 8% of women had an unmet need for contraception. The majority of married or in union Roma women aged 15–49 years (55%) made their own decisions regarding sexual relations, contraceptive use, and health care.

5.3.3.1 Descriptive Statistics for Children Aged 0–59 Months and their Mothers, North Macedonia

Roma children in North Macedonia were on average 30 months old and second born. There were more boys than girls (51 vs 49%), HAZ and WAZ scores were both below 0 (M = 0.64, SD = 1.32, and M = −0.32, SD = 1.17, respectively), while WHZ scores were above 0 (M = 0.05, SD = 1.23). Around 7% of children were underweight, 12% were stunted and 4% were wasted. Girls were less stunted than boys (10% vs 13%), but more underweight (6% vs 5%), while there was no sex difference for wasting.

Roma mothers were on average 26 years old, with age range of 16–48. Parity was 2 children per woman and birth spacing around 2 years. The majority of women were literate (58.6%) and most were in the poorest quintile.

Parental (maternal and paternal) and allomothers' direct care was moderate. The majority of mothers and allomothers provided moderate direct care (39%), while most Roma fathers engaged in low direct care (58%).

There were 443 Roma children aged 0–24 months, and 23% were unwanted. Roma children were on average 13 months old, second born, with more boys than girls (51.5% vs. 48.5%). Weight at birth was 3 kg, while 15% were born with low birth weight. HAZ and WHZ scores were below 0 (M = −0.52, SD = 1.52, and M = −0.04, SD = 1.31), while WAZ was 0.32 (SD = 1.20). 11.3% of children were stunted, 6.3% were underweight, and 3% were wasted. The majority of children (91%) lived with both biological parents.

Roma mothers were on average 25 years old, with an average of three children (range 1–8). Child mortality was 4%, and average birth spacing 13 months. More than 33% of mothers were illiterate, and most were from the poorest quintile.

5.3.4 Montenegro

MICS 5 and 6 were conducted for Montenegro Roma settlements in 2013 and 2018 (UNICEF Montenegro Roma Settlements, 2014a, 2019). There were 1399 children aged 0–59 months. For both surveys, Roma infant and child mortality estimates were not determined.

MICS 5 reported that early childbearing indicators for Roma women aged 15–19 were high, 23 percent had begun childbearing, and 20 percent already had a live birth. More than one-third of Roma women aged 20–24 years (37%) had a live birth before age 18. Use of contraception was reported by only 4 percent of Roma women aged 15–49 who were married or in a union. At the same time, almost one-half (48 percent) of the women aged 15–49 who were married or in a union had an unmet need for contraception while only 8 percent had their demand for contraception met. Among Roma women aged 15–49 years, 14 percent of women had at least one induced abortion. Among women who had abortion, 10 percent had four or more..

MICS 6 data show that 1 year prior to the survey, Roma TFR was 4.5 children per women aged 15–49 years, while in rural areas this was five. Roma adolescent birth rate for women aged 15–19 years was 161, while the percentage of women age 20–24 years who have had a live birth before age 18 was 36.

Early marriage was common in Roma settlements: 28 percent of women aged 15–19 years were married or in a union at the time of the survey. More than one-half of women (56 percent) aged 20–49 years married before age 18, while 18 percent of women aged 15–49 married below age 15.

Percentage of women aged 15–49 years, married or in a union at the time of the survey who were using any contraceptive method was 13 percent, 15 percent had their need for family planning met, while 7 percent of women had at least one induced abortion.

5.3.4.1 Descriptive Statistics for Children Aged 0–59 Months and their Mothers, Montenegro

Roma children aged 0–59 months were on average 30 months old and third born, with more boys than girls (51.1% vs 48.9%). Average HAZ and WAZ scores were below 0 (M = −0.96, SD = 1.64, and M = −0.22, SD = 1.21), while average WAZ score was 0.47 (SD = 1.35). More than 20% of children were stunted, 8% were underweight, and 3% wasted. Roma boys were more stunted (22% to 20%) and more underweight (8.3% to 6.7%) than girls, but girls were more wasted than boys (4% to 2%).

Roma mothers were on average 26 years old, with an age range 15 to 46 years. Parity was on average 4 (range 1–11). Birth spacing was 23 months. Almost 76% of mothers were illiterate, with the majority from the second quintile (23%).

Parental and allomaternal direct care was moderate. The majority of mothers provided moderate direct care (37.3%), those with low direct care- 35.2% and those with high direct care - 28%. In contrast, the majority of Roma fathers (42.6%) provided low direct care, while one-third (34%) provided high direct care. Allomothers were mostly engaged in low direct care (48%), while 30% provided high direct care.

There were 485 children aged 0–24 months, of whom 11% were unwanted. Children were on average 12 months, birthweight was 3 kg, while 13% were born with low birthweight. There were more boys than girls (51% vs 48.7%), while children were on average third born. Average HAZ and WAZ scores were below 0 (M = −0.58, SD = 1.87, and M = −0.23, SD = 1.37), while WHZ was 0.16 (SD = 1.46). 20% of children were stunted, 7% were underweight, and wasted were 6.6%. The majority of children (75%) lived with both biological parents.

Roma mothers were on average aged 25 years, with 3.45 (SD = 2.38) children per woman (range 1–15). Birth spacing was 15.53 months, while child mortality was 6%. The majority were literate (65.6%) and from the second quintile (27%).

5.3.5 Serbia

According to the MICS 5 survey for Serbian Roma settlements, the estimated infant mortality rate was 12.8 per thousand live births, while the probability of dying under age 5 was around 14.4 per thousand live births (UNICEF, 2014b).

The TFR for the year preceding the 2014 Serbia Roma Settlements MICS survey was 3.1 births per woman, while the estimated adolescent birth rate was 157. About one-quarter of Roma women aged 15–19 years already had a birth at the time of the survey. Around 9 percent of the women of this age were pregnant with their first child, and 4 percent had a live birth before age 15. Thirty percent of Roma women aged 20–49 had a live birth before age 18.

Early marriage was common: 43 percent of Roma young women aged 15–19 years were already married, 17 percent of girls and women age 15–49 were married

5.3 Sample Characteristics by Country

before the age of 15, while 57 percent of women aged 20–49 were married before age 18.

Nearly all women (95 percent) in the Roma settlements were aware of some method of contraception, 6 being the mean number of methods known by the women. Regular use of contraception was reported by 61 percent of women married or in union. The percentage of married women using any method of contraception varied from 59 percent among those with no education and 61 percent with primary education, to 71 percent for those with secondary or higher education.

TFR for the year preceding the 2019 Serbia Roma Settlements MICS 6 survey (UNICEF, 2020c) was 3.5 births per woman. The estimated infant mortality rate among children in the Roma settlements was 8 per 1000 live births, while the probability that a child will die before their fifth birthday was around 9 per 1000 live births.

The birth rate for girls aged 15–19 was 163 births per 1000 women. Almost one-third (31 percent) of women aged 15–19 years had given birth or were pregnant at the time of the survey, while 3 percent gave birth to a live-born child before age 15. More than one-third of women aged 20–24 years (38 percent) gave birth to a live-born child before age 18.

All women in the Roma settlements had heard of some type of contraceptive method, while use of contraception was reported by 60 percent of women who were married or in union. Percentage of women who were married or in union who had never used any method of contraception was 29%, the main reason being that they wanted to get pregnant (61 percent).

5.3.5.1 Descriptive Statistics for Children Aged 0–59 Months and their Mothers, Serbia

There were 2652 Roma children, with an average age of 30 months. There were more boys than girls (52% vs 48%), while the children were on average third born. Average WHZ score was 0.04 (SD = 1.26), while both average HAZ and WAZ scores were below 0 (M = −0.95, SD = 1.34, and M = −0.52, SD = 1.16). About 7% of children were underweight, more boys than girls, 17% were stunted, and 3% wasted. 20% of the boys were stunted vs 14% for the girls, while there was no difference for wasting.

Roma mothers were on average 26 years old, with age range 15 to 47 years. Parity was 3 with range of 1–15 children. Birth spacing on average was 23 months. The majority of mothers were literate (62.4%) and from the poorest quintile.

Parental and allomother direct care was moderate. Maternal direct care was mostly moderate - 46.1%, high direct care - 30%, and low direct care - 24%. Most Roma fathers (49%) engaged in low direct care, similar to allomothers (44%).

There were 1027 children aged 0–24 months, 16% of whom were unwanted. Birthweight was on average 3 kg, while 16% were born with low birthweight. There were more boys than girls (53% vs 47%), and children were on average third born. All anthropometric measures were below 0, 17% of children were stunted, around

10% underweight and 7% wasted. The majority of children lived with both their biological parents (70%).

Mothers were on average 24 years old, with average parity of three. Birth spacing was 15 months, while child mortality was 3.2%. Around one-third of the Roma mothers were illiterate (28%), and most came from the poorest quintile.

5.3.6 Descriptives and Differences Between the Countries: Roma Children Aged 0–59 Months and their Mothers

There were 7602 children from the five countries, with average age of 30 months. There were more Roma boys than girls (52% vs 48%), and children were on average third born. Average HAZ and WAZ scores were below 0 (M = −0.84, SD = 1.43, and M = −0.42, SD = 1.18), while WHZ score was positive (M = 0.09, SD = 1.28). Roma mothers were on average 26 years old, with three children and birth spacing of 2 years. Child mortality was at 7%, most mothers came from the poorest quintile, and 51% were illiterate. Parental and allomaternal direct care was moderate. Maternal direct care (categorical) was mostly moderate, while paternal and allomaternal care was low (Table 5.1).

Differences between countries with regard to Roma children and their mothers were observed for almost all characteristics, except child's age, sex, rate of low birth weight, and birth spacing. Thus, child's average age for all countries was two and a half years, with an excess of boys. Rate of low-birth-weight children ranged from 13% to 16% (for children aged 0–24 months), while average birth spacing for all countries was approximately 2 years.

For all children (aged 0–59 months) all three anthropometric measures, i.e., average HAZ, WAZ and WHZ scores differed by country. With regard to HAZ scores, Roma children from Bosnia and Herzegovina were taller than Roma children from Montenegro and Kosovo ($p < 0.05$). North Macedonian Roma children were taller than children from Montenegro ($p < 0.05$) and Serbia ($p < 0.05$).

Roma children's average WAZ scores also differed by country ($p < 0.001$). There were differences found between Roma children from Bosnia and Herzegovina and Kosovo ($p < 0.05$) and Roma children from Bosnia and Herzegovina and Serbia ($p < 0.05$), while Roma children from Bosnia and Herzegovina had higher average WAZ scores than children from Kosovo and Serbia. Roma children from Montenegro had higher average WAZ scores than children from Kosovo and Serbia ($p < 0.05$), while Roma children from Macedonia had higher WAZ scores compared to children from Kosovo and Serbia ($p < 0.05$).

There also were differences in average WHZ scores by country ($p < 0.001$). Roma children from Montenegro had higher WHZ scores compared to children from Bosnia and Herzegovina, Kosovo, North Macedonia, and Serbia ($p < 0.05$). Roma children from Kosovo had significantly lower average WAZ scores compared to Roma children from Bosnia and Herzegovina, North Macedonia, and Serbia ($p < 0.05$).

5.3 Sample Characteristics by Country

Table 5.1 Descriptive and differences between the countries: Roma children aged 0–59 months and their mothers

Children 0–59, n = 7602	Bosnia and Herzegovina	Montenegro	Kosovo	N Macedonia	Serbia	p	Mean (SD) or %
Age (in months), mean (SD)	29.56 (17.00)	30.29 (17.32)	30.08 (17.24)	30.74 (17.06)	30.23 (17.28)	0.68**	30.22 (17.21)
Sex, n (%)						0.89***	
Female	356 (46.8)	682 (48.9)	781 (48.7)	581 (49.0)	1279 (48.2)		48.4
Male	404 (53.2)	714 (51.1)	824 (51.3)	605 (51.0)	1373 (51.8)		51.6
Birth order, mean (SD)	2.93 (2.00)	2.95 (1.88)	3.35 (1.16)	2.41 (1.37)	2.60 (1.63)	<0.001***	2.83 (1.84)
Height for age z-score WHO, mean (SD)	−0.59 (1.84)	−0.96 (1.64)	−0.83 (1.19)	−0.64 (1.32)	−0.95 (1.34)	<0.001***	−0.84 (1.43)
Weight for age z-score WHO, mean (SD)	−0.28 (1.30)	−0.22 (1.21)	−0.55 (1.11)	−0.32 (1.17)	−0.52 (1.16)	0.002***	−0.42 (1.18)
Weight for height z-score WHO, mean (SD)	0.09 (1.52)	0.47 (1.35)	−0.10 (1.08)	0.05 (1.23)	0.04 (1.26)	<0.001***	0.09 (1.28)
Maternal age, mean (SD)	26.79 (6.66)	26.17 (6.22)	28.09 (6.23)	26.48 (5.58)	25.52 (5.84)	<0.001***	26.43 (6.16)
Parity, mean (SD)	3.25 (2.06)	3.40 (1.90)	3.69 (2.18)	2.69 (1.42)	3.04 (1.66)	<0.001***	3.21 (1.84)
Birth spacing	22.44 (10.01)	23.38 (10.65)	23.97 (11.72)	24.22 (11.69)	23.14 (10.17)	0.262***	23.44 (10.80)
Child mortality n (%)						<0.001****	
No	681 (94.3)	606 (94.4)	645 (88.0)	445 (94.5)	1407 (95.3)		93.5
Yes	41 (5.7)	36 (5.6)	88 (12.0)	26 (5.5)	70 (4.7)		6.5
Maternal direct care, mean (SD)	3.72 (1.87)	3.22 (1.86)	2.63 (1.67)	3.43 (1.80)	3.71 (1.44)	<0.001***	3.46 (1.65)
Paternal direct care, mean (SD)	2.27 (1.47)	3.05 (2.20)	1.56 (1.54)	2.67 (2.20)	3.00 (1.61)	<0.001***	2.70 (1.88)
Allomothers direct care, mean (SD)	3.13 (2.00)	2.96 (2.09)	2.38 (1.99)	3.21 (2.03)	3.09 (1.62)	<0.001***	2.96 (1.91)

(continued)

Table 5.1 (continued)

Children 0–59, n = 7602	Country Bosnia and Herzegovina	Montenegro	Kosovo	N Macedonia	Serbia	p	Mean (SD) or %
Maternal direct care, n (%)						<0.001****	
Low	67 (37.2)	116 (35.2)	185 (48.8)	115 (32.0)	352 (23.7)		30.6
Moderate	36 (20.0)	123 (37.3)	137 (36.1)	140 (39.0)	684 (46.1)		41.0
Higher	77 (42.8)	91 (27.6)	57 (15.0)	104 (29.0)	448 (30.2)		28.4
Paternal direct care, n (%)						<0.001****	
Low	52 (74.3)	80 (42.6)	113 (76.9)	82 (57.7)	218 (48.9)		54.9
Moderate	13 (18.6)	45 (23.9)	26 (17.7)	23 (16.2)	138 (30.9)		24.7
Higher	5 (7.1)	63 (33.5)	8 (5.4)	37 (26.1)	90 (20.2)		20.4
Alllomaternal direct care, n (%)						<0.001****	
Low	32 (50.8)	111 (47.6)	107 (56.3)	77 (39.0)	170 (44.2)		46.5
Moderate	10 (15.9)	50 (21.5)	48 (25.3)	60 (30.5)	140 (36.4)		28.8
Higher	21 (33.3)	72 (30.9)	35 (18.4)	60 (30.5)	75 (19.5)		24.6
Wealth index quintile, n (%)						<0.001****	
Poorest	222 (29.7)	202 (16.3)	414 (28.1)	282 (24.6)	746 (29.1)		26.0
Second	185 (24.7)	288 (23.2)	324 (22.0)	252 (22.0)	568 (22.2)		22.5
Middle	117 (15.6)	263 (21.2)	283 (19.2)	206 (17.9)	493 (19.2)		19.0
Fourth	122 (16.3)	249 (20.1)	215 (14.6)	211 (18.4)	384 (15.0)		16.5
Richest	102 (13.6)	238 (19.2)	236 (16.0)	197 (17.2)	373 (14.5)		16.0
Basic literacy, n (%)						<0.001****	
Illiterate	296 (45.2)	468 (75.5)	377 (54.4)	172 (41.4)	515 (37.6)		51.3
Literate	359 (54.8)	152 (24.5)	316 (45.6)	243 (58.6)	853 (62.4)		48.7
Children 0–24 months, n = 2748							
Wanted last child then, n (%)							

5.3 Sample Characteristics by Country

No	52 (18.6)	48 (10.7)	143(24.2)	100(23.2)	159 (15.8)	<0.001****	18.5
Yes	228 (81.4)	400 (82.5)	446(74.6)	330(74.5)	843 (85.2)		81.5
Weight at birth kg	3.11 (0.53)	3.17 (0.58)	3.23 (0.61)	3.11 (0.62)	3.02 (0.51)	<0.001***	3.12 (0.55)
Weight at birth kg, n (%)							
≤ 2.5 kg	41(15.1)	55(13)	74(13)	65(15.4)	165(15.7)	0.20****	14.5
> 2.5 kg	231(84.9)	367(87)	496(87)	358(84.6)	834(84.3)		85.5

*p = ≤ 0.05; **p < 0.01; *** ANOVA; **** Chi-square test

Birth order was significantly different in Roma children from different countries (p = 0.00). Serbian Roma children, on average, had lower birth order compared to children from Bosnia and Herzegovina, Montenegro and Kosovo (p < 0.05). Roma children from North Macedonia had lower birth order compared to children from Bosnia, Montenegro, and Kosovo (p < 0.05) who, in turn, had higher birth order compared to children from Bosnia (p < 0.05).

Maternal age (p < 0.001), parity (p < 0.001), child mortality (p < 0.001), literacy skills (p < 0.001), and socioeconomic status (p < 0.001) differed significantly between Roma mothers by country.

Roma mothers from Kosovo were significantly older than mothers from Bosnia, Montenegro, Macedonia and Serbia (p < 0.05) whereas Roma mothers from Serbia were significantly younger than mothers from Bosnia and North Macedonia (p < 0.05).

In the sample as a whole, there was a strongly significant correlation (r = 0.619, p < 0.001) between maternal age and parity (not shown). Roma mothers from Serbia had significantly lower parity than mothers from Bosnia, Montenegro and Kosovo, but significantly higher parity than those from Macedonia (p < 0.05). Roma mothers from Macedonia had significantly lower parity from mothers from Bosnia, Montenegro and Kosovo (p < 0.05). Mothers from Bosnia had significantly lower parity than mothers from Kosovo (p < 0.05). In turn, Roma mothers from Kosovo had the highest mortality. Socioeconomic status and maternal literacy skills were also different by country - Roma mothers from Montenegro had the highest illiteracy rates, and fewer mothers from Bosnia were from the richest quintile.

Roma maternal direct care (continuous) also differed by country (p < 0.001), where the highest maternal direct care was among mothers from Bosnia and Herzegovina, followed by Serbia, North Macedonia, Montenegro, and Kosovo. When divided into low, moderate and high, direct maternal care between the countries followed a similar order (p < 0.001). Thus, Roma mothers from Kosovo engaged in significantly less direct child care than mothers from Bosnia and Herzegovina, Montenegro, Macedonia and Serbia (p < 0.05). Serbian Roma mothers engaged significantly more in direct care than mothers from Montenegro and Macedonia (p < 0.05). Roma mothers from Montenegro engaged significantly less in direct care than mothers from Bosnia and Herzegovina (p < 0.05).

Paternal direct care was also different by country (p < 0.001)-- direct care was highest for Roma Montenegrin and Serbian fathers. Similarly, when divided to low, moderate and high direct care, paternal engagement differed by country (p < 0.001). Roma fathers from Kosovo were significantly less involved in direct childcare than fathers from Montenegro, Macedonia and Serbia. Roma fathers from Bosnia and Herzegovina were significantly less engaged in direct care than fathers from Montenegro and Serbia.

Allomaternal direct care (continuous) followed the same pattern as maternal and paternal direct care, with significant country differences regarding child engagement (p < 0.001), with North Macedonian Roma allomothers investing more than allomothers from Bosnia, Serbia, Montenegro and Kosovo, in descending order. Regarding categorical allomaternal care, there was a difference in direct care (p < 0.001), with allomothers from Kosovo engaging significantly less in direct childcare than allomothers from Montenegro and Serbia (p < 0.05).

Data were not available for parental and allomothers' frequency of activities with children, but only 19% of mothers engaged in book reading, 54% in storytelling, 61% in song singing, 88% in playing with the child, 86% in taking the child outside, and 31% in naming, counting or picture drawing with the child (not shown). Regarding paternal direct care, only 10% of fathers engaged in book reading, 30% in storytelling, 34% in song singing, 84% in playing with the child, 82% in taking the child outside, and 17% in naming, counting or picture drawing with the child. Regarding allomothers, 12% engaged in book reading, 33% in storytelling, 37% in song singing, 82% in playing with the child, 76% in taking the child outside, and 19% in naming, counting or picture drawing with the child.

For the whole sample, there were strong and positive correlations between maternal and paternal investment ($r = 0.82$, $p = 0.00$), maternal and allomaternal investment ($r = 0.45$, $p = 0.00$), and paternal and allomaternal investment ($r = 0.55$, $p = 0.00$). Thus, for instance, an increase in the mother's investment increased the father's and allomother's investment, and vice versa (a decrease in the mother's investment decreased the father's and allomother's investment, etc.), while an increase in father's investment increased allomaternal investment.

There were 2857 children aged 0–24 months, with average age of 1 year ($M = 12.16$, $SD = 7.08$) (data not shown). There were more boys than girls (52% vs 47%, $SD = o.50$) and children were, on average, third born. Around 15% of the children were born with low birthweight, 19% were unwanted, while 20% were both unwanted (child wantedness $SD = 0.39$) and had low birthweight. The majority were born to mothers from the poorest quintile. Birthweight was on average 3.11 ($SD = 0.57$ for binary birthweight ≤ 2.5 kg and > 2.5 kg, $SD = 0.36$).

The average HAZ score was -0.64 ($SD = 1.61$), while 16% ($SD = 0.38$) were stunted. Average WAZ and WHZ scores were below 0 ($M = -0.45$, $SD = 1.25$, and $M = -0.09$, $SD = 1.38$, respectively), 9% were underweight ($SD = 0.30$), and 7% wasted ($SD = 0.26$). There was also significant differences in birthweight by country, with children born in Kosovo having the highest birthweight compared to children from the other countries ($p < 0.001$), while rate of low birthweight did not differ between the surveyed countries. Roma mothers were on average 25 years old, with parity of three ($M = 2.99$, $SD = 1.87$).

5.3.7 *Roma Parental Investment for Children Aged 0–24 Months*

Weight at birth and maternal parity were used as proxies for parental (maternal) investment for the younger group of children. In addition to child quality (i.e., weight at birth) and maternal parity, being unwanted-born may also influence maternal behavior and investment.

A common underlying factor influencing not only maternal investment but also child outcomes is maternal age at childbirth. Early maternal age at childbirth

(≤19 years), but also late (≥35 years) maternal age may be associated with adverse birth and child outcomes, owing to predicted biological risks associated with extremes of reproductive age. To assess the association between maternal age at childbirth and child nutritional outcomes, the Roma mothers were divided into four groups based on age at childbirth: age at childbirth in teen years, at <19, adult - 20–24 and 25–34 years, and ≥ 35 years.

5.3.7.1 Maternal Age at Childbirth and Children's Growth and Nutritional Status

Table 5.2 presents children's nutritional status and differences by maternal age at childbirth (≤ 19, 20–24, 25–34, and ≥ 35 years of age) for Roma mothers and children.

There were 2818 Roma mothers in the sample with a live birth in the past 2 years preceding the surveys. Around 20% gave birth at ≤19 years of age, 37% at 20–24, and 25–34 years of age and only 7% at ≥35 years of age. There were no differences found in children's growth and nutritional status by maternal age at childbirth, except for birthweight (p < 0.001).

Children born to mothers who gave birth between the ages of 25–34 had a significantly higher birth weight than children born to mothers who gave birth at ≤19 years and between 20–24 years of age.

5.3.7.2 Descriptive and Differences by Children's Weight at Birth

To assess differences in investment, the sample of younger Roma children was divided by weight at birth at ≤2.5 kg vs >2.5 kg, maternal parity, dichotomized as ≤4 vs >4 births, and, finally, wanted vs unwanted children (Table 5.3).

There were 2.626 children whose birthweight data were available.

In this sample, there was a statistically significant difference regarding weight at birth by sex,, with girls more often being born with low birthweight than boys (p = 0.002).

Children's anthropometric measures also differed by birthweight. Thus, children born with low birthweight were shorter than those born >2.5 kg (p < 0.001), had lower WAZ scores (p < 0.001), and lower weight for height z scores than their normal-born counterparts (p < 0.001). Furthermore, children born with low birthweight had a higher frequency of stunting (p < 0.001), underweight (p < 0.001), and wasting (p = 0.04) compared to children born with normal birthweight.

Several maternal characteristics differed for children born with low and normal birthweight. Younger mothers tend to have low birthweight children more often than older ones (p = 0.000), birth spacing was significantly shorter for low-birth-weight children (p < 0.001), and low birthweight children tended to be born to mothers from poorer quintiles (p = 0.01).

There were no differences in child's birth order, wantedness, maternal literacy, or parity.

5.3 Sample Characteristics by Country

Table 5.2 Maternal age at childbirth and children's growth and nutritional status

Characteristics	Age at birth (≤19) n = 561 Mean (SD) or %	N	Age at birth (20–24) n = 1029 Mean (SD) or %	N	Age at birth (25–34) n = 1029 Mean (SD) or %	N	Age at birth (≥35) n = 199 Mean (SD) or %	N	p*
Birthweight	3.06 (0.54)	513	3.08 (0.56)	974	3.17 (0.58)	967	3.15 (0.64)	172	<0.001*****
Weight at birth, n (%)									0.19***
≤2.5 kg	16.4	84	15.6	152	12.9	125	16.9	29	
>2.5 kg	83.6	429	84.4	822	87.1	842	83.1	143	
Height for age z-score WHO	−0.69 (1.69)	517	−0.62 (1.58)	931	−0.67 (1.59)	930	−0.46 (1.68)	182	0.32****
Weight for age z-score WHO	−0.49 (1.18)	533	−0.41 (1.27)	964	−0.44 (1.26)	965	−0.44 (1.36)	187	0.71****
Weight for height z-score WHO	−0.10 (1.38)	515	−0.07 (1.37)	930	−0.08 (1.37)	936	−0.23 (1.38)	183	0.54****
Height for age									
≤−2SD	19.0	98	16.5	154	19.0	177	14.8	27	0.31***
>−2SD	81.0	419	83.5	777	81.0	753	85.2	155	
Weight for age									
≤−2SD	11.1	59	8.4	81	9.7	94	10.7	20	0.36***
>−2SD	88.9	474	91.6	883	90.3	871	89.3	167	
Weight for height									
≤−2SD	8.3	43	7.3	68	6.8	64	9.3	17	0.56***
>−2SD	91.7	472	92.7	862	93.2	872	90.7	166	

* Sig <0.05 ** Sig <0.01 *** Chi square ****t test ***** ANOVA

Table 5.3 Descriptive and differences by children's weight at birth

Characteristics	Weight at birth (≤2.5 kg), n = 390 Mean (SD) or %	N	Weight at birth (>2.5 kg), n = 2236 Mean (SD) or %	N	p
Sex					0.002***
Female	54.6	213	46.2	1033	
Male	45.4	177	53.8	1203	
Height for age z-score WHO	−1.38 (1.65)	353	−0.49 (1.56)	2034	<0.001****
Weight for age z-score WHO	−1.11 (1.41)	366	−0.31 (1.17)	2105	<0.001****
Weight for height z-score WHO	−0.37 (1.38)	355	−0.04 (1.36)	2037	<0.001****
Height for age					<0.001***
≤−2SD	32.9	116	14.4	292	
>−2SD	67.1	237	85.6	1742	
Weight for age					<0.001***
≤−2SD	23.8	87	6.8	143	
>−2SD	76.2	279	93.2	1962	
Weight for height					0.043***
≤−2SD	10.1	36	7.1	144	
>−2SD	89.9	319	92.9	1893	
Birth order	2.91 (1.96)	390	2.91 (1.82)	2236	0.989****
Maternal age	22.17 (4.62)	357	26.32 (5.66)	1879	0.000***
Children ever born	3.03 (1.96)	390	2.97 (1.82)	2236	0.522***
Birth spacing	8.75 (7.79)	48	15.76 (4.61)	131	<0.001****

5.3 Sample Characteristics by Country

Wealth index					0.013***
Poorest	31.3	112	25.0	560	
Second	25.1	98	23.7	529	
Middle	19.0	74	18.5	414	
Fourth	12.8	50	16.0	358	
Richest	11.8	46	16.8	375	
Basic literacy skills					0.175***
Illiterate	51.2	172	47.2	875	
Literate	48.8	164	52.8	980	
Wanted last child then					0.436***
No	20.0	78	18.3	410	
Yes	80.0	312	81.7	1826	

* Sig <0.05 ** Sig <0.01 ***Chi square ****t test

5.3.7.3 Descriptive and Differences by Maternal Parity (≤4 vs >4)

There were 2818 mothers whose parity data were available. Out of the total number of mothers (SD = 0.37), 17 percent had more than four children; however, there were several statistically significant differences regarding the number of children born (Table 5.4).

Table 5.4 Descriptive and differences by maternal parity (≤4 vs >4)

Characteristics	Parity (≤4), n = 2347 Mean (SD) or %	N	Parity (>4), n = 471 Mean (SD) or %	N	p*
Sex					0.930***
Female	47.6	1116	47.8	225	
Male	52.4	1231	52.2	246	
Height for age z-score WHO	−0.59 (1.60)	2134	−0.87 (1.68)	426	<0.001****
Weight for age z-score WHO	−0.40 (1.25)	2204	−0.64 (1.27)	445	<0.001****
Weight for height z-score WHO	−0.08 (1.38)	2130	−0.17 (1.36)	434	0.197****
Height for age					
≤-2SD	16.6	355	23.7	101	<0.001***
>-2SD	83.4	1779	76.3	325	
Weight for age					
≤-2SD	9.2	203	11.5	51	0.141***
>-2SD	90.8	2001	88.5	394	
Weight for height					
≤-2SD	7.5	160	7.4	32	0.920***
>-2SD	92.5	1970	92.6	402	
Birth order	2.27 (1.05)	2345	6.18 (1.65)	471	<0.001
Maternal age	19.71 (3.36)		27.37 (5.37)		<0.001***-
Children ever born	2.34 (1.04)	2345	6.27 (1.62)	471	<0.001
Birth spacing	14.48 (5.92)	151	12.84 (7.28)	44	0.177****
Wealth index					
Poorest	24.0	563	37.6	177	<0.001***
Second	23.2	544	26.1	123	
Middle	18.9	443	18.5	87	
Fourth	16.9	396	9.1	43	
Richest	17.1	401	8.7	41	
Basic literacy skills					
Illiterate	46.1	882	65.8	298	<0.001***
Literate	53.9	1031	34.2	155	
Wanted last child					
No	15.8	363	30.8	139	<0.001***
Yes	84.2	1933	69.2	313	

* Sig <0.05 ** Sig <0.01 *** Chi square ****t test

5.3 Sample Characteristics by Country 133

Height for age and weight for height z-scores, as well as rates of stunting, differed between children born to mothers with ≤4 vs >4 parity. On average, mothers with parity ≤4 had significantly taller children than mothers with >4 parity (p = 0.001). Furthermore, mothers with lower parity (≤4) had children with a significantly higher weight for age compared to children whose mothers had higher parity (>4) (p < 0.001). Also, lower parity mothers had children with lower rates of stunting compared to mothers with higher parity (p < 0.001).

Children born to mothers with low parity had significantly lower birth order and younger mothers than children born to high-parity mothers (p < 0.001, and p < 0.001, respectively).

Maternal literacy and socioeconomic status differed by parity, in addition, with high-parity mothers being more illiterate (<0.001) and of lower socioeconomic status than lower-parity mothers (<0.001). Another difference was found in the number of children ever born: on average, parity for high parity mothers was above six children, while for low parity mothers this was two (<0.001).

Lastly, unwanted childbearing also differed between mothers with ≤4 vs >4 children: one-third of high-parity mothers were raising an unwanted child, compared to 15% of mothers with ≤4 parity. However, this could also imply that the majority of high-parity mothers (70%) actually wanted or intended the last child/pregnancy, despite their average number of children being above six. The same results were obtained after maternal parity was divided up into ≤3 and > 3 children: 73% of women wanted the last child, even though they already had 5.23 children on average (SD = 1.65, not shown).

There were no differences in children's weight for height, wasting, underweight, and maternal birth spacing by maternal parity.

5.3.7.4 Child Wantedness

Child and maternal socio-demographic and nutritional measures distribution based on whether the child was wanted showed several statistically significant differences in child's age and sex, WAZ score, and birth order, but also in maternal age, parity, birth spacing, and by country (Table 5.5).

Thus, unwanted children had lower average WAZ scores than wanted children (p < 0.05), while more girls than boys were unwanted (p < 0.001). There was also a difference in birth order, with unwanted children having higher birth order than wanted ones (p < 0.05). Furthermore, mothers of unwanted children were older (p < 0.01) and had higher parity (p < 0.001), while Serbia and Kosovo had the highest share of unwanted children (p < 0.01).

Table 5.5 Descriptives and differences based on child wantedness

Characteristics	wanted last child (yes) Mean (SD) or %	N	wanted last child (no) Mean (SD) or %	N	p
Child's age (in months)	11.85 (7)	2246	12.65 (6.95)	502	0.02****
Height for age z-score WHO	−0.63 (1.63)	2036	−0.69 (1.53)	463	0.40****
≤ −2 SD	18.0%	366	16.2%	75	0.45***
> − 2 SD	82.0%	1670	83.8%	388	
Weight for age z-score WHO	−0.42 (1.25)	2098	−0.55 (1.25)	479	0.04****
≤ −2 SD	9.5%	201	10.0%	48	0.67***
> − 2 SD	90.5%	1905	90.0%	431	
Weight for height z-score WHO	−0.08 (1.41)	2035	−0.16 (1.24)	463	0.24****
≤ −2 SD	8.0%	163	5.6%	26	0.10***
> − 2 SD	92.0%	1876	94.4%	437	
Childbirth weight	3.12 (0.57)	2138	3.11 (0.58)	488	0.85****
≤2.5 kg	14.6%	312	16.0%	78	0.43***
> 2.5 kg	85.4%	1826	84.0%	410	
Child sex					
Male	53.4%	1200	48.2%	242	0.04***
Female	46.6%	1046	51.8%	260	
Birth order	2.77 (1.80)	2246	3.59 (2.01)	502	0.00****
Maternal age	24.73 (5.56)	2246	26.59 (6.20)	502	0.00****
Parity	2.83 (1.80)	2246	3.70 (1.98)	502	0.00****
Birth spacing (in months)	13.51 (6.84)	138	15.42 (4.38)	55	0.48****
Child mortality					
Yes	5.2%	116	5.0%	25	0.87***
No	94.8%	2130	95.0%	477	
Literacy skills					
Literate	50.6%	951	49.8%	212	0.75***
Illiterate	49.4%	927	50.2%	214	
Wealth index quintile					
Poorest	25.9%	582	28.1%	141	0.66***
Second	23.5%	528	24.5%	123	
Middle	18.8%	423	18.9%	95	
Fourth	15.8%	354	13.7%	69	
Richest	16.0%	359	14.7%	74	
Country					
BIH	10.2%	228	10.4%	52	0.00***
Monte Negro	17.8%	400	9.6%	48	
Kosovo	19.9%	446	28.5%	143	
Makedonia	14.7%	330	19.9%	100	
Serbia	37.5%	842	31.7%	159	

* Sig <0.05 ** Sig <0.01*** Chi square ****t test

5.4 Regression Models

5.4.1 Predictors of Roma Children's Birthweight, HAZ, WAZ and WHZ Scores

The estimated associations of predictors with the risk of low birthweight is shown in Table 5.6, column 1.

Children who were not wanted by their mothers at the time of pregnancy had higher odds on having low weight at birth than wanted children ($p < 0.05$). Furthermore, maternal parity, one of the measures of parental investment used in this study, was also associated with Roma children's birth weight: higher parity mothers had higher odds of having low-birth weight children than low-parity mothers. Maternal socioeconomic status and country of residence were also associated with child birthweight: children from better-off households, and those born in Kosovo, had higher odds of having normal birthweight than children from poor households and the reference country (Serbia).

When statistically significant results were put into SD units, for child wantedness ($\beta = 0.79$, SD = 0.39), 1 SD increase in the variable predicted 0.30 SD of the birthweight, and 2 SD increase predicted 0.60 SDs of the birthweight. For maternal parity ($\beta = 0.73$, SD = 0.37), 1 SD increase in maternal parity predicted 0.27 SDs of the birthweight, and 2 SD increase in parity predicted 0.54 SDs of the birthweight.

Table 5.6. shows predictors of Roma children stunting, underweight and wasting (column 2, 3 and 4, respectively). As seen from the table, being born from an unwanted pregnancy influenced on underweight only. Roma unwanted children had higher odds of being underweight than wanted children ($p < 0.05$).

Children born with low birth weight had higher odds of being stunted ($p < 0.001$), underweight ($p < 0.001$) and wasted ($p < 0.05$). Furthermore, boys had higher odds of being stunted ($p < 0.001$) and underweight ($p < 0.001$) than girls.

In addition, older children ($p < 0.001$) and those from poorer households ($p = 0.01$) had higher odds of being stunted than younger children and those from better-off households. Also, being born in North Macedonia was associated with better growth ($p = 0.00$). Furthermore, underweight and wasting were positively associated with child's age: younger children had higher odds of being underweight ($p < 0.001$) and wasted ($p < 0.001$), while those coming from the poorer households had higher odds of being underweight ($p < 0.05$).

Moving statistically significant results into SD units showed that for the results explaining stunting, for child's birthweight ($\beta = 3.04$, SD = 0.57), 1 SD increase in birthweight predicted 1.15 SDs of stunting and 2 SD increase in child's birthweight predicted 2.31 SDs of stunting. For child's sex ($\beta = 0.54$, SD = 0.50), 1 SD increase in the variable predicted 0.27 SDs of stunting and 2 SD increase predicted 0.54 SDs of stunting.

Regarding underweight, for child's birthweight ($\beta = 3.04$, SD = 0.57), a 1 SD increase in birth weight predicted 1.75 SDs of underweight and 2 SD increase in child's birth weight predicted 3.75 SDs of underweight. For child's sex ($\beta = 0.57$,

Table 5.6 The risk of low birthweight, stunting, underweight and wasting for Roma children 0–24 months

	Weight at birth ≤2.5 kg vs > 2.5 kg		HAZ-2		WAZ-2		WHZ-2	
	Exp (B) (95% C.I. for Exp(B))	p	Exp (B) (95% C.I. for Exp(B))	p	Exp (B) (95% C.I. for Exp(B))	p	Exp (B) (95% C.I. for Exp(B))	p
Child								
Weight at birth (kilograms)			3.037 (2.413, 3.822)	<0.001	4.637 (3.478, 6.181)	<0.001**	1.534 (1.116, 2.107)	0.008**
Sex								
Female	1.0 reference category		1.0 reference category		1.0 reference category		1.0 reference category	
Male	1.052 (0.862, 1.283)	0.618	0.541 (0.416, 0.703)	<0.001**	0.570 (0.408, 0.798)	0.001**	1.157 (0.800, 1.673)	0.440
Age (months)			0.968 (0.950, 0.986)	0.001**	1.059 (1.033, 1.085)	<0.001**	1.073 (1.043, 1.104)	<0.001**
Maternal age at birth	1.015 (0.994, 1.037)	0.152						
Maternal age			0.995 (0.969, 1.021)	0.700	1.005 (0.972, 1.039)	0.768	1.020 (0.981, 1.060)	0.329
Literacy skills								
Illiterate	1.0 reference category		1.0 reference category		1.0 reference category		1.0 reference category	
Literate	1.126 (0.903, 1.405)	0.291	1.047 (0.791, 1.384)	0.750	1.218 (0.855, 1.735)	0.275	1.225 (0.814, 1.843)	0.331
Parity								
≤4	1.0 reference category		1.0 reference category		1.0 reference category		1.0 reference category	
>4	0.733 (0.550, 0.977)	0.005**	0.950 (0.638, 1.414)	0.801	1.135 (0.675, 1.909)	0.633	0.996 (0.540, 1.839)	0.990
Wanted last child								
Yes	1.0 reference category		1.0 reference category		1.0 reference category		1.0 reference category	
No	0.793 (0.648, 0.970)	0.024*	0.896 (0.637, 1.261)	0.529	0.887 (0.801, 0.982)*	0.025*	0.908 (0.549, 1.501)	0.706

(continued)

5.4 Regression Models

Table 5.6 (continued)

	Weight at birth ≤2.5 kg vs > 2.5 kg		HAZ-2		WAZ-2		WHZ-2	
	Exp (B) (95% C.I. for Exp(B))	p	Exp (B) (95% C.I. for Exp(B))	p	Exp (B) (95% C.I. for Exp(B))	p	Exp (B) (95% C.I. for Exp(B))	p
Child mortality								
No	1.0 reference category		1.0 reference category		1.0 reference category		1.0 reference category	
Yes	1.175 (0.915, 1.510)	0.206	0.820 (0.472, 1.425)	0.481	0.745 (0.383, 1.449)	0.386	1.674 (0.578, 4.851)	0.342
Household wealth index								
First quintile	1.0 reference category		1.0 reference category		1.0 reference category		1.0 reference category	
Second quintile	1.024 (0.786, 1.333)	0.862	1.334 (0.954, 1.865)	0.092	1.235 (0.809, 1.884)	0.328	1.214 (0.724, 2.035)	0.463
Third quintile	0.841 (0.637, 1.110)	0.222	1.667 (1.140, 2.437)	0.008**	1.156 (0.735, 1.818)	0.531	1.050 (0.608, 1.814)	0.860
Fourth quintile	1.289 (0.906, 1.833)	0.158	1.776 (1.145, 2.755)	0.010**	1.969 (1.090, 3.559)	0.025*	1.313 (0.671, 2.571)	0.427
Fifth quintile	1.747 (1.165, 2.620)	0.007**	1.909 (1.189, 3.065)	0.007**	2.707 (1.329, 5.515)	0.006**	0.682 (0.380, 1.225)	0.200
Country (Macedonia)	0.883 (0.648, 1.203)	0.431	1.930 (1.221, 3.051)	0.005**	1.570 (0.907, 2.719)	0.107	1.156 (0.641, 2.085)	0.629
Country (Montenegro)	1.251 (0.926, 1.690)	0.144	0.709 (0489, 1.028)	0.070	1.649 (0.943, 2.883)	0.079	1.286 (0.731, 2.265)	0.383
Country (Kosovo)	1.516 (1.152, 1.994)	0.003**	1.277 (0.909, 1.794)	0.159	0.786 (0.524, 1.179)	0.245	1.550 (0.933, 2.574)	0.091
Year								
2016	1.0 reference category		1.0 reference category		1.0 reference category		1.0 reference category	
2019	1.175 (0.915, 1.510)	0.206	1.123 (0.860, 1.467)	0.395	1.197 (0.788, 1.819)	0.399	1.286 (0.871, 1.898)	0.205

*p = ≤ 0.05; **p < 0.01

SD = 0.50), 1 SD increase in the variable predicted 0.29 SDs of underweight and 2 SD increase predicted 0.57 SDs of underweight. For child's age (β = 1.05, SD = 7.08), 1 SD increase in child's age predicted 7.4 SDs of underweight and 2 SD increase in child's age predicted 14.8 SDs of underweight. For child wantedness (β = 0.89, SD = 0.39), 1 SD increase predicts 0.34 SD of underweight and 2 SD increase predicted 0.69 SDs of underweight.

Finally, in regard to wasting, for child's birthweight (β = 3.04, SD = 0.57), 1 SD increase in birth weight predicts 1.17 SDs of wasting and 2 SD increase in child's birth weight predicted 3.46 SDs of wasting. For child's age (β = 1.05, SD = 7.08), 1 SD increase in child's age predicts 7.43 SDs of wasting and 2 SD increase in child's age predicted 14.8 SDs of wasting.

5.4.2 Individual Level HAZ, WAZ and WHZ Scores

Table 5.7 provides the estimated predictors of Roma children's individual HAZ, WAZ and WHZ scores. Children who were not wanted by their mothers at the time of pregnancy tended to have lower HAZ and WAZ scores, while child wantedness had no effect on individual WHZ scores.

Thus, wanted children were taller by 0.04 standard deviations compared to unwanted children (p = 0.04). Furthermore, an increase in birth weight by 1 kg was accompanied by an increase in HAZ scores by 0.28 standard deviations (p < 0.001). Boys tended, on average, to be shorter by 0.09 standard deviations compared to girls (p < 0.001). An increase in the child's age by 1-month resulted in a decrease in HAZ of 0.15 standard deviations (p < 0.001). Children who had more than four siblings were on average shorter by 0.07 standard deviations compared with children who had 4 or fewer siblings (, p = 0.01). Children from households in the 4th and 5th quintiles were taller by 0.11 standard deviations compared with children in the first three quintiles (p < 0.001). Children from Macedonia were taller by 0.05 standard deviations compared with children from Serbia (p = 0.05).

Wanted children had higher WAZ scores by 0.05 standard deviations compared to unwanted children (p = 0.01). An increase in birthweight by 1 kg was accompanied by an increase in WAZ scores by 0.30 standard deviations (p < 0.001). Boys were on average 0.06 standard deviations lighter than girls (p = 0.01). An increase in the child's age by 1 month was followed by an increase in WAZ scores of 0.04 standard deviations (p = 0.04). Children who had more than four siblings were on average lighter by 0.08 standard deviations compared with children who had 4 or fewer siblings (p = 0.002). Children from homes in the 4th and 5th quintiles were heavier by 0.10 standard deviations compared with children from homes from the first three quintiles (p < 0.001). Children from Macedonia were heavier by 0.05 standard deviations compared with children from Serbia (p = 0.04). Children from

5.4 Regression Models

Table 5.7 Roma children individual HAZ, WAZ, and WHZ scores

	HAZ2 β (95% CI for β)	p	WAZ2 β (95% CI for β)	p	WHZ2 β (95% CI for β)	p
Child						
Wanted last child	0.043 (0.003, 0.084)	0.036*	0.054 (0.013, 0.094)	0.010**	0.013 (−0.031, 0.057)	0.563
Weight at birth (kilograms)	0.279 (0.240, 0.323)	<0.001**	0.302 (0.264, 0.346)	<0.001**	0.124 (0.081, 0.168)	<0.001**
Sex	−0.092 (−0.132, −0.051)	<0.001**	−0.058 (−0.099, −0.018)	0.005**	0.000 (−0.042, 0.043)	0.989
Age (months)	−0.147 (−0.187, −0.106)	<0.001**	0.042 (0.002, 0.083)	0.040*	0.112 (0.069, 0.154)	<0.001**
Mother						
Age	0.036 (−0.011, 0.083)	0.138	0.035 (−0.012, 0.0,82)	0.139	0.006 (−0.043, 0.055)	0.808
Literacy sjills	0.028 (−0.016, 0.072)	0.214	0.034 (−0.011, 0.078)	0.136	0.018 (−0.029, 0.064)	0.458
Parity	−0.069 (−0.118, −0.020)	0.005**	−0.075 (−0.124, −0.027)	0.002**	−0.032 (−0.084, 0.019)	0.217
Child mortality	0.033 (−0.009, 0.079)	0.122	0.025 (−0.018, 0.070)	0.250	0.014 (−0.032, 0.062)	0.530
Household wealth index	0.106 (0.065, 0.147)	<0.001**	0.095 (0.053, 0.136)	<0.001**	0.006 (−0.037, 0.050)	0.779
Country (Macedonia)	0.046 (0.001, 0.091)	0.048*	0.048 (0.002, 0.093)	0.039*	0.017 (−0.031, 0.064)	0.487
Country (Montenegro)	0.030 (−0.019, 0.080)	0.223	0.085 (0.038, 0.137)	0.001**	0.082 (0.033, 0.136)	0.001**
Country (Kosovo)	−0.009 (−0.056, 0.038)	0.704	−0.048 (−0.095, −0.002)	0.042*	−0.048 (−0.097, 0.001)	0.055
Year	0.006 (−0.036, 0.048)	0.768	0.029 (−0.012, 0.072)	0.162	0.019 (−0.023, 0.062)	0.371

*p = ≤ 0.05; **p < 0.01

Montenegro were heavier by 0.09 standard deviations compared with children from Serbia (p = 0.001). Children from Kosovo were lighter by 0.05 standard deviations compared with children from Serbia (p = 0.04).

Regarding WAZ scores, an increase in birth weight by 1 kg was accompanied by an increase in WHZ scores of 0.12 standard deviations (p < 0.001). Increase in the child's age by 1 month was followed by an increase in WHZ scores of 0.11 standard deviations (p < 0.001). Children from Montenegro were heavier by 0.08 standard deviations compared with children from Serbia (p = 0.001).

5.4.2.1 Unintended Pregnancy Differences by Child's Sex and Wantedness

To estimate the differential impact of unintended pregnancies by child sex on growth and nutritional outcomes, the sample of children aged 0–24 months was divided by sex and wantedness (table 5.8).

For unwanted children, the differences between boys and girls were mostly insignificant, except for birthweight and underweight. Unwanted boys were heavier at birth than unwanted girls, while unwanted girls had better nutritional outcomes, i.e., they were less underweight than boys.

For wanted boys and girls, boys were heavier at birth, while more girls were born with low birthweight. In contrast, wanted girls had better growth outcomes than wanted boys as they had higher HAZ scores, and were less stunted than boys.

To compare possible differences in pregnancy unwantedness, instead of using the wanted/unwanted variable, children wanted later and those not wanted at all were compared by growth and nutritional status (Table 5.9).

There was no difference in growth and nutritional outcomes between children wanted later and not wanted at all, implying that children wanted later were, in effect, unwanted children.

5.4.3 Roma Parental Investment: Children Aged 25–59 Months

Roma mothers with children aged 25–59 months were divided according to the levels of direct childcare into low, moderate and high care, to assess maternal and child characteristics and potential differences (Table 5.10).

Roma children who received high maternal direct care were, on average, second born, while children who received moderate and low maternal direct care were, on average, third born (p < 0.001). Children of high-investing mothers were also older than the rest (p < 0.001), taller (p < 0.001), less stunted (p < 0.001), heavier (p < 0.001) and less underweight (p < 0.001) than children from moderate and low-investing mothers.

5.4 Regression Models

Table 5.8 Sex differences by child wantedness for children 0–24 months

	Was the child wanted							
	Not wanted				Wanted			
	Female	Male	p		Female	Male	p	
	Mean (SD) or n (%)	Mean (SD) or %		N	Mean (SD) or %	Mean (SD) or %		N
Child weight at birth	3.04 (0.55)	3.19 (0.61)	0.005*	488	3.06 (0.56)	3.17 (0.57)	<0.001**	2138
Height for age	−0.67 (1.40)	−0.72 (1.66)	0.697	463	−0.50 (1.61)	−0.74 (1.64)	0.001*	2036
Weight for age	−0.50 (1.22)	−0.61 (1.30)	0.348	479	−0.38 (1.24)	−0.45 (1.26)	0.169	2106
Weight for height	−0.16 (1.23)	−0.15 (1.25)	0.947	463	−0.10 (1.36)	−0.06 (1.45)	0.621	2039
Child weight at birth								
<2.5 kg	45 (17.9)	33 (14.0)	0.243	78 (16.0)	168 (16.9)	144 (12.6)	0.005****	312 (14.6)
>2.5 kg	207 (82.1)	203 (86.0)		410 (84.0)	826 (83.1)	1000 (87.4)		1826 (85.4)
Height for age								
≤-2SD	34 (13.9)	41 (18.8)	0.151	75 (16.2)	144 (15.3)	222 (20.3)	0.003****	366 (18.0)
>2SD	211 (86.1)	177 (81.2)		388 (83.8)	800 (84.7)	870 (79.7)		1670 (82.0)
Weight for age								
≤-2SD	16 (6.3)	32 (14.1)	0.005****	48 (10.0)	87 (8.9)	114 (10.1)	0.383	201 (9.5)
>2SD	236 (93.7)	195 (85.9)		431 (90.0)	886 (91.1)	1019 (89.9)		1905 (90.5)
Weight for height								
≤-2SD	13 (5.3)	13 (5.9)	0.777	26 (5.6)	75 (7.9)	88 (8.1)	0.898	163 (8.0)
>2SD	231 (94.7)	206 (94.1)		437 (94.4)	873 (92.1)	1003 (91.9)		1876 (92.0)

*p = ≤ 0.05; **p < 0.01; t test***; Chi-square test****

Roma high-investment mothers were better-off (p < 0.001), older (p < 0.001) had lower parity (p < 0.001) and higher literacy skills (p < 0.001) than moderate- and low-investing mothers. Child mortality also differed between the mothers, with moderate-investing mothers experiencing fewer child deaths (p < 0.05). Paternal and allomaternal investment was higher for children whose mothers reported high child direct care (p < 0.001, and p < 0.001, respectively).

Table 5.9 Children wanted later or not wanted at all: growth and nutritional differences

	Sex								
	Female				Male				
	Not wanted	Wanted later	p		Not wanted	Wanted later	p		
	Mean (SD) or n (%)	Mean (SD) or n (%)		N	Mean (SD) or n (%)	Mean (SD) or n (%)			N
Child weight at birth	3.01 (0.56)	3.06 (0.54)	0.484***	252	3.19 (0.63)	3.18 (0.59)	0.876***		236
Height for age	−0.74 (1.36)	−0.60 (1.44)	0.453***	245	−0.75 (1.69)	−0.69 (1.64)	0.784***		218
Weight for age	−0.57 (1.13)	−0.43 (1.29)	0.359***	252	−0.62 (1.34)	−0.59 (1.25)	0.822***		227
Weight for height	−0.26 (1.24)	−0.07 (1.21)	0.244***	244	−0.15 (1.30)	−0.15 (1.20)	0.972***		218
Child weight at birth									
≤2.5 kg	27 (22.3)	18 (13.7)	0.076****	45 (17.9)	16 (13.3)	17 (14.7)	0.770****		33 (14.0)
>2.5 kg	94 (77.7)	113 (86.3)		207 (82.1)	104 (86.7)	99 (85.3)			203 (86.0)
Height for age									
≤−2SD	16 (13.8)	18 (14.0)	0.971****	34 (13.9)	22 (19.8)	19 (17.8)	0.697****		41 (18.8)
>2SD	100 (86.2)	111 (86.0)		211 (86.1)	89 (80.2)	88 (82.2)			177 (81.2)
Weight for age									
≤−2SD	7 (5.9)	9 (6.7)	0.799****	16 (6.3)	16 (13.8)	16 (14.4)	0.893****		32 (14.1)
>2SD	111 (94.1)	125 (93.3)		236 (93.7)	100 (86.2)	95 (85.6)			195 (85.9)
Weight for height									
≤−2SD	7 (6.0)	6 (4.7)	0.640****	13 (5.3)	7 (6.2)	6 (5.7)	0.867****		13 (5.9)
>2SD	109 (94.0)	122 (95.3)		231 (94.7)	106 (93.8)	100 (94.3)			206 (94.1)

*p = ≤ 0.05; **p < 0.01; t test***; Chi-square test****

There were no statistically significant differences in maternal birth spacing, child's sex, weight-for-height z scores and wasting.

Table 5.11 shows the regression model for predictors of maternal high direct care.

Taller children were more likely to be born to mothers with high investment and higher literacy, compared with shorter children and children of illiterate mothers. Maternal household wealth was also significant: children born to better-off mothers

5.4 Regression Models

Table 5.10 Maternal and child characteristics and differences by maternal direct care

Characteristics (N = 2291)	Maternal investment, direct care, n = 2732								p
	Low		Moderate		High		Total		
	M (SD) or %	N	M (SD) or %	N	M (SD) or %	N	M (SD) or %	N	
Child's age (in months)	43.46 (9.81)	729	41.91 (9.94)	890	43.66 (9.54)	672	42.92 (9.81)	2291	<0.001***
Sex									0.20****
Female	46.9	342	48.7	433	51.6	347	49.0	1122	
Male	53.1	387	51.3	457	48.4	325	51.0	1169	
Birth order	3.13 (2.01)	713	2.83 (1.92)	883	2.40 (1.52)	663	2.80 (1.86)	2259	<0.001***
Height for age z-score WHO	−1.09 (1.26)	655	−1.08 (1.26)	756	−0.76 (1.19)	611	−0.97 (1.25)	2022	<0.001***
≤−2SD	21.5	141	21.4	162	12.4	76	18.7	379	<0.001****
>−2SD	78.5	514	78.6	594	87.6	535	81.3	1643	
Weight for age z-score WHO	−0.51 (1.08)	670	−0.54 (1.14)	779	−0.29 (1.21)	627	−0.45 (1.15)	2076	<0.001***
≤−2SD	7.2	48	9.5	74	5.3	33	7.5	155	0.010****
>−2SD	92.8	622	90.5	705	94.7	594	92.5	1921	
Weight for height z-score WHO	0.17 (1.13)	653	0.11 (1.09)	755	0.22 (1.23)	605	0.16 (1.48)	2013	0.21***
≤−2SD	1.7	11	1.9	14	1.5	9	1.7	34	0.87****
>−2SD	98.3	642	98.1	741	98.5	596	98.3	1979	
Maternal age	23.61 (5.49)	715	24.84 (5.17)	886	28.23 (5.53)	663	25.59 (5.79)	2264	<0.001***
Parity	3.80 (2.03)	715	3.40 (1.93)	886	2.89 (1.54)	663	3.38 (1.89)	2264	<0.001***
Birth spacing (in months)	25.28 (10.27)	389	25.36 (10.22)	434	25.36 (10.54)	283	25.33 (10.31)	1106	0.99***
Child mortality									0.04****
No	92.6	662	95.5	846	94.4	626	94.3	2134	
Yes	7.4	53	4.5	40	5.6	37	5.7	130	
Paternal investment	1.56 (0.81)	462	3.61 (0.50)	175	5.40 (0.52)	135	2.63 (1.50)	772	<0.001***
Allomaternal investment	1.51 (0.86)	335	3.56 (0.51)	88	5.57 (0.53)	71	2.39 (1.56)	484	<0.001***
Literacy skills									
Literate	38.8	252	51.1	379	69.7	332	51.6	963	<0.001****
Illiterate	61.2	398	48.9	363	30.3	144	48.4	905	
Wealth index quintile									
Poorest	33.3	243	31.3	279	17.1	115	27.8	637	<0.001****
Second	24.8	181	27.9	248	16.5	111	23.6	540	
Middle	15.9	116	16.1	143	21.1	142	17.5	401	
Fourth	14.8	108	13.4	119	22.6	152	16.5	379	
Richest	11.1	81	11.3	101	22.6	152	14.6	334	

*p = ≤ 0.05; **p < 0.01; *** ANOVA; **** Chi-square test

Table 5.11 Predictors of maternal high investment

	Exp(B)	Sig.
Child		
Height	1.79 (1.18, 2.68)	0.005*
Age	1.01 (0.99, 1.03)	0.234
Sex		
Female	1.0 reference category	
Male	0.82 (0.59, 1.14)	0.246
Household		
Wealth index		
First, second, third quintile	1.0 reference category	
Fourth and fifth quintile	1.67 (1.18, 2.36)	0.004*
country_MN(1)	0.75 (0.44, 1.28)	0.289
countri_KOS(1)	0.51 (0.31, 0.82)	0.006*
countri_NMAC(1)	0.48 (0.25, 0.92)	0.026*
Year		
2016	1.0 reference category	
2019	0.77 (0.55, 1.07)	0.122
Mother		
Parity		
≤4	1.0 reference category	
>4	0.91 (0.59 (1.39)	0.656
Literacy skills		
Illiterate	1.0 reference category	
Literate	1.69 (1.17, 2.43)	0.005*
Allomaternal investment	1.06 (1.00, 1.33)	0.005*

*p = ≤ 0.05; **p < 0.01

had higher odds of receiving high maternal investment than the rest. Increased allomaternal investment resulted in greater odds of high maternal investment. At country level, children from Kosovo, North Macedonia and Montenegro had lower odds of high maternal investment compared with children from Serbia.

When statistically significant results were put into SD units, for maternal literacy(dichotomous) (β = 1.68, SD = 0.50), 1 SD increase in the variable predicted 0.84 SDs of direct care and 2 SD increase predicted 1.68 SDs of maternal direct care. For maternal socioeconomic status (dichotomous) (β = 1.66, SD = 0.50), 1 SD increase in the variable predicted 0.83 SDs of direct care and 2 SD increase predicted 1.66 SDs of maternal direct care. For child's height (β = 1.78, SD = 1.25), a 1 SD increase in child's height predicted 2.22 SDs of direct care and 2 SD increase predicted 4.5 SDs of maternal direct care. For allomaternal care (β = 1.06, SD = 1.91), 1 SD increase in the variable predicted 2 SDs of direct care and 2 SD increase in allomaternal care predicted 4 SDs of maternal direct care.

References

Abufhele, A., Behrman, J., & Bravo, D. (2017). Parental preferences and allocations of investments in children's learning and health within families. *Social Science & Medicine, 194*, 76–86. https://doi.org/10.1016/j.socscimed.2017.09.051

Chatterjee, E., & Sennott, C. (2021). Fertility intentions and child health in India: Women's use of health services, breastfeeding, and official birth documentation following an unwanted birth. *PLoS One, 16*(11), e0259311. https://doi.org/10.1371/journal.pone.0259311

Coall, D. A., & Chisholm, J. S. (2003). Evolutionary perspectives on pregnancy: Maternal age at menarche and infant birth weight. *Social Science & Medicine, 57*(10), 1771–1781. https://doi.org/10.1016/S0277-9536(03)00022-4

Costa, M. E., Trumble, B., Kaplan, H., & Gurven, M. D. (2018). Child nutritional status among births exceeding ideal family size in a high fertility population. *Maternal & Child Nutrition, 14*(4), e12625. https://doi.org/10.1111/mcn.12625

Čvorović, J. (2013). Serbian gypsy witch narratives: 'Wherever Gypsies Go, There the Witches Are, We Know!'. *Folklore, 124*(2), 214–225. https://doi.org/10.1080/0015587X.2013.798535

Čvorović, J. (2020). Child wantedness and low weight at birth: Differential parental investment among Roma. *Behavioral Sciences, 10*(6), 102. https://doi.org/10.3390/bs10060102

Čvorović, J. (2022a). Paternal investment, stepfather presence and early child development and growth among Serbian Roma. *Evolutionary Human Sciences, 4*, e15. https://doi.org/10.1017/ehs.2022.14

Čvorović, J. (2022b). Maternal age at marriage and child nutritional status and development: Evidence from Serbian Roma communities. *Public Health Nutrition, 25*(5), 1183–1193. https://doi.org/10.1017/S1368980022000544

De Onis, M., & Branca, F. (2016). Childhood stunting: A global perspective. *Maternal & Child Nutrition, 12*, 12–26. https://doi.org/10.1111/mcn.12231

Fessler, D. M., Navarrete, C. D., Hopkins, W., & Izard, M. K. (2005). Examining the terminal investment hypothesis in humans and chimpanzees: Associations among maternal age, parity, and birth weight. *American Journal of Physical Anthropology, 127*(1), 95–104. https://doi.org/10.1002/ajpa.20039

Gipson, J. D., Koenig, M. A., & Hindin, M. J. (2008). The effects of unintended pregnancy on infant, child, and parental health: A review of the literature. *Studies in Family Planning, 39*(1), 18–38. https://doi.org/10.1111/j.1728-4465.2008.00148.x

Gluckman, P. D., Hanson, M. A., & Beedle, A. S. (2007). Early life events and their consequences for later disease: A life history and evolutionary perspective. *American Journal of Human Biology, 19*(1), 1–19. https://doi.org/10.1002/ajhb.20590

Hall, J. A., Benton, L., Copas, A., & Stephenson, J. (2017). Pregnancy intention and pregnancy outcome: Systematic review and meta-analysis. *Maternal and Child Health Journal, 21*, 670–704. https://doi.org/10.1007/s10995-016-2237-0

Jeong, J., McCoy, D. C., Yousafzai, A. K., Salhi, C., & Fink, G. (2016). Paternal stimulation and early child development in low-and middle-income countries. *Pediatrics, 138*(4). https://doi.org/10.1542/peds.2016-1357

Knodel, J., & Van de Walle, E. (1979). Lessons from the past: Policy implications of historical fertility studies. *Population and Development Review*, 217–245.

Kost, K., & Lindberg, L. (2015). Pregnancy intentions, maternal behaviors, and infant health: Investigating relationships with new measures and propensity score analysis. *Demography, 52*(1), 83–111. https://doi.org/10.1007/s13524-014-0359-9

Kramer, K. L., Veile, A., & Otárola-Castillo, E. (2016). Sibling competition & growth tradeoffs. Biological vs. statistical significance. *PLoS One, 11*(3), e0150126. https://doi.org/10.1371/journal.pone.0150126

Marston, C., & Cleland, J. (2003). Do unintended pregnancies carried to term lead to adverse outcomes for mother and child? An assessment in five developing countries. *Population Studies, 57*(1), 77–93. https://doi.org/10.1080/0032472032000061749

Nguyen, M. (2024). The health costs of being born unwanted. *The Developing Economies, 62*(2), 115–138. https://doi.org/10.1111/deve.12387

Promislow, D. E., & Harvey, P. H. (1990). Living fast and dying young: A comparative analysis of life-history variation among mammals. *Journal of Zoology, 220*(3), 417–437. https://doi.org/10.1111/j.1469-7998.1990.tb04316.x

Silventoinen, K. (2003). Determinants of variation in adult body height. *Journal of Biosocial Science, 35*(2), 263–285. https://doi.org/10.1017/S0021932003002633

Skjærvø, G. R., & Røskaft, E. (2013). Early conditions and fitness: Effect of maternal parity on human life-history traits. *Behavioral Ecology, 24*(2), 334–341.

Sonneveldt, E., Plosky, W. D., & Stoverm, J. (2013). Linking high parity and maternal and child mortality: What is the impact of lower health services coverage among higher order births? *BMC Public Health, 13*(Suppl 3), S7. https://doi.org/10.1186/1471-2458-13-S3-S7

Stulp, G., & Barrett, L. (2016). Evolutionary perspectives on human height variation. *Biological Reviews, 91*(1), 206–234. https://doi.org/10.1111/brv.12165

Sudfeld, C. R., McCoy, D. C., Fink, G., Muhihi, A., Bellinger, D. C., Masanja, H., et al. (2015). Malnutrition and its determinants are associated with suboptimal cognitive, communication, and motor development in Tanzanian children. *The Journal of Nutrition, 145*(12), 2705–2714. https://doi.org/10.3945/jn.115.215996

Uggla, C., & Mace, R. (2016). Parental investment in child health in sub-Saharan Africa: A cross-national study of health-seeking behaviour. *Royal Society Open Science, 3*(2), 150460. https://doi.org/10.1098/rsos.150460

UNICEF. (2012). *Severna Macedonia—Istraživanje višestrukih pokazatelja (North Macedonia—MICS)*. UNICEF.

UNICEF. (2013). *Bosnia and Herzegovina Roma survey*. Multiple Indicator Cluster Survey 2011–2012. UNICEF.

UNICEF. (2014). *Roma, Ashkali and Egyptian communities in Kosovo (UNSCR 1244). Multiple indicator cluster survey 2013–2014*. Kosovo Agency of Statistics and UNICEF.

UNICEF. (2014a). *Montenegro and Montenegro Roma Settlements*. Multiple indicator cluster survey 2013. UNICEF Montenegro.

UNICEF. (2014b). *Srbija—Istraživanje višestrukih pokazatelja (Serbia—MICS)*. UNICEF.

UNICEF. (2015). Early childhood development. The analysis of Multiple Indicator Cluster Survey data. https://www.unicef.org/serbia/media/1201/file/MICS%20ECD.pdf.

UNICEF. (2019). *2018 Montenegro multiple indicator cluster survey and 2018 Montenegro Roma settlements multiple indicator cluster survey, survey findings report*. MONSTAT and UNICEF.

UNICEF. (2020a). *Kosovo multiple indicator cluster survey and 2019–2020 Roma, Ashkali and Egyptian communities multiple indicator cluster survey, survey findings report*. Kosovo Agency of Statistics and UNICEF.

UNICEF. (2020b). *Severna Macedonia—Istraživanje višestrukih pokazatelja (North Macedonia—MICS)*. UNICEF.

UNICEF. (2020c). *Srbija—Istraživanje višestrukih pokazatelja (Serbia—MICS)*. UNICEF.

Walker, R. S., Gurven, M., Burger, O., & Hamilton, M. J. (2008). The trade-off between number and size of offspring in humans and other primates. *Proceedings of the Royal Society B: Biological Sciences, 275*(1636), 827–834. https://doi.org/10.1098/rspb.2007.1511

Wells, J. C. (2018). Life history trade-offs and the partitioning of maternal investment: Implications for health of mothers and offspring. *Evolution, Medicine, and Public Health, 2018*(1), 153–166. https://doi.org/10.1093/emph/eoy014

Winking, J., & Koster, J. (2015). The fitness effects of men's family investments: A test of three pathways in a single population. *Human Nature, 26*, 292–312. https://doi.org/10.1007/s12110-015-9237-4

Chapter 6
Roma Parental Investment, Unwanted Childbearing and Child Nutritional Status in the Western Balkan Roma Communities

6.1 Investment in Children Aged 25–59 Months

6.1.1 Direct Care

Parenting behavior may be influenced by a multitude of family and child characteristics, dependent on culture but also political and economic development (Walker et al., 2011). For instance, in many countries, childcare is culturally "mother centric", with limited participation from fathers (Hosegood & Madhavan, 2010). In this Roma sample, too, there was significant sex asymmetry in parenting, evidencing the dominant prevailing patriarchal cultural milieu.

In all countries, for older children (aged 25–59 months) Roma mothers tended to invest more in offspring than Roma fathers, and in the majority of cases, with only moderate investment per offspring. In doing so, they were helped by allomothers, and to a lesser extent, by fathers. Roma allomothers and fathers tended to mirror maternal investment, as there were strong positive correlations between maternal and paternal investment, and maternal and paternal allomaternal investment. This implies that when mothers did invest in a particular offspring, allomothers and fathers invested as well, and vice versa, and when fathers invested, allomothers did so too, thus the overall investment provided benefited the children, producing better outcomes. The positive correlations may also, at least partially, reflect the influence each parent has on the other's behavior, and also on behavior of allomothers (Cabrera et al., 2014).

Across the different ecological settings, the data suggest that father investment may often be substituted with care from others (Sear, 2021). However, identification of fathers (through marriage) also increases the possibility of a human offspring to acquire far more identifiable kin than any other mammal, which may have been of preeminent importance in human cultural and biological evolution (Palmer et al.,

2005). MICS data do not provide identification of allomothers except family members older than 18 living in the same household. However, since Roma children grow up in large circle of relatives and traditionally have patrilocal residence patterns (Ena et al., 2022), it is likely that allomothers were paternal relatives. Moreover, given the Roma early marriage, it seems unlikely that older brothers, and/or especially sisters, acted as allomothers. Investment in children by paternal relatives is not uncommon. For instance, it is usually expected that uterine grandchildren are invested more in than agnatic grandchildren; however, in the absence of the daughter's children, grandparents tend to invest in their son's children as well (Danielsbacka et al., 2011). "Cooperative care" can include complementing the mother's direct care, such as playing with or teaching a child, or providing other types of resources (Starkweather et al., 2021).

Another characteristic of the Roma parental and allomaternal investment was a lack of both book reading and name counting activities. Instead, mothers but also fathers and allomothers invested in child playing activities the most. Given the general poverty of Roma, the variations in surplus investments— activities with children in the home—may be largely shaped by access to resources. The majority of Roma children grow up in unstimulating home environments, lacking not only books but also toys, and the activities with children in the home, such as reading them books or teaching them about letters and numbers, require not only actual books but also basic literacy and numeracy skills, which, as the results have shown, many Roma do not possess. Instead, Roma caregivers engaged in what they could: a form of open-ended play-based learning, consisting of play and storytelling. Studies have found that special benefits arise from playing with a parent or other caregiver: playing with a child can help with development of social skills and self-control, working memory, gross motor skills, cognitive flexibility, and regulation of emotions, amongst others (Sunderland, 2006). Roma parents and allomothers also engaged in storytelling, which in the past was a favorite entertainment but also educational activity among many Roma, young and old alike (Čvorović, 2010). The benefits of storytelling are numerous: storytelling provides a number of psychological and educational advantages, such as improved imagination to help visualize spoken words, better vocabulary, and more refined communication skills (Yabe et al., 2018). Across diverse cultural and economic settings, all these stimulation activities contribute to a child's cognitive and socioemotional development.

On the other hand, studies examining parental behavior have clearly demonstrated that higher maternal education and household wealth are associated with higher levels of investment in children. The socioeconomic context within which a family lives may strongly influence parenting behavior through differential access to resources, but also its effects on parental conditions, including health. Generally, the lower the socioeconomic status, the lower the childrearing knowledge and actual or potential investment (Fingerman et al., 2015).

The influence of socioeconomic status on parenting and consequently on child health outcomes, may vary across different ethnic groups and cultures, but research in this area remains limited (Prevoo & Tamis-LeMonda, 2017). Available studies on within-country comparisons of majority vs. minority parenting effort suggest that

6.1 Investment in Children Aged 25–59 Months

ethnic-minority parents differ from majority parents with regard to resources, parenting styles, and direct childrearing practices (Mesman et al., 2012). However, these studies also show that the association between parenting and child outcomes tends to generalize across cultures (Prevoo & Tamis-LeMonda, 2017). Thus, the studies found less child-focused communications and less maternal engagement in learning activities in ethnic-minority compared to ethnic-majority parents (Tamis-LeMonda & Song, 2012). The general conclusion, therefore, is that the association between socioeconomic status and parenting effort in ethnic minority populations remains poorly understood, mostly due to the strong focus on inter-cultural differences, which may mask variations occurring in ethnic-minority samples (Knauer et al., 2018; Prevoo & Tamis-LeMonda, 2017).

Considerable variations in parental investment/direct care existed in sample of Roma mothers from the five countries studied. Around one third of Roma mothers engaged in high direct care, while 20% of fathers did so, and these results are in contrast to the results from low-and-middle-income countries. By way of example, a study on parental engagement in 62 low-and-middle-income countries found that almost 40% of mothers, but only around 10% of fathers, provided high care (Cuartas et al., 2020). The results for allomaternal care are comparable, though (in both samples around 20%). This particular finding aligns with previous research that highlights the supportive childrearing roles of grandparents, older siblings, and other relatives in low-and-middle-income countries, and the Roma as well (Bereczkei & Dunbar, 2002). Nevertheless, Roma mothers were found to invest more compared to fathers and allomothers: the majority of mothers (41%) invested moderately in their children, while the majority of fathers and allomothers had low levels of investment (55% and 47%, respectively).

There were also country differences in parental care, with the highest maternal direct care reported among mothers from Bosnia and Herzegovina, followed by Serbia, North Macedonia, Montenegro, and, finally, Kosovo. Correlatedly, the highest paternal direct care was reported for Roma Montenegrin and Serbian fathers, while Roma fathers from Kosovo had the lowest levels of direct care. Allomaternal direct care followed a similar pattern, with allomothers from Kosovo having the lowest investment. The parental and allomaternal lowest engagement with children may most likely be explained by the characteristics of the mother and the child: Kosovo Roma mothers had the highest parity in the sample, while the sampled child had, on average, the highest birth order. The lack of resources, i.e., time for instance, may also have influenced this finding: the birth of each additional child limits the time, attention and other resources that parents, and also allomothers could invest in any one child (Lawson & Mace, 2008).

In addition to between-country differences, there were also differences between the mothers providing direct childcare — the mothers reported their investment as low, moderate or high. As expected, gradients in household wealth, as a proxy for socioeconomic status, differed between mothers engaging in low, moderate and high investment, where mothers from better-off households were more likely to engage in moderate and higher investment with the child, compared to mothers from poorer homes. Furthermore, mothers who engaged in high maternal investment differed significantly in other traits from mothers who engaged in moderate and low investment: the former were not only economically better off, but also more literate, older at childbirth and had lower parity. These are common findings from both evolutionary and economic studies of the family (Uggla & Mace, 2016; Beaulieu & Bugental, 2008; Restrepo, 2016; Fan & Porter, 2020). However, as with other studies, direct care for older children did not differ by child's sex (Cuartas et al., 2020).

In addition to access to resources due to differential household wealth, levels of investment among Roma mothers varied by age at childbirth. According to evolutionary prediction, females tend to adjust investment according to remaining age-related reproductive potential (Williams, 1966). In the present study, high-investing Roma mothers were older at childbirth compared to moderate-and-low-investing mothers.

Maternal age at childbirth may have numerous effects on offspring health outcomes (Savage et al., 2013). Early ($\leq$19 years) but also late ($\geq$35 years) maternal age at childbirth may be associated with poor birth and child outcomes due to the theoretical predicted biological risk associated with extremes of reproductive age and reproductive outcomes. Having a child in later years may be associated with adverse outcomes due to reproductive aging: the risks include poor perinatal outcomes and increased risk of mortality and cancer in adulthood (Barclay & Myrskylä, 2016). Yet, at the same time, for children born to relatively older mothers, there may be certain benefits over children born to younger mothers. Studies have demonstrated that increasing maternal age is associated with more favorable offspring phenotype, such as height, better survival outcome for multiple pregnancies, and better child health and development (Savage et al., 2013; Helle, 2008). Differences in the pre- and post-natal child-rearing environment and maternal age-related behaviors may have a role in these correlations.

For the Roma high-investing mothers, the sample child was second born, while birth spacing was a little over 2 years on average. Consistent with studies showing a positive effect of maternal age on childbirth and child health, compared to children born to moderate-and low-investing mothers, children born to high-investing mothers displayed higher HAZ, WAZ and WHZ scores, and lower rates of stunting, underweight and wasting. In addition to age and household wealth, these health outcomes may be connected to another indicator of socioeconomic status -- maternal literacy -- which was higher for high-investing mothers. It is well-established that mothers' level of education may increase their healthcare utilization during pregnancy, as well as improve child nutrition and care practices, in turn affecting children's health outcomes (Savage et al., 2013).

In the sample that included all women, from all five countries, for children aged 25–59 months, Roma mothers from Kosovo were significantly older than all others. Nevertheless, and inconsistent with the terminal investment hypothesis, Roma mothers from Kosovo engaged significantly less in direct childcare than mothers from all other countries. This apparent discrepancy maybe explained by the significantly higher parity of Kosovo mothers, being four on average. Other contributing factors may be rates of child mortality being significantly higher among mothers

6.1 Investment in Children Aged 25–59 Months

from Kosovo, with the child also, on average, being of a higher birth order than children in the rest of the countries. Regardless of the maternal age, however, these findings aligned with several evolutionary predictions regarding variability in maternal investment. For instance, maternal parity is responsible for the differentials in parental investment across and within species: studies have found that later-born children (of a higher birth order) are frequently disadvantaged relative to earlier-borns, as the offspring reproductive value tends to increase with higher age (Walker et al., 2008). This is especially true under poor conditions. Having many siblings, or as expressed in evolutionary theory, the parental trade-off between numbers of children and investment per offspring, results in overall poorer parental investment but also economic distress.

Similar results were obtained for high maternal direct care. Taller children, born to better-off and literate mothers and receiving greater allomaternal investment, had higher odds of having high-investing mothers. Children from Kosovo, North Macedonia and Montenegro had lower odds of high maternal investment compared to children from Serbia. Thus, the effects of education and socioeconomic status among Roma mothers explained the high maternal direct care of older Roma children, and these results were comparable to other studies: it is generally found that children born to literate and better-off mothers tend to receive higher maternal investment (Yadav & Bhandari, 2022).

Overall, investments by allomothers tend to be correlated with maternal and child's well-being, including improvements in growth and nutritional outcomes, but also survivorship and increased maternal reproductive success (Sear, 2015). Allomaternal direct care was lower for both Kosovo and Montenegro, in comparison to Serbia, while, in contrast, both parity and child's birth order were significantly higher for the mothers in these two countries compared to mothers from Serbia, which may help explain the differences. However, North Macedonia deviates from this pattern, and other, unaccounted factors are likely needed to explain the discrepancy. For all countries, Roma maternal and allomaternal investment were positively correlated, and given this relationship, the overall investment received has a potential to positively affect children, and thus result in better outcomes.

Roma child's height also predicted maternal high investment: mothers who provided high direct care had taller children. Reverse causality may be the most likely means through which a cross-sectional, positive association of maternal high direct care with child's height may manifest, such that the Roma mothers biased their investment towards taller, more endowed children (Čvorović, 2022a). Thus, Roma high-investing-mothers most likely favored specific children, reinforcing endowment differences among their children. This finding is consistent with most prior literature: parents tend to bias their investment towards more endowed children because of greater fitness pay-off. During early childhood, height serves as a measure of the cumulative effect of nutritional and health loads from conception, and, it being a proxy for offspring quality, may influence future health and reproduction (Kramer et al., 2016).

Indicative of the above finding is that when the results explaining maternal high investment were put into SD units, only allomaternal investment and child's height showed any significant effects.

6.2 Investment in Children Aged 0–24 Months

6.2.1 Low Birthweight

From the five countries surveyed in the sample, around 15% of Roma children were born with low birthweight, with the average being 3 kg. Serbia and Macedonia had the highest rates of low-birth-weight children and Kosovo the lowest, but the difference was not statistically significant. On the other hand, Roma mothers from Kosovo had children with the highest birthweight values compared to mothers from the other countries and, here, the difference was statistically significant. In the sample as a whole, there were more girls born with low birth weight than boys, with the difference being statistically significant. Predictors of significance for the Roma birthweight included if the child was wanted, maternal parity, socioeconomic status, and country of residence (Kosovo).

Generally, females with larger statures tend to have higher birthweight babies, while birthweight highest values are recorded in the most economically developed countries (Thomas et al., 2004). Unfortunately, MICS did not collect data on maternal size and other anthropometric measures. Previous studies found that shorter women may have reduced protein and energy stores, smaller reproductive organs and limited room for fetal development, which puts them at higher risk for adverse pregnancy outcomes as well as adverse newborn and child outcomes, such as low offspring birth size, childhood stunting, and reduced human capital (Addo et al., 2013; Wilcox, 2001). Research among Serbian Roma suggests that the effect of maternal height on the variation in children's mortality and health status seems to be continuous, even without a definite height cut-off: thus Roma mothers of short stature were more likely to experience child mortality than tall mothers, and were more likely to report having sick and low birth weight children than mothers of greater height (Čvorović, 2018).

Small body size is a response to disease and malnutrition, and may be a life-history consequence of relatively faster ontogeny in high-mortality environments (Walker & Hamilton, 2008). In addition, even though maternal stature has important implications for reproductive success, the relationship is complex, as it seems that having average or slightly above average stature is the most advantageous (Sear, 2010). In populations where the opposite may hold, short maternal stature could have been selected for as a result of the advantages of an earlier period of growth cessation and enhanced reproduction, and where low birthweight is a part of an adaptive behavior for increasing reproduction (Helle, 2008; Walker et al., 2008). These assumptions are mirrored in statistically significant differences between mothers with normal and low birthweight children. Thus, Roma mothers with low birthweight children were younger and poorer, with shorter birth spacing, higher parity but also higher child mortality, and had shorter, lighter and children with lower WHZ scores. Additionally, low birthweight children were more stunted, wasted and underweight than their normal birthweight counterparts. This may imply reduced investment in low birthweight children after birth, or, at least, a lack of increased effort to mitigate the adverse health status of children born with low birth weight. Evolutionary and economic studies both suggest that parents may be expected to shift investment according to the cues of eventual offspring fitness (Rohde et al., 2003). Thus, parents should respond to their offspring's early endowments such as health at birth, with birth weight being a very strong measure of early endowments and easily recognizable by mothers (Hsin, 2012).

A further finding from the present study was that child's sex predicted birth outcome: more girls were born with low birth weight than boys, corresponding with the results of previous studies in low- and middle-income countries (Lemlem et al., 2021). Generally, birthweight tends to be typically higher for boys, whereas girls are more likely to be born with low birthweight, especially in settings where son preference is strong (Cho, 2023). Sons might receive greater parental investment as they can benefit more from parental resources in terms of reproductive success than daughters (Gibson & Sear, 2010). This, however, is in contrast with other studies on Roma parental sex preference, where it was most often found that females were the preferred sex (Bereczkei & Dunbar, 2002; Čvorović, 2022a). For instance, the Hungarian Roma, who display varying degrees of exogamy, tend to favor differential investment in daughters due to the latter's greater opportunity for hypergamy, i.e., high fitness returns (measured in terms of numbers of grandchildren). Thus, in this case, daughters are the preferred sex as they can not only marry up, but can also provide a more valuable service in helping their parents with younger children compared with boys. Another study, based on a nationally representative sample of Serbian Roma children, found that undernutrition in Roma children under 5 years is more likely to affect boys than girls. In this study, sex differences among Roma children were observed/in nutritional status, with boys being shorter, more likely to be stunted and, on average, more wasted, suggesting that Roma boys were more susceptible to nutritional inequalities than girls of the same age, thus the sex preference in favor of girls (Čvorović, 2022a).

6.2.2 Being Unwanted

Parental investment may also vary according to another child's characteristic: that of being unwanted. For the sample as a whole, 16% were unwanted children, the majority being girls and fourth-born. Of these children, 20% were both unwanted and born with low birthweight. At country level, Serbia and Kosovo had the highest share of unwanted children. There were 16% of unwanted children in Serbia and 24% in Kosovo, while, at the same time, Kosovo had the highest maternal parity:

four children per woman on average. Thus, more Roma girls than boys were unwanted, again implying specific parental sex preference; furthermore, higher birth-order children were more likely to be unwanted than earlier-borns—in line with the evolutionary prediction regarding parental favoritism of older children.

There were no differences in HAZ and WHZ scores between unwanted and wanted children. However, the unwanted children had lower average WAZ scores than the wanted children. Given that the WAZ score represents a composite index of height-for-age (HAZ) and weight-for-height (WHZ) scores, as it takes into account both chronic and acute malnutrition, this indicated that unwanted children were more susceptible to nutritional inequalities than wanted children. In other words, for the present sample, underweight-for-age likely reflected both past (chronic) and/or present (acute) undernutrition.

These findings were further validated by the regression model explaining the risks of low birthweight. Previous research on the association between child wantedness and low birthweight showed inconsistent results (Joyce et al., 2000; Wado et al., 2014; Goossens et al., 2016). However, in this study, after adjusting for confounding factors, child wantedness predicted low weight at birth: wanted children had higher odds of being more than >2500 g at birth compared with children who were not wanted. Given that birthweight is often used as a proxy for maternal investment during pregnancy, for the unwanted children in this sample, child outcomes correlated with investment alone (Čvorović, 2020; Merklinger-Gruchala et al., 2019).

In line with previous studies, gradients in household wealth and maternal reproductive history, e.g. parity, were significantly associated with offspring birthweight (Gluckman et al., 2007). As expected, being born in better-off households resulted in lower odds of having low birthweight. In contrast, higher maternal parity was significantly associated with low infant birthweight. Mothers of unwanted children were older, and had higher parity. And although maternal age was not significant in explaining weight at birth, maternal parity in this sample had a negative effect on birthweight. In traditional societies, age and parity are often correlated, with parity predicting biological age acceleration (Fessler et al., 2005; Shirazi et al., 2020). Although insignificant in explaining weight at birth, Roma maternal age was strongly correlated with parity. Parity-related physiological changes may be considered as a measure of age, resulting in investment modifications (Fessler et al., 2005). This suggests that high parity may be an important trigger for investment, indicating an accomplished fertility or, depending on the environmental setting, maximum family size almost completed (Helle, 2008).

Furthermore, low birthweight may be also associated with either too early (≤ 19 years) or relatively late (≥ 35 years) maternal age. In the present Roma sample, however, there was no significant difference in rate of low birthweight between mothers in different age groups but, in line with previous findings, there was a difference in average birthweight, with mothers aged 25–34 at childbirth having children with the highest birthweights, on average (Fessler et al., 2005).

In contrast, some studies found that high-parity women, owing to having had numerous children, tended to have more vascularized uteri, thus leading to infants of higher birthweight (Rybo et al., 1985; Hinkle et al., 2014). In the present sample,

6.2 Investment in Children Aged 0–24 Months

this may be reflected by the finding that mothers from Kosovo were the oldest and had children with the highest birthweight compared with children from other countries, as well as children with lower odds of having low birthweight than mothers from the reference group.

In this sample, 15% of mothers with ≤4 children and an average parity of two, reported that their last child was unwanted, in contrast to almost one third of women with >4 children. This suggests that the majority of high-fertility women, or 70% —with an average parity of six—wanted the child. Thus, as the case for many women in other traditional societies, Roma women may be more concerned about having too few rather than too many children (Costa et al., 2018; Filipovic, 2017). For many women in developing countries, as for the Roma women as well, patterns of fertility are traditionally institutionalized in cultural practices and rules regulating marriage. For many Roma women, having children in marriage is the only socially sanctioned route for improvement in status (Čvorović & Coe, 2019), with many Roma women thus favoring large families.

Generally, education, status in society, and improved women's economic conditions are considered key factors in fertility reduction, in that they decrease the desire for fertility (Pritchett, 1994). In this sample, no differences were found for literacy rates and household wealth between mothers of wanted and unwanted children, but these differences were nonetheless significant between high and lower parity mothers. The differences in child wantedness between low- and high-parity mothers may be explained by the easily observed differences in socioeconomic status and maternal literacy between these women: low-parity women had greater literacy skills and were better off than the high-parity women, a common finding worldwide.

On the other hand, differences found for the group of high-parity women, i.e., between the high parity women who did not want the last child and those who did, showed that mothers of unwanted children were considerably older than mothers of wanted children (i.e., 32 vs. 26 years old). One of the distinct features of Roma reproductive practice is, relatively early cessation of reproduction: several studies among Roma have found that women tend to end reproduction in their early thirties, a finding that corroborates the official, existing data (Radovanović & Knežević, 2014; Čvorović, 2014; Gamella, 2018). This suggests that, regardless of a considerable fertile period ahead, Roma women and their partners make a deliberate decision to cease reproduction after the desired number of children is reached, either with or without the use of modern contraceptive methods.

A number of studies have shown that parents tend to balance family size against offspring success (Melia & Li, 2018). For the Roma, this may be facilitated by subsidies received from social benefits, which help to maintain fertility, feed their children, and balance the costs to maternal health and nutrition that mothers would otherwise face if relying only on their own work efforts (Čvorović, 2024).

6.2.3 Nutritional Status of Roma Children

Studies have often used child outcomes, such as birth weight, nutritional status, illnesses, or age-specific survival, as approximations of parental investment (Uggla & Mace, 2016). Thus, an assessment of growth and nutritional status of Roma children aged 0–24 months mirrors assessment of maternal investment after birth: child's growth and development are sensitive to available resources and care, while the most obvious means by which maternal investment can influence growth is via nutrition, i.e., feeding. The direction and degree of the maternal response, i.e., postnatal investment, to an unwanted child is not clear and may vary by ethnic group and socioeconomic status (Lynch & Brooks, 2013).

Some studies have found that parents generally tend to invest more resources in children with higher birth endowments, while others found no differences in parental investment based on birth weight alone (Almond & Currie, 2011; Datar et al., 2010; Hsin, 2012). Still other studies found that investment tends to vary with maternal education and socioeconomic position: for instance, lower-class parents do not respond to ability differences (Grätz & Torche, 2016), while several studies have found that higher SES mothers tend to invest more in lesser-endowed children (Fan & Porter, 2020; Cabrera-Hernández & Orraca-Romano, 2023).

One of the indicators of having a low birthweight in this sample was whether the child was wanted or not. After controlling for birthweight and household wealth as a proxy for maternal socioeconomic status, Roma children's HAZ and WAZ scores were negatively associated with child wantedness, while being born from an unwanted pregnancy only had an effect on being underweight. Thus, the results indicate that unwanted children face a significant deficit in terms of their growth and nutritional outcomes, as measured by child's height for age and weight for age. Previous studies found inconsistent relationships between child wantedness and nutritional outcomes, but in this sample, unwanted children had significantly shorter stature, lower weight and higher odds of being underweight than wanted children (Baschieri et al., 2017; Costa et al., 2018; Hajizadeh & Nghiem, 2020). Since height and nutritional status serve as indicators of health and social environment in early life, for Roma children, being unwanted may be associated with worse health outcomes (Rahman et al., 2016). The above effects were magnified for both height and weight if the child was born as a boy with low birthweight to a mother from poorer socioeconomic status and higher parity.

Two further predictors found for Roma children growth and nutritional status were child's sex and maternal country of residence. Thus, child's sex predicted individual HAZ and WAZ scores, stunting and being underweight, in that Roma girls were taller, had higher WAZ scores and were less stunted and underweight than their male counterparts. There were more Roma girls than boys being born with low birthweight, and more girls reported as being unwanted, suggesting lower maternal investment prenatally. However, girls' better nutritional status and growth suggests that Roma mothers might have shifted their post-natal investment toward daughters. Roma mothers' compensating behavior in shifting of post-natal investment toward

6.2 Investment in Children Aged 0–24 Months

less-endowed children was also found in several other studies (review in Almond & Mazumder, 2013). This was also reflected in growth and nutritional differences by child's sex: both wanted and unwanted girls had better nutritional outcomes than wanted and unwanted boys.

The present findings are consistent with previous studies where biased parental investment was associated with children's health, i.e., height and nutritional outcomes, but also sex (Alvergne et al., 2009; Čvorović, 2020; Hagen et al., 2001). Furthermore, the results agree with previous studies where large disparities were found between reported offspring sex preferences and actual parental behavior toward offspring (Lynch & Brooks, 2013; Du & Mace, 2018). Reported unwantedness of daughters may reflect the influence of the majority of cultural norms on the Roma, while the ratio of boys and girls in the sample may indicate excess infant male mortality. A recent study among less segregated Roma groups in Serbia found a change in preferences toward lower fertility and sons over daughters, probably resulting from greater exposure to the Serbian majority culture (Battaglia et al., 2021). In general, studies have shown that fathers prefer sons and mothers tend to prefer daughters, but the ultimate outcome-child's well-being depends more upon which parent controls and distributes the resources (Godoy et al., 2006). On the other hand, in terms of body development, girls often tend to cope better with less than adequate food than boys (Marcoux, 2002), and this could be an alternative explanation for the finding.

Maternal parity, a fundamental trade-off between number and size of offspring (Walker et al., 2008), was reflected by the negative association between maternal parity and children's HAZ and WAZ scores. With each additional birth, parental investment is likely reduced as parents have limited resources in terms of time, attention and money. Food insecurity may be especially important to Roma families, as they heavily rely on welfare incentives (Čvorović, 2024). Among the poor, when the family size increases, shared food and resources remain the same, thus higher birth order children, i.e., younger children, end up growing up in more scarce conditions (Draper & Hames, 2000). However, in resource limited and high-fertility settings, all children may be at risk due to the disparity between family size and available resources (Kramer et al., 2016). This was reflected in the present results: younger Roma children had higher HAZ scores than their older counterparts, while there was a positive association of child's age and WAZ and WHZ scores. Similarly, older children were more stunted, but less wasted and underweight than their younger counterparts. This may reflect maternal favoring of older children, in agreement with other studies on Roma children's growth and nutrition (Čvorović, 2022b).

However, although the results of this study results revealed statistically significant differences, when these results were put into SD units, only a few of the variables showed any large or significant effect. Thus, for Roma birthweight, not a single variable reached two or above two standard-deviations difference. In contrast, for stunting, underweight and wasting, both child's age and birthweight had a considerable effect, ranging from a difference of more than approximately two standard deviations in birthweight to more than seven standard deviation in child's age.

This implies that differences in Roma children nutritional status may be largely attributed to differences in birthweight and age.

Overall, Roma children's birthweight had a significant effect on children's growth and nutritional status, as it explained the HAZ, WHZ and WAZ scores, and also stunting, wasting, and underweight. As with other studies, birthweight has therefore emerged as one of the main specific correlates of child growth for both height and weight (Ntenda, 2019; Aryastami et al., 2017). Across various populations, birthweight tends to be correlated with the risk of mortality and morbidity, and, in addition to being a proxy for pre-natal investment, it may also influence maternal post-natal behaviors, such as child feeding and care, thus further contributing to children's negative health outcomes (Class et al., 2014; Čvorović, 2020).

Child's age is reflected in birth order, and birth order often shapes siblings' differentials, particularly in poor populations where children of higher birth order are often disadvantaged in respect of nutritional outcomes compared to earlier-born children, and also may have higher morbidity and mortality (Lawson & Mace, 2008). Studies have found that in many developing countries, children's initial average HAZ and WAZ scores tend to be close to the international standard at birth, but with a tendency to decline with age, resulting in a decreasing shift of the entire HAZ and WAZ distribution (Victora et al., 2021). This implies that children across the HAZ and WAZ range may experience slower growth in comparison with international standards (Rieger & Trommlerová, 2016). In all five countries, Roma children had a mean HAZ of less than 0 (−0.84), comparable with other studies on children's outcomes in low- and middle-income countries (Yadav & Bhandari, 2022). Maternal reproductive strategy, such as closed birth-spacing, multiple births, and inadequate diet, may cause maternal depletion and result in poor maternal and child health, particularly for younger children (Winkvist et al., 1992).

Country of residence also affected Roma children's growth and nutritional status. Roma children born in North Macedonia were taller and less stunted than children from the reference group (Serbia), while they also had higher WAZ scores, along with children born in Montenegro, compared to Serbian Roma children. Montenegrin Roma children had higher WHZ scores, while Kosovo Roma children had lower WHZ scores compared with children from Serbia. Roma mothers from North Macedonia were older and had significantly lower parity than Serbian Roma mothers, which may explain the differences in their children's respective nutritional status as both maternal age and parity influence child outcomes. Montenegrin Roma, in turn, were better-off in terms of household wealth compared to Roma in other countries, while both Serbia and Kosovo were positioned at the bottom of the household wealth indicators, this socioeconomic difference possibly explaining the results. The impact of socioeconomic status was also evident in that children from better-off households had higher HAZ and WAZ scores, and were less stunted and less underweight than their poorer counterparts. However, maternal socioeconomic status had no effect on WHZ scores or on wasting. Acute malnutrition is influenced by a range of child and maternal factors, including poor maternal nutrition, high parity, low education, poor feeding practices, low socioeconomic status, but also in-utero transfers (Thurstans et al., 2022).

Unlike in other studies, Roma maternal education (basic literacy skills in this sample) had no effect on Roma children's growth and nutritional status, for children aged 0–24 months. This result may be explained by the observation that, in general, the effect of household wealth and maternal education tends to be much stronger among older children, while the positive effect of maternal education on child's health tends to get stronger with age (Yadav & Bhandari, 2022). In addition, as Roma mothers have high illiteracy rates, this homogeneity in Roma mother's literacy may also have influenced the obtained result.

Limitations A number of limitations in the present study may have biased the results. The cross-sectional design of the MICS studies prevented causal inferences. Variables were mostly mother-reported, which may have facilitated potential reporting bias. For instance, previous studies have found that fathers generally reported having considerably higher levels of child engagement than reported by mothers, depending on numerous factors, including ethnicity, quality of the couple's relationship, and child's characteristics (Charles et al., 2018). For the older Roma children, aged between 25 and 59 months, several measures of maternal investment/direct care may not be entirely typical for the Roma, nor represent all the possible ways that mothers invest in their children. For instance, a more intimate style of parenting, consisting mainly of body contact and body stimulation but without much verbalizing, may be a more accurate measure of Roma mother–child interaction than the parenting styles measured in MICS surveys (Čvorović, 2020). In addition, the measures of maternal activities with children may have been exaggerated for older children since some activities are more commonly performed with older children.

For the younger Roma children, retrospective reporting by the mother in regard to childbearing intentions may have been prejudiced by the presence of the child (Flatø, 2018). Childbearing intention was only measured for surviving children and not for any deceased children, which may also have influenced the results. In addition, some of the indicators of maternal care measured may not be representative of all mothers and cultures, nor typify all the possible ways that mothers invest in their children (Keller, 2007). Other confounding variables such as parental height and health, gestation and previous preterm or low birthweight births, child's medical history and chronic illnesses were not available in MICS data. Future surveys should also include questions on religious differences in relation to childrearing, as religion may be an important determinant of reproductive and fertility patterns, in addition to maternal investment (Čvorović & Coe, 2019).

6.3 Instead of Conclusion: How Many Children Is Too Many

Studies looking at parental investment in early childhood from developing countries and ethnic groups are few (Abufhele et al., 2017). Anthropologists and developmental scientists agree that parenting hinges on particular environmental and cultural contexts. Since most studies have focused on Western populations, knowledge of parenting and child development may be biased in favor of contexts unrepresentative of minority populations (Lansford, 2022). Available evidence suggests that when parents are confronted with limited resources and numerous children, they may behave differently in relation to different outcomes, and so may reinforce certain inequalities but compensate for the others.

In the context of general deprivation, Roma parents were moderately invested in their children (direct care for older Roma children), and the childcare was chiefly mother-centered, albeit that this was supported to a certain extent by fathers and allomothers. Roma mothers from Kosovo engaged in less direct care than mothers from other countries, dependent upon maternal parity and child's birth order. Roma children who received high maternal direct care were taller, born to mothers with greater literacy skills, higher socioeconomic position, older in age and with lower parity compared with children born to moderate- and low-investing mothers. Greater maternal investment was reflected in better child growth and nutritional outcomes, as proxies for fitness and health: children of high-investing mothers had greater HAZ, WAZ and WHZ scores, and lower rates of stunting, underweight and wasting, than children born to other mothers. High-investing Roma mothers invested in better-endowed children, as measured by children's higher height, probably in expectation of greater fitness benefits.

Birthweight for younger Roma children was highest for children born in Kosovo, who also had the lowest rates of low birthweight, likely as a consequence of the Kosovo mothers' higher parity. Determinants of low birth weight included gradients in household wealth, maternal parity, country of residence (Kosovo) and whether the child was wanted or not. More Roma girls than boys were born with low birthweight, while, at the same time, daughters were also more reported as unwanted, in comparison with sons. The majority of Roma mothers, including those with high parity, still desired the last-born child, indicating a preference for having many children. Higher birth order children were more likely to be reported as unwanted than earlier-borns, while unwanted children were more likely to experience deficits in their growth and nutritional outcomes. The worst health outcomes were where the child was born a boy with low birth weight to a mother with low socioeconomic status and high parity. There was no significant difference in child health between children born from unwanted pregnancies and those wanted at a later time.

Roma girls were taller and had better nutritional status than boys, despite being more often born with low birth weight and reported as unwanted compared to Roma boys. As height and weight are also often used as estimates of child investment by parents, the results suggest that Roma mothers may have given higher postnatal investment to daughters than to sons. This compensating strategy of Roma mothers may be the result of their efforts to achieve equality among children and, ultimately, to improve their children's future outcomes, as well as, over the long term, reproductive success (Tracer, 2009; Costa et al., 2018; Fan & Porter, 2020).

Overall, a child's birthweight— and age are the characteristics that most closely reflect a child's growth and nutritional status. Aside from all other measured characteristics, the effects of child's birthweight and child's age may be the most influential for Roma children. Across Europe, Roma infants have the highest incidence of

6.3 Instead of Conclusion: How Many Children Is Too Many

low birthweight, generally more than double that of non-Roma, usually as a result of their poor socio-economic conditions but also genetic factors (Stanković et al., 2016, Čvorović, 2020). In addition to maternal stature and environmental limitations, weight at birth also reflects maternal reproductive strategy. In many studies across contemporary and historic populations, maternal parity may serve as a proxy for investment, and is associated with reduced odds of normal growth (Hagen et al., 2001; Walker et al., 2008). Roma maternal parity does not reach thresholds of effect significance, but, nevertheless, high fertility may be an important trigger for investment. High fertility is usually defined as five or more births per woman over the reproductive period. And even though a declining trend in Roma fertility has been observed, their relatively high and persistent fertility remains the most distinguishing characteristic of the Roma population compared to their non-Roma counterparts. Throughout Europe, the fertility of Roma women is far above the majority population average in all birth cohorts and in every country (Szabó et al., 2021; Ekezie et al., 2023).

For the younger Roma children in the sample, age was another major confounding factor in assessing the growth outcomes. HAZ and WAZ were calculated relative to age and sex, while the age range of the children included very different periods of child growth trajectories. In populations with high rates of childhood stunting, the incidence tends to increase over the first 2 years of life. Children born with low weight at birth or small-for-gestational-age may also experience catchup or rapid growth, and cross major WAZ centiles. Although birthweight was positively associated with the children's anthropometric measures in this Roma sample, that affect may have been attenuated if there were unaccounted associations between birthweight and WAZ, dependent on age at measurement.

In evolutionary models, payoffs are measured as reproductive success, while other outcomes such as mating or economic endeavors may serve as valid substitutes for guiding behaviors (Hopcroft & Martin, 2014; Hedges et al., 2016). And even though the measures used cannot directly assess long-term fitness outcomes for Roma children, body size and growth are commonly used as proxies for fitness in life history analyses. Roma invest in their children in a multitude of ways, while biased investment may be hypothetically adaptive as they include proxies of eventual offspring fitness, including child's sex, age, and height.

Overall, Roma mothers engage in both reinforcing and compensatory strategies, but are there any differences that bias in investment may create among children? Maternal compensatory behavior may be reflected in a daughter's better growth and nutritional status, compared to sons. Short height is often being associated with reduced reproductive success, especially in men, and greater odds of child mortality, and children's nutritional deficits in women (Stulp et al., 2012). However, the Roma generally smaller stature does not appear to compromise fitness. Today, the chances of survival in early childhood for contemporary Roma infants and children is higher than in the past, with fertility remaining high. Adult Roma are well fed regardless of their low socioeconomic position, while short women, despite experiencing low birth weight infants, and greater infant and child mortality, tend to have numerous surviving children (Gallagher et al., 2009; Čvorović, 2018).

Roma women share a number of characteristics with women in other high-fertility populations. As with many women in traditionally high-fertility settings worldwide, Roma women often live in poverty, frequently in segregated communities, lack adequate education, the skills for and access to jobs, and have cultural practices that encourage early, endogamous marriages and high fertility (Coe & Čvorović, 2017; Voicu & Popescu, 2009).

Unlike many other women in disadvantaged populations, Roma women living in the former Yugoslav republics have access to both education and health care, provided for them by the governments of their resident countries; however, their utilization of these services tends to be limited and sporadic (Coe & Čvorović, 2017; Janevic, 2019). Replacement in the case of child deaths, pressure to conform to cultural and local community prescribed behaviors, but also "insurance" for old age, or social status gained later in life after having numerous children, are probably related to Roma women's preferences for large families (Čvorović, 2014). Typically, Roma traditional ideals stipulate that marriage and having children are a proof of maturity and decency, and many women take great pride in having a family with several children.

In many traditional societies around the world, social status was found to have important implications for the dynamics of fertility decision-making but also outcomes, above and beyond the many other contributing factors (Shenk et al., 2016). In turn, in contemporary modern societies, there is an inverse relationship between reproductive success and "endowment" as measured by wealth, socioeconomic position, and capability (Vining, 1986). Both evolutionary and non-evolutionary studies have found that having fewer children increases the social and economic success of descendants for up to four generations but reduces the total number of long-term descendants (Goodman et al., 2012). The drive for social status, as reflected in income, heritable wealth or education, may therefore be an important factor in explaining human fertility variation and recent fertility decline: social status was found to be important for fitness across most, if not all, human societies, while it also tends to trade off with fertility, especially under conditions of heritable wealth and modern markets (Shenk et al., 2016).

In sum, therefore, fertility is mainly determined by parent's choices regarding children in relation to the socioeconomic, educational, and cultural environment the parents, but especially women, face: many women in the developing world, as well as those lacking other prospects in life, such as the Roma, may have the perception that they are better off with large families (Pritchett, 1994). Hence, in effect, for parents everywhere, having many children (high fertility) is, to a greater or lesser extent, a choice, i.e., it is endogenous (Casterline, 2010). A good example is a highly publicized case of family planning in Niger, where women on average have seven children, the highest fertility rate in the world (Kabir, 2023). Yet, despite their country experiencing conflicts, displacement, food insecurity, child malnutrition, climatic hazards, epidemics and the highest world fertility, women in Niger have reported they want even more children than they actually have – an average of nine, while the preference for the men in Niger is eleven children (Filipovic, 2017). Moreover, despite the warnings from demographers and the development,

6.3 Instead of Conclusion: How Many Children Is Too Many

environment and economic sectors, unless these women's preference changes in favor of a smaller family, it is unlikely that the fertility rate will decrease anytime soon. A similar situation obtains for the high-fertility Roma women in the five Balkan countries: high fertility preference for the large majority of women with more than three and four children was reflected in that their last pregnancy was intentional and the children were wanted, despite already having, on average, five and six children. Recent studies have confirmed the strong association between fertility preference and completed fertility, whereas fertility outcomes are explained not by external limitations (access to contraceptives) but rather by women's preferences (Gietel-Basten et al., 2024). In turn, covariation of fertility with other outcomes—social, economic, and health, including child outcomes such as infant and child mortality—may reflect intentionally chosen trade-offs rather than direct causal effects of fertility (Knodel & Van de Walle, 1979; Casterline, 2010).

External circumstances and different environmental conditions usually determine whether parents will favor quality or quantity of offspring. Per the quantity-quality trade-off model, parents must decide how much to invest in number and in quality of their offspring. Low socioeconomic status may be one of the most important indications of externally caused morbidity-mortality: living in low socioeconomic environments exposes humans to more risks, disability and death. Generally, there is a positive correlation between socioeconomic status and levels of parental investment per child, whereas a negative correlation between socioeconomic status and offspring number (Vining, 1986; Ellis et al., 2009). When environmental cues indicate high levels of extrinsic morbidity-mortality, humans tend to favor offspring quantity over quality. This implies that high parental investment per offspring would not necessarily increase the reliability of investment returns, i.e., it would not result in increased parental fitness. Therefore, parents would be better off by instead producing a relatively large number of offspring, with a limited amount of investment in each. Both evolutionary and economic models of family predict reduced parental investment in families with numerous children (Becker, 1981; Lawson & Mace, 2011). At the same time, owing to modern economic interventions, e.g. state policies, and improved public health, care, and food provision, parents may still possess adequate, or just enough sufficient resources, to support the production and growth of large numbers of offspring (Melia & Li, 2018; Čvorović, 2024).

There is widespread agreement that socio-economic development, education and the encouragement of family planning results in lower fertility. At the same time, both socioeconomic gradient and parenting can independently influence children's health and development. The negative effects of low socioeconomic status on children's well-being may be mitigated with increased parental investment, in that having fewer children and investing in base-level resources, may contribute to better child outcomes despite the low socioeconomic status (Mbuma et al., 2021).

The fertility transition has not affected all Roma women alike; there were large differences between and within the five countries studied, depending on location and level of exposure to the majority cultural norms (Čvorović, 2010; Battaglia et al., 2021). Still, irrespective of socioeconomic status, both Roma fertility and mortality remain higher than in the majority populations, but lower than was the case in premodern societies (Szabó et al., 2021; Gamella, 2018). At the same time, the rates of Roma births and deaths cannot be classified under any particular stage of the classic demographic transition (Radovanović & Knežević, 2014). For instance, an increase in average life expectancy would indicate a decline in mortality rate, especially during childhood; however, a reduction in growth of the Roma population in Europe was not found (Nestorová Dická, 2021). On the contrary, in the countries of the Western Balkans with some of the world's lowest fertility rates, relatively high fertility rates and population growth differenced the Roma from the rest.

The decision to limit family size can be considered as a deliberate decision to improve the socioeconomic position of children and their descendants, albeit that the benefit is not being reflected in fitness returns (Kaplan, 1994; Goodman et al., 2012). The ability of parents to influence their children's socioeconomic status is much greater in complex societies with heritable wealth and heritable statuses (Borgerhoff Mulder et al., 2009). Roma, on the other hand, have no middle-class to aspire to. The Roma in the former Yugoslav republics do not possess the endowments and assets they need or the ability to generate economic gains and climb the socioeconomic ladder, while their returns of education are low (Robayo-Abril & Millán, 2019). Few Roma have inheritable resources, e.g. land, property, occupations, or livestock. Instead, the majority have little schooling or vocational skills, and many of them are unemployed, relying mainly on welfare benefits to survive (Čvorović, 2024). Even for those groups that have managed to become relatively wealthy or at least better off, fertility tends to follow the traditional pattern (Čvorović, 2014; Gamella, 2018). At the same time, investments in schooling and health care as well as other forms of assistance, including benefits in cash transfers, are provided by the welfare state and is available particularly to families of low socioeconomic status, increasing with family size (Čvorović, 2024). Thus, Roma populations may not need to sacrifice reproduction for cultural or socioeconomic goals as much as the average European with higher-than-average socioeconomic status (Bereczkei, 1998).

Among Roma women, there is a close relationship between wanted and actual fertility: a case of having too few children, rather than too many. Having numerous children means not only a large number of births by the end of a woman's reproductive period, but a constantly high rate of pregnancies at a young age, narrowly spaced births, unplanned pregnancies at certain point, and also, in the absence of contraception and/or abortions, unwanted births. Globally, unintended births contribute to unwanted population growth, which in turn may compromise provision of social services (Dutta et al., 2015). On the other hand, for Roma children, being unwanted tends to be associated with worse health outcomes, yet the biological significance of these outcomes may be negligible, not only in early childhood but also later in life. Parents tend to balance the costs and benefits of investment by taking decisions that maximize fitness, and when they decrease investment in a particular offspring, the costs fall upon the development of the child, while the parents only lose the potential future benefits (Alonso-Alvarez & Velando, 2012; Nettle, 2010). Conversely, when the Roma mothers in the sample increased their investment in unwanted daughters, they not only mitigated their adverse childhood conditions but also improved their chances to survive and reproduce later on.

References

Abufhele, A., Behrman, J., & Bravo, D. (2017). Parental preferences and allocations of investments in children's learning and health within families. *Social Science & Medicine, 194*, 76–86. https://doi.org/10.1016/j.socscimed.2017.09.051

Addo, O. Y., Stein, A. D., Fall, C. H., Gigante, D. P., Guntupalli, A. M., Horta, B. L., et al. (2013). Maternal height and child growth patterns. *The Journal of Pediatrics, 163*(2), 549–554. https://doi.org/10.1016/j.jpeds.2013.02.002

Almond, D., & Currie, J. (2011). Killing me softly: The fetal origins hypothesis. *Journal of Economic Perspectives, 25*(3), 153–172. https://doi.org/10.1257/jep.25.3.153

Almond, D., & Mazumder, B. (2013). Fetal origins and parental responses. *Annual Review of Economics, 5*(1), 37–56. https://doi.org/10.1146/annurev-economics-082912-110145

Alvergne, A., Faurie, C., & Raymond, M. (2009). Father–offspring resemblance predicts paternal investment in humans. *Animal Behaviour, 78*(1), 61–69. https://doi.org/10.1016/j.anbehav.2009.03.019

Alonso-Alvarez, C., & Velando, A. (2012). Benefits and costs of parental care. In N. J. Royle, P. T. Smiseth, & M. Kölliker (Eds.), *The evolution of parental care* (pp. 40–46). Oxford University Press.

Aryastami, N. K., Shankar, A., Kusumawardani, N., Besral, B., Jahari, A. B., & Achadi, E. (2017). Low birth weight was the most dominant predictor associated with stunting among children aged 12–23 months in Indonesia. *BMC Nutrition, 3*, 1–6.

Barclay, K., & Myrskylä, M. (2016). Advanced maternal age and offspring outcomes: Reproductive aging and counterbalancing period trends. *Population and Development Review*, 69–94. https://www.jstor.org/stable/44015615

Baschieri, A., Machiyama, K., Floyd, S., Dube, A., Molesworth, A., Chihana, M., et al. (2017). Unintended childbearing and child growth in northern Malawi. *Maternal and Child Health Journal, 21*, 467–474. https://doi.org/10.1007/s10995-016-2124-8

Battaglia, M., Chabé-Ferret, B., & Lebedinski, L. (2021). Segregation, fertility, and son preference: The case of the Roma in Serbia. *Journal of Demographic Economics, 87*(2), 233–260. https://doi.org/10.1017/dem.2020.8

Beaulieu, D. A., & Bugental, D. (2008). Contingent parental investment: An evolutionary framework for understanding early interaction between mothers and children. *Evolution and Human Behavior, 29*(4), 249–255. https://doi.org/10.1016/j.evolhumbehav.2008.01.002

Becker, G. S. (1981). *A treatise on the family*. Harvard University Press.

Bereczkei, T. (1998). Kinship network, direct childcare, and fertility among Hungarians and Gypsies. *Evolution and Human Behavior, 19*(5), 283–298. https://doi.org/10.1016/S1090-5138(98)00027-0

Bereczkei, T., & Dunbar, R. I. (2002). Helping-at-the-nest and sex-biased parental investment in a Hungarian Gypsy population. *Current Anthropology, 43*(5), 804–809. https://doi.org/10.1086/344374

Borgerhoff Mulder, M., Bowles, S., Hertz, T., Bell, A., Beise, J., Clark, G., et al. (2009). Intergenerational wealth transmission and the dynamics of inequality in small-scale societies. *Science, 326*(5953), 682–688. https://doi.org/10.1126/science.1178336

Cabrera, N. J., Fitzgerald, H. E., Bradley, R. H., & Roggman, L. (2014). The ecology of father-child relationships: An expanded model. *Journal of Family Theory & Review, 6*(4), 336–354. https://doi.org/10.1111/jftr.12054

Cabrera-Hernández, F. J., & Orraca-Romano, P. P. (2023). Inequality in the household: How parental income matters for the long-term treatment of healthy and unhealthy siblings. *Journal of Family and Economic Issues, 44*(3), 674–692. https://doi.org/10.1007/s10834-022-09858-9

Casterline, J. B. (2010). Determinants and consequences of high fertility: A synopsis of the evidence. World Bank. https://documents1.worldbank.org/curated/en/389381468147851589/pdf/630690WP0P10870nants0pub08023010web.pdf. Accessed June 2023.

Charles, P., Spielfogel, J., Gorman-Smith, D., Schoeny, M., Henry, D., & Tolan, P. (2018). Disagreement in parental reports of father involvement. *Journal of Family Issues, 39*(2), 328–351. https://doi.org/10.1177/0192513X16644639

Cho, H. (2023). Son preference and low birth weight for girls. *Journal of Demographic Economics, 89*(4), 553–563. https://doi.org/10.1017/dem.2022.13

Class, Q. A., Rickert, M. E., Lichtenstein, P., & D'Onofrio, B. M. (2014). Birth weight, physical morbidity, and mortality: A population-based sibling-comparison study. *American Journal of Epidemiology, 179*(5), 550–558. https://doi.org/10.1093/aje/kwt304

Coe, K., & Čvorović, J. (2017). The health of Romanian Gypsy women in Serbia. *Health Care for Women International, 38*(4), 409–422. https://doi.org/10.1080/07399332.2017.1292278

Costa, M. E., Trumble, B., Kaplan, H., & Gurven, M. D. (2018). Child nutritional status among births exceeding ideal family size in a high fertility population. *Maternal & Child Nutrition, 14*(4), e12625. https://doi.org/10.1111/mcn.12625

Cuartas, J., Jeong, J., Rey-Guerra, C., McCoy, D. C., & Yoshikawa, H. (2020). Maternal, paternal, and other caregivers' stimulation in low-and-middle-income countries. *PLoS One, 15*(7), e0236107. https://doi.org/10.1371/journal.pone.0236107

Čvorović, J. (2010). Roast chicken and other Gypsy stories: Oral narratives among Serbian Gypsies. Hamburg, Peter Lang.

Čvorović, J. (2014). *The Roma: A Balkan underclass*. Ulster Institute for Social Research.

Čvorović, J. (2018). Influence of maternal height on children's health status and mortality: A cross-sectional study in poor Roma communities in rural Serbia. *Homo, 69*(6), 357–363. https://doi.org/10.1016/j.jchb.2018.11.00

Čvorović, J. (2020). Child wantedness and low weight at birth: Differential parental investment among Roma. *Behavioral Sciences, 10*(6), 102. https://doi.org/10.3390/bs10060102

Čvorović, J. (2022a). Maternal age at marriage and child nutritional status and development: Evidence from Serbian Roma communities. *Public Health Nutrition, 25*(5), 1183–1193. https://doi.org/10.1017/S1368980022000544

Čvorović, J. (2022b). Paternal investment, stepfather presence and early child development and growth among Serbian Roma. *Evolutionary Human Sciences, 4*, e15. https://doi.org/10.1017/ehs.2022.14

Čvorović, J. (2024). The impact of welfare on maternal investment and sibling competition: Evidence from Serbian Roma communities. *Journal of Biosocial Science, 56*(3), 560–573. https://doi.org/10.1017/S0021932023000184

Čvorović, J., & Coe, K. (2019). Happy marriages are all alike: Marriage and self-rated health among Serbian Roma. *Bulletin of the Institute of Ethnography SASA, 67*(2), 341–359. https://doi.org/10.2298/GEI1810310001C

Danielsbacka, M., Tanskanen, A. O., Jokela, M., & Rotkirch, A. (2011). Grandparental child care in Europe: Evidence for preferential investment in more certain kin. *Evolutionary Psychology, 9*(1), 3–24. https://doi.org/10.1177/147470491100900102

Datar, A., Kilburn, M. R., & Loughran, D. S. (2010). Endowments and parental investments in infancy and early childhood. *Demography, 47*(1), 145–162. https://doi.org/10.1353/dem.0.0092

Draper, P., & Hames, R. (2000). Birth order, sibling investment, and fertility among Ju/'hoansi (!Kung). *Human Nature, 11*, 117–156. https://doi.org/10.1007/s12110-000-1016-0

Du, J., & Mace, R. (2018). Parental investment in Tibetan populations does not reflect stated cultural norms. *Behavioral Ecology, 29*(1), 106–116. https://doi.org/10.1093/beheco/arx134

References

Dutta, M., Shekhar, C., & Prashad, L. (2015). Level, trend and correlates of mistimed and unwanted pregnancies among currently pregnant ever married women in India. *PLoS One, 10*(12), e0144400. https://doi.org/10.1371/journal.pone.0144400

Ekezie, W., Hopwood, E., Czyznikowska, B., Weidman, S., Mackintosh, N., & Curtis, F. (2023). Perinatal health outcomes of women from Gypsy, Roma and traveller communities: A systematic review. *Midwifery*, 103910. https://doi.org/10.1016/j.midw.2023.103910

Ellis, B. J., Figueredo, A. J., Brumbach, B. H., & Schlomer, G. L. (2009). Fundamental dimensions of environmental risk: The impact of harsh versus unpredictable environments on the evolution and development of life history strategies. *Human Nature, 20*, 204–268. https://doi.org/10.1007/s12110-009-9063-7

Ena, G. F., Aizpurua-Iraola, J., Font-Porterias, N., Calafell, F., & Comas, D. (2022). Population genetics of the European Roma—a review. *Genes, 13*(11), 2068. https://doi.org/10.3390/genes13112068

Fan, W., & Porter, C. (2020). Reinforcement or compensation? Parental responses to children's revealed human capital levels. *Journal of Population Economics, 33*(1), 233–270. https://doi.org/10.1007/s00148-019-00752-7

Fessler, D. M., Navarrete, C. D., Hopkins, W., & Izard, M. K. (2005). Examining the terminal investment hypothesis in humans and chimpanzees: Associations among maternal age, parity, and birth weight. *American Journal of Physical Anthropology, 127*(1), 95–104. https://doi.org/10.1002/ajpa.20039

Filipovic, J. (2017). Why have four children when you could have seven? Family planning in Niger https://www.theguardian.com/global-development-professionals-network/2017/mar/15/why-have-four-children-when-you-could-have-seven-contraception-niger. Accessed July 2024.

Fingerman, K. L., Kim, K., Davis, E. M., Furstenberg, F. F., Jr., Birditt, K. S., & Zarit, S. H. (2015). "I'll give you the world": Socioeconomic differences in parental support of adult children. *Journal of Marriage and Family, 77*(4), 844–865. https://doi.org/10.1111/jomf.12204

Flatø, M. (2018). The differential mortality of undesired infants in sub-Saharan Africa. *Demography, 55*(1), 271–294. https://doi.org/10.1007/s13524-017-0638-3

Gallagher, A., Čvorović, J., & Štrkalj, G. (2009). Body mass index in Serbian Roma. *Homo, 60*(6), 567–578.

Gamella, J. F. (2018). Marriage, gender and transnational migrations in fertility transitions of Romanian Roma women. Intersections. *East European Journal of Society and Politics, 4*(2), 57–85.

Gibson, M. A., & Sear, R. (2010). Does wealth increase parental investment biases in child education? Evidence from two African populations on the cusp of the fertility transition. *Current Anthropology, 51*(5), 693–701. https://doi.org/10.1086/655954

Gietel-Basten, S., LoPalo, M., Spears, D., & Vyas, S. (2024). Do fertility preferences in early adulthood predict later average fertility outcomes of the same cohort?: Pritchett (1994) revisited with cohort data. *Economics Letters*, 111975. https://doi.org/10.1016/j.econlet.2024.111975

Gluckman, P. D., Hanson, M. A., & Beedle, A. S. (2007). Early life events and their consequences for later disease: A life history and evolutionary perspective. *American Journal of Human Biology, 19*(1), 1–19. https://doi.org/10.1002/ajhb.20590

Godoy, R., Reyes-García, V., McDade, T., Tanner, S., Leonard, W. R., Huanca, T., et al. (2006). Why do mothers favor girls and fathers, boys? A hypothesis and a test of investment disparity. *Human Nature, 17*, 169–189. https://doi.org/10.1007/s12110-006-1016-9

Goodman, A., Koupil, I., & Lawson, D. W. (2012). Low fertility increases descendant socioeconomic position but reduces long-term fitness in a modern post-industrial society. *Proceedings of the Royal Society B: Biological Sciences, 279*(1746), 4342–4351. https://doi.org/10.1098/rspb.2012.1415

Goossens, J., Van Den Branden, Y., Van der Sluys, L., Delbaere, I., Van Hecke, A., Verhaeghe, S., & Beeckman, D. (2016). The prevalence of unplanned pregnancy ending in birth, associated factors, and health outcomes. *Human Reproduction*, 1–13. https://doi.org/10.1093/humrep/dew266

Grätz, M., & Torche, F. (2016). Compensation or reinforcement? The stratification of parental responses to children's early ability. *Demography, 53*(6), 1883–1904. https://doi.org/10.1007/s13524-016-0527-1

Hagen, E. H., Hames, R. B., Craig, N. M., Lauer, M. T., & Price, M. E. (2001). Parental investment and child health in a Yanomamö village suffering short-term food stress. *Journal of Biosocial Science, 33*(4), 503–528. https://doi.org/10.1017/S002193200100503X

Hajizadeh, M., & Nghiem, S. (2020). Does unwanted pregnancy lead to adverse health and healthcare utilization for mother and child? Evidence from low-and middle-income countries. *International Journal of Public Health, 65*, 457–468. https://doi.org/10.1007/s00038-020-01358-7

Hedges, S., Mulder, M. B., James, S., & Lawson, D. W. (2016). Sending children to school: Rural livelihoods and parental investment in education in northern Tanzania. *Evolution and Human Behavior, 37*(2), 142–151. https://doi.org/10.1016/j.evolhumbehav.2015.10.001

Helle, S. (2008). Why twin pregnancies are more successful at advanced than young maternal age? A potential role of 'terminal reproductive investment'. *Human Reproduction, 23*(10), 2387–2389. https://doi.org/10.1093/humrep/den305

Hinkle, S. N., Albert, P. S., Mendola, P., Sjaarda, L. A., Yeung, E., Boghossian, N. S., & Laughon, S. K. (2014). The association between parity and birthweight in a longitudinal consecutive pregnancy cohort. *Paediatric and Perinatal Epidemiology, 28*(2), 106–115. https://doi.org/10.1111/ppe.12099

Hopcroft, R. L., & Martin, D. O. (2014). The primary parental investment in children in the contemporary USA is education: Testing the Trivers-Willard hypothesis of parental investment. *Human Nature, 25*, 235–250. https://doi.org/10.1007/s12110-014-9197-0

Hosegood, V., & Madhavan, S. (2010). Data availability on men's involvement in families in sub-Saharan Africa to inform family-centred programmes for children affected by HIV and AIDS. *Journal of the International AIDS Society, 13*, S5–S5. https://doi.org/10.1186/1758-2652-13-S2-S5

Hsin, A. (2012). Is biology destiny? Birth weight and differential parental treatment. *Demography, 49*, 1385–1405. https://doi.org/10.1007/s13524-012-0123-y

Janevic, T. (2019). Romani maternal and child health: Moving from documenting disparities to testing progress and interventions to achieve equity. *International Journal of Public Health, 64*, 981–982. https://doi.org/10.1007/s00038-019-01255-8

Joyce, T. J., Kaestner, R., & Korenman, S. (2000). The effect of pregnancy intention on child development. *Demography, 37*(1), 83–94. https://doi.org/10.2307/2648098

Kabir, K. (2023). Niger is Africa's fastest growing country—how to feed 25 million more people in 30 years. The Conservation. https://theconversation.com/niger-is-africas-fastest-growing-country-how-to-feed-25-million-more-people-in-30-years-198321. Accessed June 2024.

Kaplan, H. (1994). Evolutionary and wealth flows theories of fertility: Empirical tests and new models. *Population and Development Review*, 753–791. https://doi.org/10.2307/2137661

Keller, H. (2007). *Cultures of Infancy*. Lawrence Erlbaum Associates Publishers.

Knauer, H. A., Ozer, E. J., Dow, W., & Fernald, L. C. (2018). Stimulating parenting practices in indigenous and non-indigenous Mexican communities. *International Journal of Environmental Research and Public Health, 15*(1), 29. https://doi.org/10.3390/ijerph15010029

Knodel, J., & Van de Walle, E. (1979). Lessons from the past: Policy implications of historical fertility studies. *Population and Development Review*, 217–245. http://www.jstor.org/stable/1971824

Kramer, K. L., Veile, A., & Otárola-Castillo, E. (2016). Sibling competition & growth tradeoffs. Biological vs. statistical significance. *PLoS One, 11*(3), e0150126. https://doi.org/10.1371/journal.pone.0150126

Lansford, J. E. (2022). Annual research review: Cross-cultural similarities and differences in parenting. *Journal of Child Psychology and Psychiatry, 63*(4), 466–479. https://doi.org/10.1111/jcpp.13539

References

Lawson, D. W., & Mace, R. (2008). Sibling configuration and childhood growth in contemporary British families. *International Journal of Epidemiology, 37*(6), 1408–1421. https://doi.org/10.1093/ije/dyn116

Lawson, D. W., & Mace, R. (2011). Parental investment and the optimization of human family size. *Philosophical Transactions of the Royal Society B: Biological Sciences, 366*(1563), 333–343. https://doi.org/10.1098/rstb.2010.0297

Lemlem, G. A., Mezen, M. K., Atinafu, A., & Abitew, Z. A. (2021). Maternal factors associated with low birth weight in governmental hospitals of Wollo District, Northeast Ethiopia: A cross sectional study. *PAMJ-One Health, 4*(18). https://doi.org/10.11604/pamj-oh.2021.4.18.27861

Lynch, J. L., & Brooks, R. (2013). Low birth weight and parental investment: Do parents favor the fittest child? *Journal of Marriage and Family, 75*(3), 533–543. https://doi.org/10.1111/jomf.12028

Marcoux, A. (2002). Sex differentials in undernutrition: A look at survey evidence. *Population and Development Review, 28*(2), 275–284. https://doi.org/10.1111/j.1728-4457.2002.00275.x

Mbuma, V., Lissner, L., & Hunsberger, M. (2021). Parental investment can moderate the negative effects of low socioeconomic status on children's health: An analysis of Kenyan national data. *Journal of Global Health Reports, 5*, e2021097. https://doi.org/10.29392/001c.29462

Melia, N. V., & Li, N. P. (2018). *Quantity versus quality of offspring. Encyclopedia of evolutionary psychological science.* Springer. https://doi.org/10.1007/978-3-319-16999-6_1989-1

Merklinger-Gruchala, A., Jasienska, G., & Kapiszewska, M. (2019). Paternal investment and low birth weight—the mediating role of parity. *PLoS One, 14*(1), e0210715. https://doi.org/10.1371/journal.pone.0210715

Mesman, J., van IJzendoorn, M. H., & Bakermans-Kranenburg, M. J. (2012). Unequal in opportunity, equal in process: Parental sensitivity promotes positive child development in ethnic minority families. *Child Development Perspectives, 6*(3), 239–250. https://doi.org/10.1111/j.1750-8606.2011.00223.x

Nestorová Dická, J. (2021). Demographic changes in Slovak Roma Communities in the new millennium. *Sustainability, 13*(7), 3735. https://doi.org/10.3390/su13073735

Nettle, D. (2010). Dying young and living fast: Variation in life history across English neighborhoods. *Behavioral Ecology, 21*(2), 387–395. https://doi.org/10.1093/beheco/arp202

Ntenda, P. A. M. (2019). Association of low birth weight with undernutrition in preschool-aged children in Malawi. *Nutrition Journal, 18*, 1–15. https://doi.org/10.1186/s12937-019-0477-8

Palmer, C. T., Steadman, L., & B. & Coe, K. (2005). More kin: An effect of the tradition of marriage. *Structure and Dynamics, 1*(2) .

Prevoo, M. J., & Tamis-LeMonda, C. S. (2017). Parenting and globalization in western countries: Explaining differences in parent–child interactions. *Current Opinion in Psychology, 15*, 33–39. https://doi.org/10.1016/j.copsyc.2017.02.003

Pritchett, L. H. (1994). Desired fertility and the impact of population policies. *Population and Development Review, 20*, 1–55. https://doi.org/10.2307/2137605

Radovanović, S., & Knežević, A. (2014). *Romi u Srbiji (Roma in Serbia, census)*. Republički zavod za statistiku.

Rahman, M. M., Rahman, M. M., Tareque, M. I., Ferdos, J., & Jesmin, S. S. (2016). Maternal pregnancy intention and professional antenatal care utilization in Bangladesh: A nationwide population-based survey. *PLoS One, 11*(6), e0157760. https://doi.org/10.1371/journal.pone.0157760

Restrepo, B. J. (2016). Parental investment responses to a low birth weight outcome: Who compensates and who reinforces? *Journal of Population Economics, 29*(4), 969–989. https://doi.org/10.1007/s00148-016-0590-3

Rieger, M., & Trommlerová, S. K. (2016). Age-specific correlates of child growth. *Demography, 53*(1), 241–267. https://doi.org/10.1007/s13524-015-0449-3

Rohde, P. A., Atzwanger, K., Butovskaya, M., Lampert, A., Mysterud, I., Sanchez-Andres, A., & Sulloway, F. J. (2003). Perceived parental favoritism, closeness to kin, and the rebel of the family: The effects of birth order and sex. *Evolution and Human Behavior, 24*(4), 261–276. https://doi.org/10.1016/S1090-5138(03)00033-3

Robayo-Abril, M. & Millán, N. (2019). Breaking the cycle of Roma exclusion in the Western Balkan. The World Bank. https://documents1.worldbank.org/curated/fr/642861552321695392/pdf/Breaking-the-Cycle-of-Roma-Exclusion-in-the-Western-Balkans.pdf. Accessed September 2024.

Rybo, G., Leman, J., & Tibbin, E. (1985). Epidemiology of menstrual blood loss. *Serono Symposia Publications 25*, 181–193.

Savage, T., Derraik, J. G., Miles, H. L., Mouat, F., Hofman, P. L., & Cutfield, W. S. (2013). Increasing maternal age is associated with taller stature and reduced abdominal fat in their children. *PLoS One, 8*(3), e58869. https://doi.org/10.1371/journal.pone.0058869

Sear, R. (2010). Height and reproductive success: Is bigger always better? In U. Frey, C. Störmer, & K. Willführ (Eds.), *Homo Novus—a human without illusions* (The Frontiers collection) (pp. 127–143). Springer. https://doi.org/10.1007/978-3-642-12142-5_10

Sear, R. (2015). Evolutionary contributions to the study of human fertility. *Population Studies, 69*(Suppl 1), S39–S55. https://doi.org/10.1080/00324728.2014.982905

Sear, R. (2021). The male breadwinner nuclear family is not the 'traditional' human family, and promotion of this myth may have adverse health consequences. *Philosophical Transactions of the Royal Society B, 376*(1827), 20200020. https://doi.org/10.1098/rstb.2020.0020

Shenk, M. K., Kaplan, H. S., & Hooper, P. L. (2016). Status competition, inequality, and fertility: Implications for the demographic transition. *Philosophical Transactions of the Royal Society B: Biological Sciences, 371*(1692), 20150150. https://doi.org/10.1098/rstb.2015.0150

Shirazi, T. N., Hastings, W. J., Rosinger, A. Y., & Ryan, C. P. (2020). Parity predicts biological age acceleration in post-menopausal, but not pre-menopausal, women. *Scientific Reports, 10*(1), 20522. https://doi.org/10.1038/s41598-020-77082-2

Stanković, S., Živić, S., Ignjatović, A., Stojanović, M., Bogdanović, D., Novak, S., et al. (2016). Comparison of weight and length at birth of non-Roma and Roma newborn in Serbia. *International Journal of Public Health, 61*, 69–73. https://doi.org/10.1007/s00038-015-0736-1

Starkweather, K. E., Keith, M. H., Prall, S. P., Alam, N., Zohora, F., & Emery Thompson, M. (2021). Are fathers a good substitute for mothers? Paternal care and growth rates in Shodagor children. *Developmental Psychobiology, 63*(6), e22148. https://doi.org/10.1002/dev.22148

Sunderland, M. (2006). *Science of parenting: Practical guidance on sleep, crying, play, and building emotional well-being for life*. Dorling Kindersley.

Stulp, G., Verhulst, S., Pollet, T. V., & Buunk, A. P. (2012). The effect of female height on reproductive success is negative in western populations, but more variable in non-western populations. *American Journal of Human Biology, 24*(4), 486–494. https://doi.org/10.1002/ajhb.22252

Szabó, L., Kiss, I., Šprocha, B., & Spéder, Z. (2021). Fertility of Roma minorities in central and Eastern Europe. *Comparative Population Studies, 46*, 10.12765/CPoS-2021-14.

Tamis-LeMonda, C. S., & Song, L. (2012). Parent-infant communicative interactions in cultural context. *Handbook of psychology: Developmental psychology, 6*, 143–170.

Thomas, F., Teriokhin, A. T., Budilova, E. V., Brown, S. P., Renaud, F., & Guegan, J. F. (2004). Human birthweight evolution across contrasting environments. *Journal of Evolutionary Biology, 17*(3), 542–553. https://doi.org/10.1111/j.1420-9101.2004.00705.x

Thurstans, S., Sessions, N., Dolan, C., Sadler, K., Cichon, B., Isanaka, S., et al. (2022). The relationship between wasting and stunting in young children: A systematic review. *Maternal & Child Nutrition, 18*(1), e13246. https://doi.org/10.1111/mcn.13246

Tracer, D. P. (2009). Breastfeeding structure as a test of parental investment theory in Papua New Guinea. *American Journal of Human Biology: The Official Journal of the Human Biology Association, 21*(5), 635–642. https://doi.org/10.1002/ajhb.20928

Uggla, C., & Mace, R. (2016). Parental investment in child health in sub-Saharan Africa: A cross-national study of health-seeking behaviour. *Royal Society Open Science, 3*(2), 150460. https://doi.org/10.1098/rsos.150460

Victora, C. G., Christian, P., Vidaletti, L. P., Gatica-Domínguez, G., Menon, P., & Black, R. E. (2021). Revisiting maternal and child undernutrition in low-income and middle-income countries: Variable progress towards an unfinished agenda. *The Lancet, 397*(10282), 1388–1399.

References

Vining, D. R. (1986). Social versus reproductive success: The central theoretical problem of sociobiology. *Behavioral and Brain Sciences, 9*, 167–216. https://doi.org/10.1017/S0140525X00021968

Voicu, M., & Popescu, R. (2009). Roma women-known and unknown. *EURoma Network*. https://www.euromanet.eu/upload/80/83/Research_Report_Roma_Women_engl_09___OSI-Romania_.pdf

Wado, Y. D., Afework, M. F., & Hindin, M. J. (2014). Effects of maternal pregnancy intention, depressive symptoms and social support on risk of low birth weight: A prospective study from southwestern Ethiopia. *PLoS One, 9*(5), e96304. https://doi.org/10.1371/journal.pone.0096304

Walker, R. S., Gurven, M., Burger, O., & Hamilton, M. J. (2008). The trade-off between number and size of offspring in humans and other primates. *Proceedings of the Royal Society B: Biological Sciences, 275*(1636), 827–834. https://doi.org/10.1098/rspb.2007.1511

Walker, R. S., & Hamilton, M. J. (2008). Life-history consequences of density dependence and the evolution of human body size. *Current Anthropology, 49*(1), 115–122. https://doi.org/10.1086/524763

Walker, S. P., Wachs, T. D., Grantham-McGregor, S., Black, M. M., Nelson, C. A., Huffman, S. L., et al. (2011). Inequality in early childhood: Risk and protective factors for early child development. *The Lancet, 378*(9799), 1325–1338. https://doi.org/10.1016/S0140-6736(11)60555-2

Williams, G. (1966). *Adaptation and natural selection: A critique of some current evolutionary thought*. Princeton University Press.

Wilcox, A. J. (2001). On the importance—and the unimportance—of birthweight. *International Journal of Epidemiology, 30*(6), 1233–1241. https://doi.org/10.1093/ije/30.6.1233

Winkvist, A., Rasmussen, K. M., & Habicht, J. P. (1992). A new definition of maternal depletion syndrome. *American Journal of Public Health, 82*(5), 691–694. https://doi.org/10.2105/AJPH.82.5.691

Yabe, M., Oshima, S., Eifuku, S., Taira, M., Kobayashi, K., Yabe, H., & Niwa, S. I. (2018). Effects of storytelling on the childhood brain: Near-infrared spectroscopic comparison with the effects of picture-book reading. *Fukushima Journal of Medical Science, 64*(3), 125–132. https://doi.org/10.5387/fms.2018-11

Yadav, S., & Bhandari, P. (2022). Age heterogeneities in child growth and its associated sociodemographic factors: A cross-sectional study in India. *BMC Pediatrics, 22*(1), 384. https://doi.org/10.1186/s12887-022-03415-x